Liberal Hearts and Conservative Brains

Liberal Hearts and Conservative Brains

◆

The Correlation between Age and Political Philosophy

Ron Lipsman

iUniverse, Inc.
New York Lincoln Shanghai

Liberal Hearts and Conservative Brains
The Correlation between Age and Political Philosophy

iUniverse books may be ordered through booksellers or by contacting:

iUniverse
2021 Pine Lake Road, Suite 100
Lincoln, NE 68512
www.iuniverse.com
1-800-Authors (1-800-288-4677)

ISBN: 978-0-595-46320-6 (pbk)
ISBN: 978-0-595-90615-4 (ebk)

Printed in the United States of America

To Dave Eig and Elliot Goodman,
conversations with whom over many years reassured me that the appellation
politically conservative Jew *is not an oxymoron;*
to Nelson Markley and John Osborn, who performed the same service
*for **politically conservative professor**;*
and to the late Arieh Rigevsky, for thirty years of inspirational guidance.

Contents

Acknowledgments

I would like to acknowledge my debt to three groups of people. First is the group of five to whom I have dedicated the book. They were and are an inspiration for me. Next, I am grateful to all my liberal friends, colleagues and relations, both in academia and among my co-religionists, who over many years have treated me to a never-ending stream of ideas for collectivist and government-oriented solutions to virtually every problem that plagues American society. In my political discussions with them, I never had any need for straw men. Finally, my deepest gratitude goes to my father Irving and his brother Seymour. I am sure that, as my drift to the right began and intensified over the years, I was a great disappointment to them. They probably reckoned it an unfair reward for their having introduced me to and sparked my interest in political affairs. They were classic New Deal liberals who came to grips, painfully, with the realization that I worshipped at a different political altar. But they never held it against me—the love and affection they bestowed upon me until the end of their lives remains a treasure for me.

Preface

I have spent a tremendous portion of my adult life in two worlds. One world is academia, the university, and the inhabitants I have associated with most intimately in that world are, like me, mathematics faculty. The other world is that of Jewish America. My family, my neighbors, my friends, my social contacts, even many of my colleagues, have been Jewish in large proportion. I am extremely comfortable in these worlds. One of America's great gifts is that it allows its citizens a freedom of association that affords a wide latitude to choose among myriad possibilities. It is possible to pursue one's associations in depth without compromising one's place as an upstanding member of American society. I vote, shop, travel, pursue a career, discharge my civic responsibilities (e.g., serve on juries), attend sporting and cultural events, all alongside my fellow Americans, most of whom inhabit other worlds (e.g., law enforcement officials, construction trades people, evangelicals, stamp collectors, political bloggers, NASCAR enthusiasts, etc.) and we all cohabit easily, simultaneously treasuring this great country that embraces us all.

As I said, I am comfortable in my two worlds. I love mathematics and the academic life in which I pursue it. Like my fellow mathematicians, I enjoy patterns, logical thought, abstraction and computation. Like my fellow professors, I value the search for truth and beauty, and I cherish the freedom to pursue the strands of investigation that I choose—which is the hallmark of an academic life—rather than be assigned to a project team investigating a specific scientific phenomenon as I would be in the corporate or industrial world. I am comfortable in my academic milieu and I exhibit behavioral patterns and thought processes that are typical of my academic colleagues.

I also treasure my Jewish life. From as early as I can remember, I enjoyed learning about Jewish history, participating in Jewish festivals, taking pride in the achievements of Jewish people, and reveling in the fact that America has provided the warmest home and greatest opportunity for the Jewish people in our millennia-long wanderings around the Earth. Gentiles are skeptical when Jews claim that they can recognize other Jews on the scantest of physical evidence. Nevertheless, it's true. And it helps to account for the comfort zone I feel in their presence. As with my academic world, my Jewish world is filled with characters that think and behave like me—we celebrate the same holidays, uphold like values, esteem the same traditions of scholarship and worship the same God. It is indeed very comfortable.

But there is one corner in both of my worlds in which I am out of kilter with my cohabitants—political philosophy. Scores of my friends and associates, in both worlds, see me as an anomaly. They are overwhelmingly liberal—and I am conservative. I wasn't always. Until roughly the age of 30, I was in lockstep with my two brethren politically. What happened? Why didn't it happen to them? Moving from a liberal to a conservative philosophy as one grows older is a fairly commonly observed phenomenon—at least in many (perhaps most) of the different worlds in America. But not in my two worlds. I will attempt to explain why that might be so in this book.

Having said that, I actually will not provide the explanation until the third and final part of the book. In the first two parts, I will examine more generally whether my political trek from port to starboard is indeed a typical journey for Americans as they age, and why or why not one might expect it to be typical. In short, I will examine the legitimacy of a correlation between age and political philosophy. And although I won't examine that correlation as it applies to my two worlds until the final chapters of the book, I will, throughout the book, constantly adopt three perspectives—academic, Jewish and personal—as I present my arguments, test my hypotheses and draw my conclusions.

CREDENTIALS

Recently, I published YOU CAN DO THE MATH: *How to Overcome your Math Phobia and Make Better Financial Decisions.* The book, a financial self-help manual for the math-challenged people of America, was my first foray outside the realm of academic publishing. In fact, I am Senior Associate Dean and Professor of Mathematics at the University of Maryland. In addition to YOU CAN DO THE MATH, I have published eleven other books dealing with mathematics and computing, and I am the author of more than 70 scientific research articles and the editor of numerous mathematical research volumes.

How does this qualify me to write about political matters? Strictly speaking, it doesn't. But in fact, I have always been interested in political and social issues. Long recognized, and chided incessantly for being one of a handful of political conservatives in the vast liberal academic regime that dominates American universities, I have extensive experience defending the conservative viewpoint in informal writings and conversations on campus. Now I test those convictions in my first entry into formal political literature. During my academic career, I have been storing up many of the ideas expressed in this book. It is a pleasure and a relief to finally let them out. I believe their poignancy and originality, and the passion with which I express them, will more than compensate for my "rookie status." And, by the way, I use a little mathematical reasoning to help me reach my conclusions in the second part of the book.

OUTSIDE THE STANDARD MODE

Most contemporary political books promote exactly one of the liberal or conservative agendas. This usually entails an attendant attempt to explain why the other agenda is misguided. This book will differ from that mode in several respects. First, it will offer a, hopefully, fair comparison of the agendas. Next, although it will quickly be evident that *my* poker chips are on the conservative side of the table, I will at least entertain the notion that I am betting a losing hand. Also, the book presents a rather comprehensive and coherent enumeration and compartmentalization of the current central tenets of the two agendas. And finally, I will explore the correlation of these agendas with age. All of this is rather different from the usual book that either examines specific political battles, eras, individuals or events, or evolves quickly into a political diatribe on the superiority of one philosophy over the other.

SPECIAL FEATURES

- **Fairness.** I will suspend value judgments from the main presentation of the liberal and conservative agendas in the first part of the book. Although I freely admit that I am an adherent of the conservative philosophy, I see no purpose in allowing that potential bias to color my outline of the two agendas. I will confine the expression of *my* personal preferences largely to those portions of the book that are …

- **Personal.** Throughout the book, in sections that are clearly marked, I will trace my personal experiences as I made my own journey from the liberal to the conservative side of the ledger. The personal vignettes and stories will often, but not always, have a Jewish or academic underlying theme.

- **Style.** I seek to avoid the appearance of a weighty political tome, replete with cross references, annotations and data from statistical surveys. I prefer to present the book more in the style of a long op/ed piece rather than as an academic government and politics text. Thus, there is only an occasional footnote, a relatively short bibliography and virtually no citation of polling data. This makes for easier reading and a more lively and entertaining experience. Nevertheless, the treatment is …

- **Comprehensive.** Fundamental statements of the two competing philosophies are developed, the philosophies are identified by two dozen specific issues that define the respective agendas, issues which are then organized into five broad compartments around which is studied …

- **Correlation.** The relationship between the agendas and the age of their adherents. The idea of such a correlation is not new, but its exploration in the context of the developed issues and compartments allows for a systematic examination of the correlation and affords the possibility of a prediction of our political future.

A NEW AGE?

Most conservatives believe that the country's political and cultural agendas have been driven *almost exclusively* by liberals from the time of the Roosevelt era—and many would specify that of Teddy, not Franklin. That statement becomes false with the advent of the Reagan presidency, but only to the extent that the exclusivity is over, the liberal dominance continues in many ways to this day. Now, some might argue that we are on the verge of a historic shift, indeed that the tide has already turned. After a century in which liberal thought and practice has governed our politics, dominated our cultural institutions, and called the social tunes, we stand at the dawn of a nascent conservative age in America. Is it so? Through an examination of the liberal/conservative divide and its relation to age, I will attempt to answer that question.

Introduction

The quote, "If you are young and not *liberal*, then you have no *heart*; but if you are old and not *conservative*, then you have no *brain*," is most often attributed to Disraeli or to Churchill—although its true ownership remains cloudy. In this book, we shall examine the worthiness of that assessment of the correlation between age and political philosophy as it applies to the people of the United States in the first decade of the 21st century. First of all, is it reasonable to expect the imagination and political passions of America's youth to be fired by the ideas and axioms of modern liberalism, and is it equally reasonable to expect the middle aged and elderly population to adhere to the more conservative tenets of political thought? If so, does the reality match the expectation? Do most people complete a journey, as they advance in years and accumulate experiences, from the left end of the political spectrum to the right side of that spectrum? In fact, I have made the journey myself—from a classic, dyed-in-the-wool, liberal in my teens and 20s to a rock-hard conservative in middle age, and now senior citizen status. Am I typical? If not, why not?

These are the questions that I shall explore in this book. In order to do so, I begin in Part I with a description of what I perceive are the core or touchstone issues and positions that separate a liberal philosophy from a conservative one. I will identify 24 such issues. (The number is not meant to be iron-clad—others might produce more, still others, fewer.) The 24 issues are identified in tabular form in Chapter 1. For example, the first issue is *government spending*, wherein clearly the liberal position is in favor of extensive government expenditures, whereas the conservative position favors limited government spending. Other issues involve taxes, welfare, foreign affairs, abortion, diversity, gun control, capital punishment, etc. Please consult the list for a fuller accounting.

Next, I shall backtrack slightly in Chapter 2 and examine *dictionary definitions* of the terms liberal and conservative. While useful, the definitions are a little too vague or general. Therefore, I rework them in five different ways, incorporating into the basic definitions, respectively, the notions of human nature, religion, government, history and business. This results in the formulation of five fundamental statements that encapsulate what I understand as a liberal, or a conservative, view of the world. As you will see, they differ sharply, and so throughout the book I use the term *liberal/conservative divide*. Nevertheless, the country is not coming apart at the seams, and I illustrate that by offering a dozen areas of commonality or points of agreement between the two political communities. Next, in Chapter 3, I continue the exploration of the liberal/conservative divide by presenting a compartmentalization of the two dozen touchstone issues. I group the 24 of them into five broad categories or compartments, two of which have to do with the assignment of roles:

- The role of the government in the country
- The role of the USA in the world,

and three of which have to do with personality factors:

- Absolutist or Relativist
- Opportunist or Egalitarian
- Pragmatist or Idealist.

I will discuss how each of the issues fits into its respective compartment in Chapter 4—although, as we shall see, there are some overlaps. The first part of the book concludes in Chapter 5 with a concise history of the liberal/conservative divide in the USA during the twentieth century.

In Part II there is an examination of the issues and compartments in the context of age. Is it reasonable to associate the liberal stance on the touchstone issues with a young age or youthful outlook? Is it appropriate to associate a conservative viewpoint with a mature or experienced personality? We shall examine in depth in Chapters 6 and 7 those issues and compartments where this is indeed the case, as well as some where it is not. Our overall conclusion is that, indeed, there is a correlation between age and political philosophy—although, it is not as strong as the opening quote might suggest. Our work also leads to the renewed observation that there is a rather substantial divide or dichotomy between the liberal and conservative positions on the issues. Chapter 8 presents an assessment of the relative strengths at the present time of the liberal and conservative camps. In fact, the bitterness and animosity between the two camps seems to be as great as any time in our nation's history. It is not clear whether conservatives "hated" Clinton any more than liberals "hate" Bush, but it is clear that the depths of feelings were/are not imaginary. In Chapter 9, I briefly compare the current division to those in other periods in US history. Then I concentrate on a comparison with the situation in the early twentieth century when the roles were reversed, that is, liberals were gaining power at the expense of conservatives.

Finally, in Part III, we shall confront the fact that not all youth are liberal, but more seriously the fact that many middle-aged and elderly Americans are not conservative. If there were no substance to the correlation, then neither of these phenomena would be particularly surprising. But if one accepts my assertion (in Part II) that the correlation is legitimate, then the existence of the former (i.e., conservative youth) may be nothing more than a manifestation of precocity (sayeth the Right), or it may be unfair parental influence (as a Leftist might surmise). Either way, it does not disprove the correlation as a conservative youth may maintain or strengthen her conservative principles as she ages. But the latter phenomenon (i.e., liberal elders) is more problematic. It flies in the face of the correlation. A stark, controversial and short explanation would simply be, "people who refuse to grow up." I shall go deeper and offer five possible reasons why this "anomaly" occurs, ranging from immaturity (as the Right might charge) to idealism maturing into wisdom (as the Left would assert). I also offer some special insights into the "aging liberal" phenomenon for my two special communities (Jews and academic faculty). All of the preceding is in Chapters 10 and 11. I conclude the book in Chapter 12 with a glimpse into the future and a prediction of the relative strengths of the liberal and conservative communities in the coming decades.

To recapitulate, we have four objectives in this book:

1. to argue for a correlation between age and political philosophy, which asserts that young people tend to gravitate toward liberalism while older people are usually more comfortable with conservatism; and that, additionally, among the people who change their political preference over time, more go from liberal to conservative than vice versa; and finally, to assess the strengths of these trends;

2. to examine the most interesting counter-examples to these trends—namely, premature conservatives and aging liberals—and to explain what motivates them;

3. to present a history of the liberal/conservative divide and then to augment it with an assessment of its current status as well as a prediction of its future;

4. to describe, through personal vignettes (found at the conclusion of each chapter), the experiences that resulted in my conversion from liberal to conservative.

PART I
The Differences Between Liberals and Conservatives

1

The Two Dozen Touchstone Issues

Who is liberal? Who is conservative? What words, beliefs or actions define a person as liberal? What policies, manifestos or position papers characterize their authors as conservative? We had better have a good understanding of the answers to these questions if there is to be any hope of achieving the book's goals set down in the Preface and Introduction. In fact most Americans have a clear intuitive sense of the political leanings of the politicians and political organizations to which they are exposed. When they hear a politician speak, or read a newspaper editorial or examine a party's position paper, they quickly come to a conclusion as to whether the stance they just encountered represents a liberal or conservative way of thought. As such politicians and political organizations get pegged rather quickly as to their positions in the political spectrum—from ultra-liberal, to liberal, moderate (or centrist), conservative or ultra-conservative. But sometimes the labels and reputations can be confusing or even misleading. The current Bush administration is widely regarded as conservative, even ultra-conservative by some. Yet its record on the growth of government, deficit spending and immigration control could easily be characterized as liberal. Its predecessor, the Clinton administration, was routinely tagged with the liberal label, yet it pursued welfare reform, free trade and (relative) fiscal restraint in a way that would garner laurels from a conservative audience.

So, perhaps we really do need to pin down more precisely what constitutes liberalism/conservatism and liberal/conservative thought and policies. But to do so we need to decide which, among several methods, is the best way to do that—especially in relation to our ultimate goal of correlating age to political axioms. Indeed, there are various ways to formulate a set of answers to the questions that opened this chapter. A logician or philosopher might attempt to write down (perhaps long and elaborate) dictionary-type definitions of the two words, liberal and conservative, and then characterize words, beliefs, deeds, policies, etc. according to which of the two definitions they best satisfy. A very simple example might be:

A liberal is someone who believes in the perfectibility of man and that society must therefore be structured so as to foster the best possibility of man advancing toward that state of perfection; whereas a conservative accepts that man is inherently flawed, and therefore society must be arranged so as to minimize the mistakes he can make and the damage he can wreak.

Another possibility is to identify a small number—perhaps no more than one—of issues, whereby the individual's words, actions or beliefs addressed to these issues determine his locus in the continuum of positions between liberal and conservative. For example, for some people, if you are pro-abortion, you are liberal and if you are pro-life then you are conservative. End of story.

Yet a third method would be to examine the host of organizations to which you belong, newspapers and magazines to which you subscribe and parties that you support. That roster defines your political philosophy. For example, if you are a member of the American Civil Liberties Union (ACLU), People for the Ethical Treatment of Animals (PETA) and People for the American Way; if you subscribe to the Nation, the New York Review of Books, the New York Times and listen to CBS News; if you vote for candidates put forth by the Democratic Party; then you are most certainly liberal. On the other hand, if you are a member of the Heritage Foundation, the National Rifle Association and the National Association of Scholars; if you subscribe to the Weekly Standard, Commentary and the Washington Times and listen to Fox News; if you vote for candidates sponsored by the Republican Party, then no one would mistake you for anything but a conservative. Well this form of definition is a little like guilt by association, but it has its merits. It affords a classification without any deep analysis of philosophy or ideology. You are identified essentially by the company you keep.

In a similar vein, you might use the pantheon of political gods whom you worship. Thus if you read the books and approve of the words of Adam Smith, William Buckley, Friedrich Hayek, Russell Kirk, John Locke, Edmund Burke and Ronald Reagan, then you are most certainly of the conservative persuasion. But if you are moved by the scribblings and ideas of John Dewey, Voltaire and

Rousseau, Franklin Roosevelt, Lyndon Johnson, John Maynard Keynes or Karl Marx, then you are most assuredly marked as a liberal.

Our method for specifying liberalism and conservatism will draw to some extent on all four of the preceding schemes. We'll start by codifying the intuitive approach. We'll do this by listing 24 specific issues—I call them *touchstone issues*—such that one's position on these issues will, at the beginning of the twenty first century in the USA, reveal with near certainty, whether one leans to political starboard or port. This is considerably less formal than supplying a rigorous definition or a basic statement of philosophy according to which we would measure political temperature, but it is how our country's citizens generally distinguish between liberals and conservatives, that is, by the positions they espouse on the touchstone issues. When we listen to a presidential debate, watch the nominating conventions, read the newspaper accounts of stump speeches, we look for code words and phrases, and hints as to where the candidate comes down on "the issues"; most of us don't try to match the contents to the thoughts of Engels or de Tocqueville. If we know which side a candidate takes on 6-10 fundamental issues, we feel we know her political pedigree, and we vote accordingly. It may not be the most axiomatic or deductive method, but it works for the American people.

However, we must not lose sight of the basic goal in the book—namely, to attempt a correlation between age and political philosophy. Arranging our understanding of the differences between liberals and conservatives by locating them on the touchstone issues will turn out not to be the most effective way to pursue that goal. That will become clear as we explore each of the 24 issues briefly later in this chapter. So in Chapter 2, we will seek a dictionary-type definition of the liberal and conservative philosophies. In fact I will offer five. And although they are very useful in understanding political differences, they are in some sense too abstract for our attempt at a correlation. Therefore, in Chapters 3 & 4, we will reformulate them into a set of five categories, or compartments, motivated by the five definitions. We will see how the touchstone issues fit into these compartments (not always so perfectly it will turn out). Moreover, it is from this compartmentalization of the issues that we will obtain a structure for addressing the question of whether there is a meaningful correlation between age and political philosophy. That analysis will occur in the second part of the book. The third part of the book will measure whether reality matches the proposed correlation.

The Two Dozen Issues

I am about to present a list of 24 issues. You are certainly anticipating most if not all of them—abortion, taxes, the war against radical Islam, etc. But rather than list them as such, I will present instead a table with two columns. Each row in the table will highlight one issue and the two columns in that row will establish the generally accepted liberal and conservative positions on the specific issue, respectively. Taken as a whole, the table offers a mighty compelling illustration of the vast differences between liberals and conservatives. We will center our discussion of those differences around the table, and we will use it throughout the book. However, as we shall see, it will not be the best vehicle for correlating political positions to the age of their adherents. Here is the table:

Things that liberals generally favor	Things that conservatives generally favor
Extensive government spending	Limited government spending
High taxes	Low taxes
More government regulations	Fewer government regulations
Welfare	Welfare reform
Low military spending	High military spending
UN preeminence in settling intl. disputes	US leadership in settling intl. disputes
Multilateral agreements and treaties	US sovereignty as paramount in setting policy
Abortion	Pro-life
Homosexual rights	Strictly heterosexual marriage
Diversity, i.e. special favors for certain groups	Equal rights before the law
Protection for targeted industries	Free trade
Minimum wage laws	No government edicts on wages
Judicial activism	Judicial restraint
Environmental activism	Envir. concern, tempered by economic reality
Animal rights	Human rights
Wall between Church and State	Religious morality infusing laws of the State
Amnesty for illegal aliens	Deportation for illegal aliens

Social justice	Rugged individualism
Rehabilitation for criminals	Punishment for criminals
Abolishment of capital punishment	Appropriate use of capital punishment
Gun control	Concealed gun permits
Constitution as a living document	Strict interpretation of the Constitution
Group rights	Individual rights
Broadening the culture to accommodate the browning of America	Preserving traditional American culture

There is no particular order to the list, no item intended to be more important than any other. And although the list is quite comprehensive I do not mean to suggest it is complete. There are undoubtedly other issues that divide liberals from conservatives, and some of you may be red hot at this point upon noticing the omission of your favorite issue. Examples that come to mind include: outsourcing of American jobs overseas, support for the United Nations, re-importation of prescription drugs, the war against illegal drugs, censorship, and the use of the Senate filibuster to prevent executive and judicial appointments. There are others. No list could possibly be exhaustive. However, I contend that my list is robust enough to accomplish three objectives:

1.   Catch issues in all the major categories of political discourse—foreign affairs, defense, finance, trade, culture, law, religion, medicine and science;

2.   Be comprehensive enough so that the identification of a position in even half of these issues will certainly pin down the political leanings of any holder of those positions;

3.   Begin to suggest a small set of embracing categories, into which the issues can be pigeon-holed, that are conducive to a study of correlation between age and political philosophy.

Succinct Summary Statements

My next task is to expound somewhat on the two dozen issues. I do not want to write a treatise on each issue, explaining why, for example, the liberal position on that issue is consistent with a basic liberal philosophy. After all, we have not stated an overarching liberal or conservative philosophy—at least not yet. Rather

I will attempt in several sentences, for each side on each issue, to provide a capsule summary of the conservative or liberal position on the issue, and in this way begin to identify the umbrella categories that will arise later in Part I.

In fact it is a challenging exercise to fashion these succinct summary sentences. Composing a short, cogent and convincing explanatory statement for each side of each issue forces one to go rapidly to the crux of both the stance on and the underlying principles for an issue—for both sides of the debate. Now you might contend that it shouldn't be so difficult for me to do that as I am an ardent proponent of one side, and I inhabited the other side for the first half of my life. I should have a good understanding of both sides. Hopefully so. In fact my goal in constructing these pithy descriptions was to do so in such a manner that if you didn't know which side of the divide I came down on, you would not be able to tell from my descriptions. Did I succeed? Read on.

But before you do, a word about *pronouns*. For centuries, when describing the actions of an unnamed individual in the English language, it was sufficient—and grammatically correct—to write, "the average theater attendee was in his 30s and he saw an average of three plays per year," safe in the knowledge that the "he" in question represented a generic theater patron, female as well as male. No longer! Today we must employ grammatical monstrosities such as "he or she," or "him or her," or (s)he or s/he, or even the incorrect "they." I find the following mode more acceptable. As the story unfolds, one alternates between the masculine and feminine pronouns in a systematic, yet arbitrary way. Not only does it preserve grammatical correctness, it occasionally introduces a bit of whimsy and even irony into the presentation. Thus in what follows in this chapter, the liberal role will be assumed by a male and the conservative counterpart by a female.

- **Government spending.** A liberal is comfortable advocating increased government spending because he views the programs, structures and equipment that the spending buys as essential for the improvement of society, and which would not come into existence if left to the devices of individuals, the business community, or civic and religious organizations. He also believes government spending improves the economy by creating jobs. A conservative, on the other hand, is sure that the programs and departments run by government agencies are wasteful, mismanaged and resistant to change—largely because the personnel who manage them are spending other people's money and so are not motivated to be efficient. She prefers that the tasks they manage be left to the market forces of the private sector where companies, and their managers, must please customers or go out of business.

- **Taxes.** A conservative is comfortable advocating lower government taxes because she believes that lower taxes will spur economic development since it places more money in the hands of business to invest, invent and modernize and in the hands of consumers to save, invest or spend. This is consistent with her propensity towards smaller government in general, as the lower the tax rates, the less government can expand. A liberal, on the other hand, favors higher taxes in order to fund the expanded government enterprises he advocates. He also strongly favors steeply progressive taxes in order to diminish the social inequities he feels are inherent in a society that allows dramatic differences in the wealth level of its citizens. The conservative would counter that the progressive income tax structure punishes those who succeed and curtails incentives for the most bold and innovative people to develop new products and create new wealth.

- **Government Regulations.** Our liberal fellow advocates robust government regulation of various aspects of American health, consumer goods, utilities, business transactions, indeed of virtually all facets of US life, business and culture because left to themselves, the citizenry's interests are too diverse and unfocused to arrive at policies and practices that would benefit the general welfare. Specialists and concerned government officials can see the big picture more readily and are better positioned to establish fair rules that all citizens and companies should play by. Not so says our conservative gal, it is impossible for any bureaucrat to fathom the wishes and needs of tens of millions of Americans with diverse interests. The good intentions of government bureaucrats lead to inconsistent application of complex rules, wasteful policies that hamper economic development and intrusions on the life and business of the citizenry—often to the extent of violating our constitutional rights. We are better off letting the profit motive motivate business to play by sound rules rather than by imposing whimsical and often counterproductive regulations from a well-intentioned, but meddling central command.

- **Welfare.** The conservative views the plethora of government welfare programs as massive disincentives to work. She asserts that if the government will pay women to have babies and fathers not to work, then that is exactly what they will do. She believes that private organizations like religious and civic charities are better equipped to help and inspire disadvantaged people. The liberal, again motivated by his discomfort with financial disparities within society, believes it is the fundamental responsibility of the government to aid those who are less fortunate. He is not impressed by the decline in welfare cases brought about by the welfare reform initiative of the last decade, but rather is incensed by the increasingly desperate condition of those it has left behind.

- **Military Spending.** The liberal sees expenditures for the military as money that could be put to far wiser use in domestic and international social programs for the betterment of Americans and all mankind. He also believes that war is a retrograde method for dealing with international disputes, and that the maintenance and deployment of large military forces are destabilizing to the cause of world peace. The conservative is less sanguine about the intentions of America's enemies. She regards as well spent the money required to create the most powerful and flexible US military force possible for deflecting threats and dealing with intractable foes such as Osama bin Laden. She wishes that is could be otherwise, but knows that unilateral disarmament will cost far more in the long run than the dollars we spend on the military. Those larger costs will be in the form of great harm to our homeland, economy and liberties.

- **International Conflict Resolution.** Our conservative lady views with suspicion the United Nations, which she considers an unholy conglomeration of nations, too many of which are led by bloodthirsty tyrants, corrupt gangsters and Marxist stooges, none of whom subscribe to the fundamental principles of Western Civilization. According to her, that organization is morally bankrupt and is unqualified to settle disputes that involve our national interests. For those, the US must take the lead. The liberal gentleman counters that the US has no corner on morality, and that unless our allies in particular (NATO) and the world in general (the UN) make common cause with us when we engage countries (or other entities) in disputes, then we have no justification for unilateral military action. He rarely enunciates it, but he increasingly believes that the concept of the sovereign nation-state grows antiquated and its replacement by an enlightened world order is inevitable.

- **Multilateralism vs. Unilateralism.** A liberal would be comfortable signing the Kyoto Protocol on Climate Change, adhering to the judgments of the International Court of Justice, and allowing US soldiers to come under the jurisdiction of the International Criminal Court (ICC). He sees these treaties, which on first inspection might seem harmful to US interests, playing an important role in converting America from the sole, but despised superpower into a shining example of a strong nation helping to lead the world's people toward unity, peace and harmony with the Earth. A conservative is aghast at the prospect of the Kyoto Protocol crippling our economy, the International Court of Justice declaring that we have no right to seal our borders against illegal immigrants, and that the actions of American soldiers defending our freedom might be deemed criminal by the ICC. She believes that the President should present and the Senate should ratify only treaties that advance the welfare and interests of the United States of America. She believes that the USA was the first country in the history of the world to organize and run itself according to a rule of law endorsed and enforced by all its people, that it has the privilege, honor and duty to spread this gospel to all the nations of the world, and that it should not subvert its own special mission by allowing its purposes to be thwarted by noble-sounding multilateral agreements that do not serve our interests.

- **Abortion.** A conservative, if motivated primarily by religious beliefs, is almost certainly going to be strongly anti-abortion. She believes that life begins at conception and that abortion is the taking of a human life—murder is not too strong a word to describe the practice in her thinking. But even a non-religious conservative is likely to oppose abortion on demand, as Roe v. Wade has mandated, because she sees it as the most extreme manifestation of a culture of death (abortion, assisted suicide, euthanasia) that threatens traditional American culture. And she believes Roe v. Wade was bad constitutional law in that it invented a legal concept (right to privacy) that is not present (in penumbras or otherwise) in the U.S. Constitution. A liberal will feel just as strongly in the opposite direction. A women's right to choose whether to terminate her pregnancy, he will counter, is a reflection of the highest form of individual rights protected by the Constitution—namely, her right to control her own body. He believes that the abortion of a fetus is not equivalent to the taking of a human life, certainly if the fetus is not viable, and that the rights of the pregnant woman far outweigh those, if there are any, of the fetus.

- **Homosexuality and Marriage.** A liberal believes that society has no more right to discriminate against anyone on the basis of sexual orientation than it does on the basis of race, gender, religion, ethnic origin or physical capabilities—namely, there is no such right in *any* of these instances. He believes that homosexuality is an involuntary personality trait (analogous to, say, left-handedness), and that stable, long-term homosexual relationships are as beneficial to society as stable, long-term traditional marriages. Therefore, they should be encouraged. The assignment of second-class status to homosexual families, especially if fostered by religious precepts, is an unholy reflection of ancient narrow-mindedness, he asserts, and the elevation of the status of homosexual relationships through legalized marriage will be a hallmark of great progress in an enlightened American society. But a conservative believes that marriage is an institution, established millennia ago, whose basic ground rules have remained constant over that time: one man and one woman, until death does them part. She recognizes that the latter is an ideal to strive for and a commandment to fulfill, not a guarantee. But she views the former as immutable, an arrangement with unquestioned benefit for the participants, the children that result, and the society that blesses and nurtures them. Regardless of whether she views homosexuality as morally wrong according to scripture, unnatural in the sense of contrary to nature's laws, or an alternate lifestyle with no particular stigma, she feels that homosexual marriage, like polygamy, or other combinations of humankind, cannot be sanctioned with the accolade of marriage.

- **Diversity.** While the conservative gal acknowledges the historic wrong perpetrated on American blacks, and the legal and cultural obstacles that were faced by women, she argues that these have been addressed by changing the laws of the land (e.g., the 13th, 14th, 15th and 19th amendments to the Constitution and the civil rights laws of the 1960s). She approves the general agreement, arrived at more than a generation ago, that additional redress would be made in the form of "affirmative action," but she understood that to mean: *all other things being equal,* a position (or promotion or whatever) would go to the black or woman. However, affirmative action has morphed into reverse discrimination, it shows no sign of ever ending, and it has been applied to groups (e.g., Hispanics) who have never suffered any legal discrimination. Reverse discrimination, like discrimination in its original forms, is wrong and unconstitutional. Moreover, it taints the successful minority person's achievements, even if those successes are legitimately earned. All individuals should be treated equally before the law. Group rights are an abomination in violation of our individual constitutional rights. Our liberal guy does not agree. He is deeply disturbed by the inequities he perceives in our country between males and females on one hand, and between white people and people of color on the other. He sees the causes as historical (slavery), cultural (religions that foster male dominance), accidental (immigrant families are generally lower on the food chain) and malevolent (KKK). These inequities must be rooted out and eliminated—if necessary, by building artificial advantages for the disadvantaged groups in standard practices like school admissions, awarding of government contracts, hiring and promotions, and awards and prizes. While these practices may inconvenience members of formerly advantaged groups in society, that is a small price to pay for temporary measures that will redress historic wrongs.

- **International Trade.** When a liberal sees the importation of a product, manufactured at a lower cost in another country, which causes the loss of a domestic job, he believes the cure is to place additional duties on the imported good so as to equalize the cost and save the American worker's job. He furthermore suspects that American business is in collusion with international suppliers in order to cut costs by either holding down domestic salaries or outsourcing jobs to companies overseas. He sees international trade as a zero sum game that must be vigorously supervised and regulated by the U.S. Government. The conservative views international trade through the same prism that she observes the American economy—that is, a private market of buyers and sellers, each trying to maximize their own gain by trading aggressively but, in the vast majority of instances, fairly. Markets wax and wane, products come in and out of fashion, nations (or regions of a country) vary in their ability to produce a good efficiently. The market is far better suited, through the normal pricing mechanism, to gauge the worth of goods, the desirability of products and the amounts in which they should be produced. Protectionist tariffs restrict free trade by propping up inefficient industries and by impeding the flow of workers to better jobs in more efficient and modern sectors of the market. Adam Smith's invisible hand works just as well internationally as it does domestically. The government's heavy hand is just as deadening internationally as it is domestically.

- **Wage Regulations.** The existence of minimum wage laws is seen by a conservative as a particularly egregious example of government intervention in the market. She asserts that if we truly believe that our economy should be a free market system, then the government's role, albeit important, should be limited to: ensuring that contracts are honored, prosecuting and punishing those who fail to do so, and pursuing policies that maintain the strength and viability of the currency. But decisions on what to produce, where and how to produce it, what to sell it for, when to stop producing or whether to produce other items, and what to pay those who participate in the production, these are all decisions that must be left in the hands of the producers. The answers to these questions provided by the magic of the market (through the pricing mechanism) are far superior to those supplied by government bureaucrats. But, counters the liberal, the market system inexorably leads to inequities. The disparities between those who prosper, often beyond reason, and those who flounder, often beyond their control, are unjust. He believes a fair and just society must implement methods to smooth out those inequities. The government must play the part of the referee, not only to ensure that the playing field is level, but that the outcomes of the game are fair and equitable. The

NFL strives for parity; the U.S. economy should do no less. Minimum wage laws are a small part of that fair play mechanism. We could do much more—for example, capping the pay of corporate executives.

- **The Role of the Judiciary.** A liberal considers the judiciary to be the most important part of the US legal system. It is the final arbiter, the last bastion between the citizen and any possible tyranny that could be imposed by the executive or legislative branches of government. It is also ideally suited to blunt the excessive power or influence that might be exerted by other segments of society—for example, business, religion, or ethnic majorities. He believes that one of the most important developments in the history of the country was the emergence of the courts' power of judicial review in the early nineteenth century, and that it is the exercise of this power by the courts that has enabled our country to move forward over the last two centuries, unshackled by old laws, customs and practices. The conservative sees the exercise of judicial powers as excessive. In short, she complains that the judiciary is often legislating from the bench and thereby usurping the powers granted to the other branches of government. She feels that the proper role of the judiciary is to interpret the Constitution and legislative laws, and to adjudicate disputes. It is not to make the laws of the land. She views the actions of judges and courts such as court-ordered bussing, nullification of ballot initiatives legally approved by voters, wanton declarations that legislative acts are unconstitutional, the discovery of group rights not granted in the federal or state constitutions, and finally the setting aside of criminal convictions on the flimsiest evidence that supposedly represents a denial of the criminal's rights, she sees all of these as judicial tyranny.

- **The Environment.** The conservative, as the appellation implies, is inclined to conserve and protect the Earth's environment—its air, water and natural beauty. However, she recognizes that the desire to do so often comes into conflict with an equally natural desire to improve the human condition—by, for example, building bigger and better homes, improving transportation, developing new sources of energy, manufacturing new products. Resolving that inherent conflict is a delicate balancing act that challenges her and her fellow conservatives. She approaches the problem objectively, aware that Mother Nature is sometimes more harmful to humans than we are to her—viz., blizzards, earthquakes, volcanic eruptions, avalanches, tsunamis. The liberal approaches the problem in a more religious way. To him, the Earth is sacred and all human desires do not measure up to the absolute requirement of preserving the natural resources and balances of the Earth's ecosystems. Finding energy sources, building roads, and manufacturing trucks rank much lower in the pecking order for him than keeping the air and water clean, preserving the rain forests and protecting wildlife. Mankind's instincts for self-preservation and advancement must not be allowed to interfere with humanity's sacred duty to protect the environment.

- **Animals.** We are all God's creatures, admonishes the liberal; mankind's claim on the Earth's bounty does not exceed those of the animal kingdom. As part of our sacred trust to preserve the environment, mankind is also duty bound to preserve and protect animal wildlife. Moreover, the liberal insists, we should treat our domesticated animals with the same respect. In particular, animals should not suffer at the hands of humans. The conservative, at times taking her cue from the biblical command to humans to "exercise dominion over the Earth," and respectful of animals as God's creatures, nevertheless does not accord them the same rights as humans. She has no problem with the use of animals in scientific or medical research, and does not feel guilty about eating or wearing them, provided humane and sanitary practices are adhered to in the process. She values the beauty of the peacock, the grace of the leopard, the power of the elephant, but if confronted with a choice between the welfare of an animal and the improvement of the human condition, her preference is unquestionably the latter.

- **Religion.** A conservative believes that the Bill of Rights grants us freedom of religion, not freedom from religion. The founders were religious people who wanted to guarantee all Americans the freedom to worship in any form they chose. The main objective was to ensure that no religion would be anointed the official state religion of the country. The founders always imagined, as our conservative lady believes has been borne out, that a democratic America would only survive and prosper if its peoples had strong morals grounded in religion. She sees the banishment of religion from the public square as contrary to the history of our nation, a development that will weaken its fabric. On the other hand, the liberal desires that the wall between Church and State—an idea plucked from the writings of Jefferson—should be set as high as possible. He worries that any State sanction of religion could lead us down a path toward religiously inspired sectarian conflict of the kind that plagued Europe for centuries. He cites the Muslim Middle East as a place where the intermingling of religion and State has lead to militarism and fanaticism, and counsels that we are not immune from that virus if we allow the commingling of religion and government. Rather, he believes religion is purely a private matter, that the State should be completely secular, and the two should have virtually nothing to do with one another.

- **Immigration.** The liberal takes pride in the fact that the US is a nation of immigrants, believes that our strength is due in no small measure to the talented people drawn to our shores from all over the world, and sees the increased diversification of our population and culture, through the continued immigration of peoples from underdeveloped nations, bringing about a change in America from a WASP-dominated society into a truly peaceful and harmonious polyglot of the world's ethnic identities. He is not terribly troubled that much of the immigration is illegal—first, because it may hasten the onset of his future vision of America, and second because it jibes with his growing belief in the eventual demise of the sovereign nation-state. For these reasons, he favors conferring all the rights of American citizens on immigrants—legal or otherwise. The conservative is also proud of America as an immigrant nation. But she is worried about current immigration for several reasons. First, she considers the granting of any legal status to illegal immigrants as a reward to people who broke US law. Second, she worries that new and recent immigrants—legal or otherwise—are purposely not being inculcated with classic American culture and fears this will lead to a fragmentation of American unity and Balkanization of our nation. Third, the level of immigration is too high for the country to properly digest all the immigrants, even if we had the right attitude on acculturation. Finally, there is too much emphasis on family reunification and not enough on skills and education. She feels we should continue to rescue politically persecuted refugees, but instead of summarily admitting third cousins of current alien residents, we should be encouraging the arrival of people who can contribute economically and socially to the country. She endorses the continuation of America as a land of immigrants, but immigration should be measured, legal and with greater emphasis on potential societal contributions.

- **Leitmotif.** What is the basic idea, guiding principle, or recurring theme that best describes what America stands for? A conservative might sum it up in the phrase *rugged individualism*. The individual is paramount in American philosophy, history and culture. She is certain American society is set up so that the individual is free to pray as she chooses, associate with whom she wishes, vote freely, engage in commerce and finance with maximum latitude, and express her ideas without fear of retribution. In short, she is unfettered in her pursuit of life, liberty and happiness—provided of course that she does not interfere with the corresponding rights of others.

What makes it rugged is that although the opportunities are endless and the road is open, the outcomes are never certain. They depend on the individual and, to some extent, fate. The liberal would likely identify the concept of *social justice* instead. Not daunted by the conservative's labeling of that phrase as a euphemism for socialism, he believes that America has projected—although perhaps not as strongly as it could—the idea of a socially just society, which for him means that: not only are people created equal, but society ensures that they are treated equally; neither poverty nor wealth should influence one's standing before the law; since unchecked rugged individualism inevitably leads to disparities and inequities among peoples and groups, mechanisms must be put in place to level them out; and finally not only do all people and groups enjoy equal opportunity in education, business, sports and entertainment, and politics, but the mosaic of participants in these endeavors must faithfully mirror the face of the country ethnically, racially and gender-wise. The most important words in the English language are justice, mercy and compassion.

- **Treatment of Criminals.** The liberal man sees criminal behavior as a failing of society. Conditions of poverty, discrimination or social injustice have driven an individual past the breaking point resulting in the commission of a crime intended by the perpetrator to ameliorate those circumstances. The best way to attack the crime problem, according to our liberal, is on the one hand, to alleviate the conditions that caused the criminal behavior and on the other hand, to rehabilitate the criminal through training and education that will help him to cope with society's failings. He sees mandatory stiff sentences, harsh prison conditions, and plea bargains that incarcerate people for longer than is warranted, as counterproductive and unfair to people who have fallen prey to the traps laid by an often unjust society. The conservative woman has a more simplistic view of criminal behavior. The rules are clear for everyone, she asserts, if you break them you must be punished. She has more concern with the rights of victims than the rights of criminals—especially as the latter routinely deprive the former of their right to life, liberty or happiness. She promotes vigorous police protection of the citizenry, aggressive prosecution of criminals, and long prison sentences for violent offenders. She believes that one of the prime functions of a just society is to provide maximum protection for its law abiding citizens and the swift and prolonged removal from their midst of those who disturb domestic tranquility.

- **Capital Punishment.** Given her attitude toward the treatment of criminals, it is not surprising that the conservative supports capital punishment. She believes that society has the right to exact the severest punishment on those who commit the most heinous crimes. She sees capital punishment not so much as a deterrent to future acts, but rather as a form of retribution against those who have been convicted of committing vicious, premeditated murder. She would gladly throw the switch on Osama bin Laden. But the liberal is strongly opposed to capital punishment. He feels that the practice is barbaric (state-sanctioned murder) and inconsistent with the morals of an enlightened society. He is appalled at the thought of the execution of an innocent person and argues that just as our legal system is geared (through the requirement for unanimous jury verdicts) to risk the acquittal of 10 guilty people if it will prevent the conviction of an innocent one, similarly, we must forego executing 100 people who are "obviously" guilty of capital offenses if it will avoid the killing of an innocent person. Executing Osama bin Laden will not restore to life the 3,000 innocent lives he snuffed out. Capital punishment is indeed not a deterrent and vengeance is a backward motive.

- **Gun Control.** One way to combat crime, advocates the liberal, is to take away the criminals' weapons. If strict controls were placed on the manufacture and sale of guns and rifles, it would drastically decrease the number of these weapons on the streets and reduce crime. Equally importantly, it would cut down on the number of dreadful gun incidents that occur in homes and businesses, either accidentally or in anger because a weapon was available. He points out that we license cars and drivers, marriages, and many other common activities and arrangements; we should license and strictly regulate dangerous weapons as well. Sounds good, says the conservative, but there is a dangerous flaw in the argument—namely, all studies show that the cities in America with the strictest gun control laws have the highest rates of violent crime, and that the jurisdictions that have legalized the holding of concealed guns have seen their crime rates plummet. She cites this as proof of the trite sounding phrase, "if you outlaw guns, then only the outlaws will have them." Moreover, we are granted the right to bear weapons in the Second Amendment to the Constitution, a right that cannot be taken away by well-intentioned liberals. The founders feared that an unarmed citizenry would be easy prey for a well-armed government. We would be foolish to test the theory by surrendering our weapons.

- **The Constitution.** The conservative views the Constitution in a biblical way, somewhat like an Orthodox Jew regards the Old Testament. It may not be the word of God, but it is the fundamental document, drafted by our wise and prescient founders, that established legal, political and social rules which have sustained and nurtured our nation for 220 years, that established a system of government which is the envy of and the model for the civilized world, and that is amendable, but only by a precise process that requires a broad political consensus among the populace. It is not a "living document" that grows legal limbs and hidden branches, which await discovery by modern lawyers and judges. It is the job of jurists to interpret how the original laws of the Constitution are to be applied to new and difficult legal and political challenges that emerge, not to use the Constitution or phantom clauses in it to create law from the bench. The liberal does not agree. While he acknowledges that the Constitution is an inspirational, seminal and revolutionary document that created a new kind of nation, one must recognize its limitations. First, it was written long ago and did not foresee the enormity and complexities of twenty-first century American life. Second, it is flawed by its accommodation of slavery, neglect of women's rights, and imposition of arcana like the Electoral College. It is extraordinarily helpful in providing first principles, but it also supplies hints and guides to new interpretations that arise naturally more than two centuries after its original conception. In short, its genius and value lie not in its immutability, but in its flexibility and adaptability.

- **The Origin and Nature of Rights.** Both conservatives and liberals accept that the basic political rights of all Americans are stipulated in the first ten amendments to the Constitution, the Bill of Rights. They differ in their emphasis on which of the rights enumerated therein are most important, their interpretation of the meaning and implications of those rights, exactly to whom the rights are granted—individuals or groups, and granted by whom. The liberal tends to focus on the first, fourth and eighth amendments. From those he extrapolates rights to: decent housing, a fair-paying job, freedom from the influence of religion, immunity from any intrusion by the government on any aspect of what he sees as his private life, and the right not to be treated too harshly by his government in the prosecution of crimes. The conservative's attention is directed more toward the second, fifth, ninth and tenth amendments. From these she expects the rights to: defend herself from aggression, pursue business interests and acquire property free from unwarranted government supervision or intervention, equal treatment as an individual before the law in every way, protection from an overly intrusive government that should be concerned only with the specific powers granted to it in the Constitution. Although the Constitution and the Bill of Rights speak of the "right of the people," liberals often interpret this to mean in a group sense, whereas conservatives are insistent about it meaning individual rights. And finally, the liberal sees the rights granted by the Constitution itself, and therefore by extension, by the government. Some conservatives understand the rights granted in the Constitution to be, as indicated by Mr. Jefferson in the Declaration of Independence, "endowed by their creator," that is, ultimately the rights are conferred by God. Other conservatives focus on a different Jeffersonian phrase, "consent of the governed," to conclude that the rights are granted by the people themselves.

• **American Culture.** The conservative feels a deep attachment to traditional American culture. By that she means an affinity for and an allegiance to: the British tradition of law, a Calvinist work ethic, a strong role for religion in private and public life, traditional marriage and family, pride and trust in the military, respect for private property, a limited government that is as invisible as possible to the individual, pursuit of the fine arts, literature and music of Western Civilization, and an economic and social system that is devoid of classes and in which an individual encounters a level playing field that allows her to advance as far as her talents permit. The basic tenets of the culture were established in the seventeenth and eighteenth centuries and held firm throughout the nineteenth and much of the twentieth. During that time vast waves of immigrants from Western and Eastern Europe, as well as from other parts of the world, adopted and practiced the culture as strongly as the descendants of the Mayflower did. It is a marvelous culture that has helped to sustain American democracy, prosperity and freedom. Not only should long-standing Americans not turn their backs on it, it is entirely reasonable to expect new immigrants, wherever they originate, to adopt it as fervently as their predecessors did. The liberal believes somewhat differently, namely that as America browns and its composition continues its reorientation from white to peoples of color, from Protestant and Roman Catholic to other religions, from European extraction to Asian, African and Latin American, its culture must evolve if it is to remain a viable and vibrant nation. In particular, its culture must incorporate and celebrate elements of: non-Christian religions, secular humanism, homosexual lifestyles—including marriage, forms of art, literature and music whose origins are outside the Anglo-European sphere, international law, commitment to non-violence and peaceful negotiation, the complete freedom of the individual to pursue his private interests—even if they offend his neighbor, as long as they don't harm his neighbor, and a wise and benevolent government that helps to perfect society by elevating its weakest components and by checking the excesses of corporate power. The liberal asserts that proponents of the traditional culture too easily gloss over its transparent flaws: its willingness to look the other way when black Americans were—and in some quarters still are—treated as second class citizens, its assignment of subservient roles to women, its countenance of discrimination against Jews up to the middle of the twentieth century, and its aggressive and hostile components that have caused many people around the world to hate us. The infusion into the USA of peoples of color and the different cultures they bring have changed America for the better—but not nearly enough. We must hasten the day when not only is our political system admired around the world, but so too is our culture. We can achieve that by making it more ecumenical, less business-oriented, more humanistic, less militaristic.

The earliest political memories I have are from the summer of 1953. The Rosenbergs were executed in June and the Korean War armistice was signed in July. Actually, I have listened to family stories all my life about how my parents trained me to stick out my tongue at the radio during the presidential campaign of 1948 whenever Governor Dewey was mentioned and to sputter, "Phooey on Dewey." It was thought cute, but to be honest I don't remember doing it—it was just too long ago. I recall being an attentive student in school when American history and/or government was taught but I don't really remember thinking about politics until approximately age 15, when I was a sophomore at the Bronx High School of Science in New York. It was at this time that my father's brother bought me a subscription to the New York Times. It was his bible (and would remain so for the rest of his life, which lasted until 2002).

I read the Times daily throughout high school, then college (at the City College of New York), and graduate school (at the Massachusetts Institute of Technology) and finally during my postdoctoral years at Yale University. I finally gave it up when I moved in 1969 to suburban Washington in order to assume a faculty position at the University of Maryland. Of course I replaced it with the Washington Post so I barely broke stride. In any event I was a Times devotee for nearly a decade and a half.

In all that time I don't ever recall reading any story and thinking that it was slanted, biased or other than totally objective and completely on target. Nor do I remember ever reading any column or editorial and thinking what I was reading was anything but enlightened, eminently sensible, and worthy of consideration. How could it be otherwise? The New York Times was as reliable as the Bible, probably more so.

The messages I recall receiving from the Times during those years were that: (i) retrograde southern Democrats and corporate-controlled Republicans, both of whom were bigots and reactionaries, had held the country in their iron grip for generations and were holding back progress; (ii) their grip was broken in the 1960s and the new order was ushering in a more just and humane society; (iii) the Cold War declared by Churchill was nothing more than a competition between competing ideologies as to how best to organize society and the economy, that it was not clear that we had the superior or winning position, and that we had better be careful in prosecuting this "war" as we might be the cause of a nuclear holocaust and the annihilation of the world. It was never pointed out: that Roosevelt's New Deal was implemented despite the aforementioned iron grip, nor that the Eisenhower administration made no effort to undo it; that the Soviets were as evil and murderous as the Nazis; that John Kennedy, charming and glamorous as he and his wife might be, was a womanizing, pain-pill popping, mob-acquainted lightweight, who was probably not nearly as "progressive" as they made him out to be, and may very well have been in over his head; and finally that Lyndon Johnson was a vulgar megalomaniac whose Great Society Ponzi schemes would likely bankrupt the nation when the bills came due several generations hence. They still haven't fessed up on that last one.

To be honest, I accepted every word I read in the Times as if it was from the mouth of God. In doing so I was only imitating my uncle, and just about everyone else in my family. We were immigrants and first and second generation Jewish Americans with a propensity to accept what the New York Times fed us unquestioningly. We were a classic ethnic family in the best sense: close-knit, food-oriented, raucous in our celebrations, demonstrably Jewish, ambitious, and quarrelsome about a lot of things—although mainly sports and business. However, our political worldview, on the other hand, was pretty homogeneous—across the generations. I shan't say too much about this historical and ongoing Jewish affinity for the Left; that irrefutable allegiance has been addressed by many. But I will examine later why it perseveres across the generations, as that is particularly germane to the topic of this book. Suffice it to say here that, in my New York Times phase, I was idealistic, passionate about social justice, convinced that the oligarchy that ran the country in the 1950s had to be overthrown, and deliriously happy when it was overthrown in the 1960s. I was thinking with my heart at the time—just as one would expect of a politically-minded young person.

2

Fundamental Statements of Conservative and Liberal World Views

We examined two dozen issues in the last chapter and observed that one's position on them, or most of them, or even on only a substantial number of them, more than suffice to locate an individual in the corridors of political philosophy—from ultra-conservative to ultra-liberal. The capsule summaries of the two positions on each issue provide succinct descriptions of the core positions of a liberal or conservative, but—keeping our focus on the prime purpose of the book—we must ask: where in any of the statements is the relation, implied or otherwise, of the opinion or position to the age of its adherents? What does your opinion on interpreting the Constitution have to do with how old you are? Exactly how does your opinion on the role of the judiciary correlate with the number of birthdays you have celebrated? And whether you think money is well spent or not on a smart missile system reveals precisely what about how many years it is since you graduated from high school? I could make similar statements for many of the other touchstone issues. Thus, it is not evident why your age should play a significant role in arriving at the positions you hold on these issues—regardless of whether those positions are on the Left or Right.

The touchstone issues are an excellent means to identify whether you are liberal or conservative. They are less helpful in determining why. For that we must begin to investigate more systematically the underlying philosophy or belief system that leads one to adopt consistently liberal or conservative positions on the touchstone issues. We will do that in this chapter in two ways. First, we shall write down the classic dictionary definitions of the words *liberalism* and *conservatism*. When you see the definitions you'll nod your head and say, "Yea, that about sums it up." But after a few moments thought you'll realize that while the definitions faithfully capture a few of the critical principles undergirding the two isms, they are too general and unspecific to enable us to make much progress toward our goal of correlating those principles with the age of their adherents. The second step in this chapter is therefore to provide some anchors for the general definitions and then to refine and embellish them in relation to those anchors. We will specify five such anchors and then develop five corresponding fundamental definitions—I prefer to call them *world views*—of liberalism and conservatism. As we shall see, those statements will get us closer to out goal, but not quite there. We'll move another step closer in the next chapter as we reformulate the world views into five categories that will serve as compartments for the two dozen touchstones issues.

But before we plough into that, I want to present an important diversion. Recall that the first part of this book is entitled, "The Differences between Liberals and Conservatives." The contents of Chapter 1 make it abundantly clear that those differences are substantial indeed. The differences are wide, they occur across the spectrum of human endeavor: politics, finance, defense, diplomacy, medicine, race, religion, trade, jurisprudence, the environment, immigration, societal organization, culture, crime, human rights, law, and more. And the differences are deep in that the distance between the stances are in many instances seemingly irreconcilable, the opinions are held with great passion, and each side is not only firmly convinced of the wisdom of its position, but also of the sheer stupidity, ignorance and danger of the other side's convictions.

One is left aghast; wondering if there is indeed any common ground. Surely there must be. Despite the depth and breadth of the chasm between the opinions, generally liberals and conservatives are not beating up or killing each other. For the most part, the debate, while heated, has remained civilized. This reflects on the one hand the long tradition of tolerance that characterizes America. But it also reflects the fact that indeed there is some common ground. And for later purposes, I would like to identify that common ground more specifically. So here comes my roster of the issues that I see constituting the common ground, that is, the issues on which both liberal and conservative Americans see eye-to-eye or hold the same values. I will present this roster of one dozen points of commonality like I did the two dozen touchstone issues—namely, state the issue and in a few sentences establish the key points and ideas around which the agreement occurs. The list is surprisingly extensive—and probably no more exhaustive than the roster of differences in Chapter 1. My purpose in including it here—aside from the fact that I will make some use of it later—is to cheer you up gentle reader. For, when you read a polemical book that espouses one side or the other of the political discourse that splits the nation, the natural end result is anger or rage. But in reading my (at least thus far) neutral presentation, a more likely result could be sadness or even despair at the irreconcilable chasm. The forthcoming list should show you that it's not as bad as it seems. There is still some pretty strong glue holding the republic together.

Unlike the list in Chapter 1, the order of the items in this list holds some significance. I tried to organize the list by placing at its head those ideas that I see as most important and/or most clearly commonly held. Here's a table listing the items, after which come the descriptions.

Things that liberals and conservatives generally agree upon
Patriotism/Love of Country
Respect for the Law
Devotion to Family
Optimism/Faith in America
Prosperity/Economic Progress
Love thy Neighbor
Tolerance
Civilian Control of the Military
Don't Tread on Me
Your Home is Your Castle
Veneration of Education
Leisure

- **Patriotism/Love of Country.** First and foremost, I believe that the vast majority of Americans, independent of their political stripes, love their country. We may differ on what aspects of the nation best reflect its ideals and how to improve those parts that don't, but we are in general agreement that the creation of the United States was a step forward in human history, that the US has been a beacon of liberty to the world, and that we are blessed and thankful to be living in the land of the free and the home of the brave.

- **Respect for the Law.** We take pride in the fact that we live in a society that is governed according to the rule of law. Sometimes our interpretations of the law may differ, but the overwhelming majority of Americans reveres our Constitutional government, respects and abides by its laws, aspires to an ideal in which all citizens have equal legal rights and looks with disfavor upon attempts by individuals or groups to circumvent the law.

- **Devotion to Family.** Even those who seek to redefine the family preach that strong family life is important for the health and welfare of society. And for those whose understanding of the word is the traditional one, it goes without saying that their allegiance to family is unwavering. Strong, stable family units are seen by all as the key component that gives strength and vitality to American communities. Americans of all political persuasions persistently rank the family as one of, if not the most important part of their lives. Devotion between family members is rarely fractured by political differences.

- **Optimism/Faith in America.** Americans are characteristically an optimistic people. They are happy to be American citizens and they are confident that the country will find ways to solve its problems, make progress in meeting its challenges and continue to serve as a positive example to the world. That optimism runs deep regardless of political persuasion.

- **Prosperity/Economic Progress.** Americans work hard, admire and seek to emulate those who prosper, are exceedingly charitable toward those who are less successful, and trust that the great economic engine that drives our economy will sustain its momentum. They may differ on the need for wealth distribution, but most see no great virtue in poverty and avidly pursue jobs, careers and work assignments that have the capability to propel them upward economically.

- **Love thy Neighbor.** Americans believe strongly in solid neighborhoods and they value highly a good neighbor. The neighbor's political proclivities are not nearly as important as his willingness to pitch in, strengthen the neighborhood, help to promote good schools and keep an eye on your house when you are away. The commitment to neighborhood in cities, suburbs and even rural areas is strong among all Americans, independent of their political views.

- **Tolerance.** We are a tolerant nation. It's codified in our founding documents and is fundamental to whom we are as a people. The tolerance extends to religion, culture and of course politics. It is sometimes difficult for us as we hold strong opinions that often don't jibe well. But both Left and Right are agreed that if we cease to be tolerant of our fellow citizens, then that is the beginning of the end of the American way of life.

- **Civilian Control of the Military.** This notion has been so deeply embedded in our fiber as a people that we don't even really think about it. But it was a unique idea in the world when we dreamed it up. And fortunately, Sinclair Lewis not withstanding, it has never been doubted. There is no quarrel between Left and Right at all on this issue.

- **Don't Tread on Me.** This is more than a patriotic slogan. It is also deeply ingrained in us as a people. We are tolerant, good neighbors and optimistic, but we are also fiercely independent and protective of our turf. We may have differences about how to prosecute the war against radical Islam, but I warrant there are no more than a handful of Americans who do not yearn for Osama's scalp. That monster underestimated the ferocity of our response when he trod on us.

- **Your Home is Your Castle.** Americans love and prize their homes. The percentage of our population that owns one exceeds that of other nations. We fix them up, decorate them with pride, tend our gardens and nurture our children in them. This is true without regard to political world view. We even factor this tendency into our tax laws. The goal of a decent, comfortable and private home is common to all political points of view.

- **Veneration of Education.** Americans are debating whether the classic government-run public school systems are failing our children. But we are not questioning the importance of the debate. Namely, all Americans seek (for themselves and their children) a good education, take pride in our institutions of higher learning to which the world's students flock, and generally assume that there is no such thing as too much education. We may differ on what and how to teach, but we are agreed that a quality education should be available to us all.

- **Leisure.** Americans work hard, very hard. But they play hard too. The wide variety of diversions in the form of sports, entertainment, parks, shopping venues, and the other myriad ways in which we fill our non-work time—with family and friends—is valued by all Americans. Sometimes we actually organize or frequent clubs that match our political tastes, but that is a small portion of the leisure pie. Generally, we treasure the tremendous variety of leisure activities available to us all.

There, do you feel better now? The USA is not coming apart at the seams. There are actually a host of values that we agree on. But of course there are also plenty on which we don't. And while it is the latter that we are focused on in this book, we should not lose sight of the former. It will help us to be optimistic that however the political argument progresses, whether one side or the other emerges triumphant or we remain relatively deadlocked, the common ground will keep us strong. And we must also remember our purpose here—namely, to consider the question: does age play a role in the formation of our views in the areas that are not part of the common ground?

Having concluded this pleasant diversion into areas of common ground, we resume the examination of our differences. As we've said, the touchstone issues reveal that the differences are wide and deep. We have also noted that the issues cut a wide swath across the scope of human endeavor: politics, finance, defense, diplomacy, medicine, race, religion, trade, jurisprudence, the environment, immigration, societal organization, culture, crime, human rights, and law. Nevertheless, there is a remarkable consistency in the way people line up. Generally, conservatives take the side I have identified as the conservative position in most, if not all, of the issues, whereas liberals take the opposite side just as often. Why do our birds of a political feather flock so closely together? Why isn't there more of a mix-and-match phenomenon? What basic philosophy, fundamental principles, or core beliefs underlie the liberal's world view so much so that he—subscribing to that philosophy, those principles or beliefs—is inexorably drawn to the positions labeled as liberal on these 24 very distinct issues? Ditto for conservatives. What about her basic philosophy, fundamental principles or core beliefs account for her adopting the conservative positions with such frequency? Can we identify that philosophy? Can we enumerate those principles and beliefs?

In order to answer those questions, we start with dictionary definitions of the terms, liberalism and conservatism. Which dictionary shall we pull from? In fact it does not matter much. The Webster's Seventh New Collegiate Dictionary (1972) in my bookcase says essentially the same thing that one finds on Merriam-Webster Online (see www.webster.com). Here are the words:

> **Liberalism. A political philosophy based on belief in progress, the essential goodness of man, and the autonomy of the individual.**

> **Conservatism. A political philosophy based on tradition and social stability, stressing established institutions, and preferring gradual development to abrupt change.**

No one could misread the essential flavor of these short definitions, but at the same time they are a little too vanilla to accommodate our purpose in this book. Moreover, they are vague enough to be misleading in exactly the way that I indicated in the opening paragraph of Chapter 1. Namely, the Bush Administration, which is viewed as rather conservative, has advocated immigration policies that many would view as socially destabilizing; has revamped federal agencies in a way that has not been done in more than 60 years; and has embarked on a course of action in the Middle East (and elsewhere) that would not exactly avoid "abrupt change." On the other hand, leading liberals in Washington are vehemently opposed to new (dare I say progressive) ideas like privatization of Social Security or school vouchers; say things about members of the Bush Administration that cause one to doubt their fundamental belief in the goodness of man; and advocate speech codes that hardly advance the autonomy of any individual. Actually, I have a minor quibble with the final liberal principle, *autonomy of the individual*. For liberals today, it generally refers to the individual's autonomy from the government in moral matters, but that autonomy is suspended in economic matters. More on that will emerge in later discussion. For now, let us continue by noting that these definitions are not nearly specific enough to afford any kind of correlation with age. Despite the fact that they look reasonable and have a ring of accuracy, they just will not suffice for our purposes. They are not definitive enough to help us determine why a person is liberal or conservative, or why that should have anything to do with the person's age.

Thus we will try to deepen the definitions somewhat. We'll do that by specifying what I like to think of as *anchors*. Then we shall reformulate the definitions by using the anchors to render more concrete or specific the very general principles in the definitions as originally stated. The five anchors are: human perfectibility, religion, protection, preservation/progress, and business/wealth. What they will be anchored to is one or more of the phrases enumerated in the definitions of the two terms, liberalism and conservatism. Here are the anchored definitions.

1. **Human Perfectibility or the Nature of Man.** We first try to anchor our basic dictionary definitions by focusing on the fundamental nature of man—as referred to in the phrase "essential goodness of man" that appears in the definition of liberalism. The liberal adherent takes that idea as absolutely indisputable. Namely, man is intrinsically a good creature whose imperfections—which manifest themselves in the form of violence, greed, promiscuity, and so on—are not due to his underlying nature, but are always attributable to a fault in the arrangement of soci-

ety—whether legal, cultural or economic—that has caused the individual to deviate from his inherent good nature. Thus man engages in crime not because he is evil, but because of economic injustice. He is lustful and promiscuous because Victorian-style repression confines him to a sexual straight jacket out of which he inevitably bursts. He commits violent acts if he is unable to obtain proper treatment to control temporary violent urges—and of course if we had a decent universal health care system, this would not happen. If impediments like social and economic injustice, racial and ethnic prejudice, and artificial constraints on individual freedom of expression were removed, then man's intrinsic goodness would elevate society to a higher level of equality and tranquility.

The contrary point of view, adopted by conservatives, is that human beings are flawed creatures, who are incapable of achieving perfection, no matter how the political or social world around them is organized. It's not that woman is inherently bad or evil, it's just that life is incredibly complex and unpredictable, human impulses are often selfish and parochial, and in the general scope of things, when faced with a crisis that requires a good decision—or a decision to do good—it's pretty much of a crap shoot as to which side any particular individual is liable to come down on. The best we can hope for is that people will come to understand that actions, which benefit the most people, are also most likely to benefit the individual—or her family, clan, neighborhood, country—and so she will be moved by self-interest toward doing the right thing. Over time traditions are built up that encourage good behavior. These salutary traditions emanate from religious morals, ethical principles and time-tested legal and social rules and organizations. These foundational tools, not mankind's perfect or perfectible nature, are what guarantee a fair and orderly society. It is foolhardy to rely on the innate goodness of human beings. We should rely instead on classic and time-tested social institutions to tame the human beast, albeit of course not to cage her.

We can sum up these contrasting points of view in our first anchored definition—which happens to coincide with the sample definition given in Chapter 1.

A liberal is someone who believes in the perfectibility of man and that society must therefore be structured so as to foster the best pos-

sibility of man advancing toward that state of perfection; whereas a conservative accepts that woman is inherently flawed, and so society must be arranged so as to minimize the mistakes she can make and the damage she can wreak.

2. **Religion or the Nature of God.** This time we look in the original definitions to the words "tradition" and "established institutions" to find our second anchor. The conservative woman sees the long and hallowed Judeo-Christian religious structures as prime examples of such traditions and established institutions. She believes that the morals that have guided our nation's destiny are derived from these religions, and that many of the legal precepts that are established in our founding documents (viz., the Constitution, the Declaration of Independence, the Bill of Rights, and the Federalist Papers) have their origin in the biblical sources of these two great religions. She thinks that a functioning democracy requires a virtuous citizenry whose morals are grounded in religious faith, and failing same, their democracy is liable to degenerate into tyranny or anarchy.

    The liberal agrees that democracy requires a virtuous citizenry, but he does not accept that the moral foundation must be found in Christianity or Judaism. A strong foundation can be built around people who derive their virtue from their commitment to Islam, Buddhism, other religions, or indeed to other ethical belief systems divorced from organized religion. Deists, agnostics and even atheists may qualify. What matters is not how long your "church" has been around, or how large its membership is, or whether it traces its roots to Europe in the last two millennia, but rather whether it animates its devotees to virtuous behavior, respect for the rule of law and a forward looking vision of human progress. A sole reliance on religious tradition to ensure virtue is unnecessary, and perhaps unwise, especially if we acknowledge the myriad atrocities committed over the millennia in the name of religion—an unfortunate practice, which continues to this day, even if the religion in whose name the atrocities are committed has changed. We sum up this discourse in the second anchored definition.

    A conservative believes that a just society is impossible unless the people have strong morals and that the morals must derive their standing from deep religious principles and faith; whereas a liberal, while acknowledging that faith may be important to the individual,

believes that state-sanctioned religion is a danger that our founders sought to protect us from, and a just society is the result of virtuous citizens acting with the help of a benevolent government.

3. **Protection or the Nature of Government.** Now we look to the phrase "social stability" for our third anchor. The liberal surveys the history of man and sees the average fellow unmercifully oppressed by marauding armies, unscrupulous landowners, greedy merchants, unforgiving clergymen, bigoted ethnic group leaders, and corporate robber barons. To whom is the poor fellow to turn for protection? The liberal believes it is the job of a wise and benevolent, and yes powerful government to protect the little guy. The government achieves this objective by leveling all playing fields and erecting legal barriers against the exploitation of the few and the weak by the many and the strong. It is wonderful to welcome to our shores the poor huddled masses, but they are going to get their fannies kicked if the government doesn't continue to look out for them after they get here. And even for those who were already here, too often they are afflicted by illness, a lousy upbringing, rotten neighborhoods, outmoded job skills and hundreds of other misfortunes not of their own making. In an enlightened country like the United States, they should be protected from their natural predators (landlords, bosses, professionals, e.g.). No one else can provide this protection like the government can.

The conservative also takes a long view. But she observes a sorry history of tyranny and terror perpetrated by kings and commissars, princes and praetorians, Caesars and czars and every other manner of dictatorial ruler. That is, she sees the greatest threat to the average guy coming not from the quarters that the liberal fears, but from the government. She gives thanks that our forefathers invented a system in which the average citizen is protected by the legal structure of the government from the power of the government. In the long history of the world—to this day—it is a citizen's government that poses the greatest threat to her life, liberty and happiness. The genius of the founders was that they recognized this fact and sought to do something about it. We would be extremely foolish to lose sight of it a mere two and one-quarter centuries later. Our summation this time leads to the following definition.

A liberal believes it is the fundamental responsibility of the government to protect him from the rapacious appetite of organized

groups that seek to amass power at the expense of the common man—examples being corporations or conglomerations of business entities, religious movements, and ethnic alliances; whereas a conservative relies on the legal and cultural foundations of society to protect her from the government which, with its natural powers to tax, conscript, confiscate property, and incarcerate, always poses the greatest threat to the liberty and prosperity of the individual.

4. **Preservation vs. Progress or the Nature of Time.** In this fourth reformulation we take our cue from three expressions in the original definitions: progress, gradual development and abrupt change. Also we continue to alternate the order of presentation, so this time the conservative lady goes first. While she acknowledges that change is inevitable, and that many changes that sweep over our lives improve them (e.g., better surgical procedures, improved transportation, and new technological goodies), she avers that many changes also alter our lives for the worse (e.g., traffic congestion, processed foods, nuclear missiles). More importantly, she warns that in our pall-mall rush to introduce progressive new ideas and institutions, we often fail to appreciate how established institutions and ideas have formed the bed rock of our civilization for generations. The classic political principles of our founders, the religion of our ancestors, the cultural traditions of our forbearers, these are the true foundations of our society. We should revere and preserve them. They give us strength and inspiration. We should discard no more than tiny pieces of them and even then only with the greatest caution. We can welcome new ideas and cultures, but we should graft them onto our basic institutions, not treat them as substitutes for those institutions.

You're going overboard says the liberal. Our traditions are often a straight-jacket, not an inspiration. Just because something is old does not necessarily mean that it is good. The ideas and ideals laid down by our ancestors were suitable for their times, they may not be for ours. The liberal is not necessarily anxious to automatically throw away all old things, but he believes fervently that organisms that don't progress, that try to stand pat, will inevitably stagnate and die. He chastises conservatives on this point when he observes that this is precisely the attitude conservatives usually adopt concerning business—that is, companies that stand pat are always blown away by those that are dynamic, progressive and innovative. So too for societies. America is fortunate that its culture is continually replenished by that of its new immigrants. We should embrace those opportunities, progress with the times, and be receptive to new peoples and practices that will help to enrich our country's culture. The fourth discussion is then summarized in the following definition.

A conservative is one who believes that ideas and institutions that have withstood the test of time, that are forces for good in society, and that promote unity, shared history and common values among the people should be honored, defended and preserved, and changes to them should be contemplated with extreme caution; whereas a liberal believes that only dynamic, adaptable societies that embrace and encourage change can prosper and survive, and that swift progress, in all aspects of human endeavor, is what keeps a society alive and vibrant.

5.   **Business and Wealth or the Nature of the Economy.** The fifth and final reformulation actually does not use any of the phrases or expressions in the original definition for inspiration. Yet, so much of the division between liberals and conservatives is grounded in the financial realm that we would be remiss not to include a reformulated definition based on that domain. So here goes. This time the liberal is first and he asserts that, although he rejects the socialist idea that all property and business should belong to the State, he also rejects its logical opposite—namely, that government should remain completely aloof from the nation's economy, trusting that a reliance on free markets will guarantee the greatest good for the largest number. In fact he believes the history of unfettered free market capitalism teaches that its practice leads instead to a small percentage of fabulously wealthy individuals who tyrannize and exploit the vast majority of lowly paid working people. Those who are most agile, or perhaps most ruthless, will inevitably concentrate power in their own hands and will inexorably be drawn to exercise it for their own betterment, irrespective of the plight of their workers. The government must intervene in the process, to whatever degree is required, in order to overcome such blatant unfairness.

Puleez, responds the conservative. The market is far better at distributing opportunity and wealth than any self-indulgent bureaucrat. An economy in a country as large and complex as the United states requires millions and millions of independent decisions every day by entrepreneurs, manufacturers, workers, managers, suppliers, and distributors; decisions about prices, wages, allocations, distribution routes, insurance, and much more. It is impossible, truly impossible, for a centralized bureaucracy to make these decisions simultaneously and continuously in all economic sectors. Moreover, if they do, their collectivist actions must inevitably, as F. Hayek asserted in *The Road to Serfdom*, lead to tyranny as they decide who benefits at who's expense, and the like. The market is infinitely wiser and more impartial at effecting such decisions. Indeed, it may be that the risks inherent in a free market system for a single individual are not insignificant, and some individuals do not prosper, but the history of the twentieth century has proven beyond any doubt that free markets, not government planning, guarantee the greatest good for the largest number. We summarize the discussion in the final anchored definition.

The liberal is deeply suspicious of unchecked free market capitalism, believing that its fierce competition results in grievous inequities in the wealth of the citizenry, and thus demands that these inequities be smoothed out by an engaged federal government empowered to monitor, adjust, influence and reorder the country's business and financial structures in order to create a more equitable distribution of wealth; whereas the conservative believes that free market capitalism is what accounts for the great wealth of our country, and that all the collectivist (socialist-leaning) government programs that were enacted in the twentieth century have been colossal failures, which punish success, discourage industriousness, encourage laziness and fraud, and generally interfere in the smooth functioning of the market economy.

We have formulated some core belief statements, or world views, subscription to which account for the attitudes liberals ands conservatives adopt on the touchstone issues. We first stated them very simply in the basic definitions of liberalism and conservatism set down at the outset of this chapter. Then we supplied somewhat more complicated, in-depth formulations in the five world views statements that we developed out of the basic definitions. From the latter—especially if taken in totality—we obtain a rather vivid portrait of the thinking that lies at the foundation of a conservative or liberal belief system.

But, repeating our oft-stated query, do these formulations lend themselves to an examination of a correlation between the belief systems and age? The answer: we're moving in the right direction, but we're not quite there yet. You can begin to see places in the five world view statements where it is reasonable to posit a correlation to age. For example, in the first one, built around perfectibility, you might assert that the liberal position is idealistic, while the conservative position is cynical. Certainly idealism is a quality more often associated with youth than old age, and the reverse is true for cynicism. Looking next at the second statement, concerned with religion, it is plausible to claim that religious orientation tends to be more prevalent among older people than among youth. And finally, working with the fourth statement, a reasonable comment would be that respect for tradition often comes with maturity, while dynamism is usually manifested by the young. Well these assertions are a bit glib and the associations are rather tenuous, but—like I said—we're moving in the right direction. We'll move further along in the next chapter when we develop more embracing categories, or compartments, that combine views of the world with what I will call *mental frameworks*. We shall locate the touchstone issues within these compartments and then in Part II conduct an analysis of the role of age in relation to them.

The next major political memory that I have, after 1953, is of the capture and trial of Adolph Eichmann in 1960-61. It's not that I wasn't politically aware during the 1950s—especially after I began my addiction to the New York Times—it's just that nothing that happened gripped me personally until the Eichmann affair. In retrospect the 1950s were a wonderful time to come of age in America. Post-War American life was flourishing, educational and career opportunities were opening everywhere, Americans were becoming suburbanized and motorized. Although I remember diving under my school desk (to avoid Soviet H-bombs, what a joke!), the national trauma over Sputnik, and the stirrings of widespread discontent at the ongoing shame of segregation, I remember more vividly the kindly and reassuring face of Ike, Ozzie and Harriett's happy home and Don Larsen's perfect game.

The optimism for the future and the zest for life that I felt as a teenager at the end of that decade were jarred when I came face to face with the unspeakable evil and horror of Adolph Eichmann and what he signified. Like many young American Jews I was vaguely aware that a great tragedy had befallen my people two decades earlier in Europe, but it was on the periphery of my consciousness. Reading the New York Times reports of Eichmann's trial, I could no longer confine those events to the periphery of my consciousness. The Israelis' capture of Eich-

mann was inspiring, the unfolding story of Nazi brutality and depravity was beyond belief, and the testimony of the survivors was gut-wrenching. As it has done for many Jews in the second half of the twentieth century, the revelation of the Holocaust raised powerful emotions in me that have endured all my life. Moreover, many ideas and attitudes that crystallized for me as a consequence of Eichmann's trial are with me still. To cite a few: There is evil in the world and pretending that it does not exist only abets its power; to occupy a weak position in relation to one's enemies invites not mercy, but slaughter; appeasement is ALWAYS the height of folly and brings about the exact event one sought to avoid by trying to appease the aggressor; Israelis are a gutsy bunch of people who, if not a new kind of Jew, are certainly different from any seen for many centuries.

However, in addition to these wise conclusions that I drew from observing the Eichmann affair, I also reached two conclusions which, in retrospect, were incorrect; and also there was another important deduction that I was unable to make at the time. My incorrect conclusions were the following. First, I believed, since the New York Times told me so, that Nazism was a tyranny of the Right, not at all related to Soviet Communism on the Left, whereas of course they were two sides of the same wretched coin—collectivist, brutal, and evil totalitarian systems that were equally antithetical to everything symbolized by the United States. Second, I thought at the time that the United Nations, not Israel, would have been a more appropriate venue for Eichmann's prosecution since his and the Nazis' crimes were against "all humanity." It was not evident only 15 years after its founding that the U.N. would degenerate into the corrupt and ineffective organization it has become. And no one, save perhaps Hitler himself, was more deserving to meet justice at Jewish hands than Eichmann.

The deduction I failed to make was to appreciate the complicit role played by Western Civilization in the Holocaust. This is a difficult issue for me. As it should be clear already to the reader, I love my country and am proud of its historic achievements. But it is not perfect. Despite definitive knowledge of the Nazi plan to exterminate the Jews of Europe—indeed the world, the US government did precious little to prevent the heinous crimes by which the Germans implemented their plan. Other warts we cannot deny: the indelible abomination of slavery, which still stains our moral standing; the less than compassionate treatment of American Indians in the eighteenth and nineteenth centuries; and the cruel internment of Japanese American citizens during WWII are also blots on our ledger. But America has made great efforts to atone for these past misdeeds. And I believe that through its strong support of Israel, its construction and *patronage of the National Holocaust Museum, the incredibly hospitable home it has provided to its Jewish citizens, and the prosecution of Nazi war criminals and reconstitution of the German nation as a peaceful member of the community of nations, America has atoned for its failure to do what it could have done 65 years ago to rescue European Jewry. I am considerably less impressed by the atonement efforts of France and a few other European nations—whose complicity was far worse.*

3

Compartmentalizing the Issues

In the last chapter we looked at dictionary definitions of the terms liberal and conservative, and then we "anchored" those definitions by tying them to five different concepts around which one could construct a view of how the world works. In each case we saw that liberals and conservatives had very different views of how the world works—regardless of the way it is anchored. Moreover, we began to see connections between age and some of the world views. But not every view supports such a connection. In particular, consider the third and fifth—namely, who protects whom from what, and how do we organize our economy? If you look closely at the discussion of the former in Chapter 2, you will see that one's world view in that instance depends heavily on one's historical perspective. One looks back through time, decides who has been oppressing whom for the most part, and then forms an opinion on the societal structure best designed to minimize, or even eliminate that oppression. It is not at all evident what, if anything, that opinion should have to do with the age of its adherent. Next, let's observe that how you would like the economy structured is largely a function of your faith in free markets. The more you trust them, the more conservative you will lean; the less you trust them, then it's toward liberal that you will list. But your attitude in this regard has no obvious tie to your age. It more than likely depends on what you learned in school, observed at home or experienced on your own in the business world.

So although one's stance on the five world views pins down rather strongly one's position in the liberal versus conservative universe, the correlation to age is not strong. Therefore, we need to move beyond them in order to correlate political philosophy with age. Thus we are going to reformulate again.

The world views arose out of the original dictionary definitions. Instead, I want to take as motivation the touchstone issues, which we have seen really determine, even if they do not define, the liberal and conservative positions in American life. The goal is to establish a set of categories, which will turn out to be a combination of world views and mental frameworks, into which we can compartmentalize the touchstone issues. Moreover, these categories or compartments, unlike the pure world views, or the touchstone issues themselves, will lend themselves to a correlation with age. As I said, the compartments—again five in number—are of two varieties, world views and mental frameworks. The distinction between the two is as follows. A world view is external to the individual; it is how a person sees the world through a prism such as religion or financial matters or government. Mental frameworks are internal, somewhat like personality traits, for example, whether a person is intrinsically optimistic, fatalistic, or pacifistic. The world view concept was explored in Chapter 2, but let us be more specific now about mental frameworks. As I said, they can be likened to a personality trait, but of a specific kind. I certainly don't mean personality traits like: gregariousness vs. shyness, or stinginess vs. generosity. Those are ingrained traits, which likely remain unchanged throughout life. I am thinking more along the lines of optimist vs. pessimist, or realist vs. dreamer. These are traits or attitudes that can change as life goes on—perhaps more than once. That said, here are the five compartments that we will use throughout the book to study the relationship between political philosophy and age.

How you view   A. The Role of the Government in the Country,
                B. The Role of the USA in the World;
Whether your mental framework is more accurately described as
                C. Absolutist or Relativist,
                D. Opportunist or Egalitarian,
                E. Pragmatist/Realist or Idealist/Utopian.

We defer to Part II the use of these five compartments to study how well or how poorly political stance correlates with age. In the remainder of this first part we shall do two things with the compartments. In this chapter we examine each of them, show that—like the touchstone issues in Chapter 1 and the world views in Chapter 2—there are very well-defined and distinct positions that liberals and conservatives occupy in each compartment. In the next chapter, we perform the important task of fitting the touchstone issues into the compartments. We will conclude this chapter with some observations on consistency and predictability. Those observations will support the following two assertions. First, the places occupied in the various compartments by a conservative lady, in relation to the world views in Chapter 2, are consistent; namely, she experiences no internal conflict between her opinions on multiple issues—ditto for the liberal gentleman. Second, if a fellow identifies himself as liberal, you can predict with great confidence where he stands in any compartment—and ditto for the conservative gal.

In our forthcoming examination of the compartments we continue with the alternating style adopted earlier. Recall that the liberal guy went first in describing the touchstone issues in Chapter 1. He went first again in describing the world views in Chapter 2, but that was only because there was an even number of issues. Since there were an odd number of world views, the conservative gal gets to go first this time.

A. The Role of the Government in the Country

Both conservatives and liberals attach great importance to the role that government, especially the federal government, should play in the affairs of the nation. But they differ sharply on the exact nature of that role. A conservative believes that the government's primary duties are to: ensure that the country is governed according to the rule of law as established in the Constitution; defend the citizens from foreign enemies; protect the sanctity of private property; ensure that the currency is sound; guarantee that the liberty of individuals is not infringed upon; and in general carry out the limited set of duties assigned to it in the Constitution. But she sees the roles and responsibilities the feds have taken on far surpassing those enumerated above. In fact, she shudders with horror when contemplating the behemoth that the federal government has become, vastly out of line with the intentions of the founders. Today, the federal government plays a massive and often disruptive role in education, health, housing, welfare, food and drug regulation, land use, transportation, intrastate finance, business (small and large), local law enforcement, environmental issues, and numerous other arenas of American life, all with precious little justification to be found for any of it in the Constitution. All three branches of the government are complicit in this power grab. Not that "the people" are innocent in this tragedy. Segments of society clamor for government programs and resources to benefit that segment, often oblivious to the fact that competing segments are doing likewise. Eventually we have benignly-intentioned but massive intervention by the government in almost all aspects of society. The conservative lady worries that the benign intentions will lead to tyrannical outcomes as the government expands its intrusive, often chaotic, usually inefficient, and eventually counterproductive influence into corners of American life that are completely beyond the jurisdiction assigned to it by the Constitution.

In pursuing these inappropriate activities, the government frequently shirks the important duties it is required to perform. It should ensure that all citizens enjoy equal rights before the law, not anoint special groups with favored legal status. It should defend our countrymen and our borders from foreigners (including illegal aliens) who too easily cross our borders and then find succor from government officials who grant them legal documents (e.g. driver's licenses), declare that they are entitled to the same services as citizens and pontificate that aliens are performing a valuable service by taking jobs that citizens shun. It should keep the currency strong rather than weaken it with profligate spending that runs up outrageous deficits, which it attempts to correct by imposing high taxes that further cripple the economy. The conservative believes that the proper responsibility of the government, aside from the duties very precisely specified in the Constitution, is to "provide for the common defense and protect the general welfare" in the classic, limited sense that our founders intended, not in the unlimited, overbearing, disruptive and dangerous manner that has become common today.

When a conservative reviews the history of our country and its people, and contemplates the role of government, the things she is most proud of are: its initial acts during the Revolutionary era that established a remarkable new kind of political arrangement, which survives and inspires to this day; the bold way it expanded our frontiers and facilitated property ownership and business activities that led to the freest and most prosperous nation in the history of the world; its ability to correct flaws and injustices, e.g. by abolishing slavery, advancing the rights of women, and compensating Native Americans and Japanese Americans for past grievances; its heroic role in leading the civilized world in the destruction of Nazism and Communism, and its willingness to do it again against Radical Islam; and welcoming, assisting and assimilating generations of legal immigrants, thereby swelling the ranks of free and productive American citizens. These are the achievements of our country and its government that make us unique and great. Not government programs and agencies like: Head Start, No Child Left Behind, Social Security, Medicare and Medicaid, Smart Growth, Volunteers for America, the EPA, etc., etc. These programs help some people, but at great cost—and not just financial cost, but also in the disruption to the republic caused by assigning tasks to the government that properly belong elsewhere. We have reached the stage where it is virtually treasonous to suggest that programs like Social Security or Medicare might be better, more efficiently and cost effectively performed by the market. In rare moments she ponders the feasibility of dismantling the government leviathan and devolving its programs to the private sector. This would require a revolutionary reorientation in public attitude, but if it happened, thinks our conservative lady, the government could then focus more diligently on its proper, assigned roles.

There is very little in the previous discussion with which a liberal would agree. He believes it is exactly the country's willingness to empower the government to correct wrongs and imperfections in society that has made our country so great. He believes that the laissez-faire doctrines of the nineteenth century led to robber barons, great wealth for a small number of individuals and families, and a grinding, dehumanizing poverty of body and spirit for everyone else, that is, for laborers, farmers, shopkeepers, and office and factory workers who constituted the insignificant cogs of the industrial revolution. It was only with the advent of muckraking efforts by social reformers a century ago that working conditions and public attitudes began to change. The last straw in unbridled capitalism was the excesses of the early twentieth century that led to the Great Depression, and thence to government intervention, which resulted in the widespread prosperity that we enjoy today—although there are still far too many imbalances in wealth and power that remain to be corrected. If not for the New Deal of Roosevelt and the Great Society of Lyndon Johnson, America would be a land of much greater inequities, a country whose profile would be more reminiscent of America in 1890 than it looks today.

And so the liberal sees a very intensive and extensive role for government in the workings of modern American society. He interprets the general welfare clause much more expansively than the conservative view indicated above. In particular, he sees an America in which, were it stripped of Social Security, Medicare and all the other items in the list above, would be laden with a surfeit of poor and sick elderly, exploited laborers, peoples of color held down by an oppressive WASP hegemony, women with limited opportunities, and vast deficiencies in educational, career and business opportunities for those who lacked access to the corridors of power in the country. While a harsh view, he does not necessarily ascribe the motives of the power brokers to intrinsic evil, it's just the nature of the world and of capitalism—the rich get richer, and the strong get stronger, unless there is a force to countermand it. That force is the U. S. Government.

When the liberal ponders the long sweep of U.S. history, he is ashamed by the institution of slavery, furious at what he sees as the second-class status to which women were consigned, angry at the exploitation of undocumented Hispanic workers, incredulous at the ongoing oppression of the gay community, and finally distrustful of the captains of industry who conspire to keep wages low, outsource jobs overseas, and keep huge percentages of their company's profits for themselves through unscrupulous stock options and other financial legerdemain. He is most proud of America when it overcomes these blots on its history and better lives up to the ideal enunciated by Jefferson that all "men" are created equal. The long history of civilization shows that the average little guy cannot overcome his oppressed state on his own. It was the genius of America to set up a powerful and enlightened government that could reverse this awful trend. It is a difficult assignment. It requires the full engagement of government. If we support and empower the government, we can fulfill our destiny, which is to achieve complete freedom and equality for all our people.

B. The Role of the USA in the World

This compartment differs from the previous in the following respect. The discussion there identifying the liberal and conservative corners of the compartment would have likely been as appropriate 50 years ago as it is today. The liberal and conservative views of the role of government are largely unchanged for at least half a century, perhaps as much as a century. On the contrary, their respective views of the role of the USA in the world have definitely undergone significant movement during that time span. A rather oversimplified description of that shift would assert that in the early and middle twentieth century, liberals were internationalists and conservatives were isolationists, whereas today the roles are reversed. Indeed, Wilsonian liberals enthusiastically entered World War I in order to "make the world safe for democracy." Liberals flocked to Spain in the 1930s to fight fascism and then led the great struggle to defeat Nazi Germany. Truman took us into the Korean War, John Kennedy risked a nuclear confrontation to evict Soviet missiles from Cuba, and Lyndon Johnson and his ultra-liberal administration fought communism in Vietnam. During this extended period, the mantra of Taft and other conservatives called for us to mind our own international business and let the bloodthirsty tyrants of the world beat each other up. Vietnam cured the liberals of their aggressive internationalism—witness the pacifism of George McGovern and Jimmy Carter. On the other hand, the conservatives have been moving in the opposite direction, originally under Reagan and his successor, and increasingly so under his successor's son. It is not my purpose to analyze these seismic shifts. While they are fascinating from a historical standpoint, I am more interested in the current differences between liberals and conservatives, that is, their respective positions in regard to international issues at the outset of the twenty first century. Thus we shall concentrate on their mindsets now, how they mesh with the other compartments, and what is the relationship to age.

Liberal guy goes first. He reviews the dismal score of international relations throughout history and sees a never-ending saga of war, bloodshed and internecine violence. Surely humankind can do better. He believes that the United States, as the leading country in the world, should have as its first international priority the obligation to move the world toward peaceful resolution of conflicts. From this core belief follows all the components of his view on the role that the USA should play in the world.

First and foremost, we should make common cause with our natural partners. Those natural partners are the democratic nations of the world, but especially the liberal democracies of (Western) Europe. When we work together with them on problems that arise we are an irresistible force. Therefore, we should do everything possible to arrive at multilateral agreements and democratic alliances that approach conflict resolution in a unified fashion. If, on the other hand, we act unilaterally, then we lose moral force and international legitimacy. In fact, whenever possible, our alliances should be even broader—including the UN, the nations of Latin America, far eastern democratic nations, etc. In this way we can achieve great things: help to guide China toward a more liberal and democratic future; reign in rogue regimes like those in Iran, Syria and North Korea; help to foster development in countries in the Middle East and Africa; and strike at terror by influencing the regimes that harbor terrorists.

Second, force is an absolute last resort, and should rarely, rarely ever be deployed. Throughout history, nations have too easily resorted to violence. It is a prime imperative for America to set a moral example for the world, and help to guide it toward a more peaceful future, by eschewing the use of force unless our nation is in mortal danger. The recent choice to go to war in Iraq is a tragic illustration of a flawed policy that does not embrace this imperative. Saddam Hussein posed no mortal danger to the United States. We should have found a way to corral him without resorting to war.

Third, America, as one of the richest countries in the world, has an obligation to the poorer nations—not unlike the obligation that the wealthiest Americans have to their less fortunate countrymen. The United States has not done nearly enough to help the peoples of poor third world nations. Working through multilateral entities like the UN, the International Monetary Fund (IMF) and the World Bank, and in conjunction with our allies, we should increase our foreign aid to less developed nations.

Implicit in all of the previous is the liberal fellow's increasing belief in the decreasing viability and legitimacy of the sovereign nation-state. He sees the world progressing toward an era in which the particularism and chauvinism of individual nations will give way to regional, and perhaps global, unification of the world's people. National armies, currencies and borders will eventually wither away to be replaced by a more unified and peaceful organization of the world's people. In this regard, the European Union and the nascent United States of Europe is a trail blazing step in the right direction. The US should respect and cooperate with this new entity and not seek to thwart it.

The conservative gal remarks that we are no closer to agreement in this compartment than we were in the first. She too surveys the bloody history of international relations, but comes to a different conclusion. Her core beliefs are described thus. Nations, like human beings, have a propensity to disagree—sometimes violently. In dealing with that reality, the US has two obligations. The first is to be as militarily and economically strong as possible so that we can defend ourselves and our allies from the designs of our enemies. The second is to do what we can to make the world like us—in the following sense. It is a proven fact that, as modern liberal democracies have evolved over the last two centuries, the number of instances in which two have gone to war with each other is remarkably few. Some maintain the number is zero. The commitment to freedom, the tendency toward tolerance, and the respect for private property that characterize liberal democracies all engender powerful motivation to avoid war, to settle disputes peaceably between like-minded nations. Thus the second obligation is to do all we can to help establish and nurture liberal democracies around the globe.

If we fulfill the second obligation, then as a natural consequence, the level of conflict in international relations will inevitably decrease. But until we reach that nirvana, we cannot ignore the evil and malevolence in the world. And so unfortunately, because of our first obligation, we may have to resort to force to defeat it. The conservative lady has no compunction about labeling the likes of Osama bin Laden and Mullah Omar as evil. In the one place on Earth where their kind has ruled unchecked—Afghanistan—their record of oppression, persecution of females, disrespect for civilization and propensity for bloodshed and intolerance, was ghastly, and should give pause to anyone who contemplates their ruling anywhere else or the ability to find peaceful coexistence with them. Indeed they pose a mortal danger to their neighbors, to us, to our allies, and indeed to the entire world. They must be defeated. There are no other options. End of story. It is our obligation to lead the battle against them, and then to spread liberty, democracy, rule of law and free markets to whichever lands we chase them from.

The conservative woman also has strong sentiments about how the US should relate to poor countries. They are summarized by the statement: misguided welfare never works—neither internationally or domestically. We have learned that if you pay people to engage in counterproductive behavior—e.g., to have babies out of wedlock, not to work, and not to support their families, then that is exactly what they will do. When we stopped paying for these things (welfare reform), the amount of such counterproductive (anti-social) behavior dropped precipitously. In a similar vein, if you infuse a country with cash as a reward for not respecting private property, for not establishing the rule of law, for not creating a market economy, or for organizing the society around an unaccountable authoritarian regime, then that is exactly what they will do with the cash. Instead of corrupting governments and their leaders with foreign aid, we should: trade with them, encourage them to establish consistent and transparent legal systems, and boycott and criticize them if they deny basic freedoms (press, assembly, worship, etc.) to their people. Like domestic welfare reform helped countless people, who were thought incapable, to stand on their own two feet, international welfare reform will free developing countries to do likewise. It is said that the greatest barometer of the worthiness of a government is how it treats its own people. We should trade as equals with those that treat their people fairly, and shun and ostracize those that don't. That will be far more effective than increasing foreign aid.

Finally, conservatives are highly suspicious of "world governments." The UN, like the League of Nations before it, is a colossal failure. Countries led by tyrannical regimes sit on its human rights councils, its peacekeeping missions bring little peace, many of its officials are hopelessly corrupt, and its perfidy in treating Israel alone disqualifies it as an impartial organization. We should expel it from our shores and replace it by a League of Democratic Nations.

C. Absolutist or Relativist

Now we turn from world views to mental frameworks. As we do let us keep in mind, as we peer into the minds of our political antagonists, that the context is political philosophy, not general psychology. We are interested in intrinsic intellectual proclivities as they relate to an individual's political view of the universe, not pure personality traits. We will have three of these frameworks. In each we will give a brief elaboration of how we understand the dual terms that frame the mindset. Then we shall give several manifestations of each. It is not until the next chapter that we explore where the touchstone issues fit into the frameworks, although I confess that some of the issues appear in the manifestations.

In the rotation it is the turn of our conservative lady. And in the opposing terms of this framework, she appears as the *absolutist*. By that I mean that the conservative lady sees (political) choices in stark terms. When contemplating political positions, policies and programs, she tends to frame issues in terms of black and white, good and evil, right and wrong, true or false. It does not leave much room for nuance. Instead to her, the choices are clear, the rules are specific, the axioms are explicit, and the consequences are evident.

To illustrate, consider the different types of governmental forms in our world. For her, there is absolutely no question that the liberal democracies are the best and that the rest—be they authoritarian, totalitarian, oligarchic or monarchial—represent at best retrograde governing structures that hold back their people's progress and at worst, tyrannical regimes that pose a grave threat to their neighbors, to liberal democracies, and most severely to their own people. She does not confuse "good" with "perfect"; she recognizes that liberal democracies are not perfect. But that recognition does not cloud her judgment or shake at all her firm conviction that liberal democracies are the right way to organize society. She has little sympathy for and pays little mind to all the others, seeing them as anywhere from inefficient to repressive to evil. She is unwavering in her belief that history is on the side of liberal democracy.

Let us give two more examples. The conservative lady has a virtually biblical respect for the US Constitution. She views it as an incredibly wise, remarkably insightful, and even divinely inspired founding legal document that has and should forever determine the way our country is governed. She believes that it has more than stood the test of time and that allegiance to it is the fundamental testament to what it means to be an American. It is not totally perfect, but it has a (suitably complicated) self-correcting mechanism—namely, constitutional amendments. There is no room in her thinking for compromise in this matter. The Constitution is the binding, seminal and ultimate law of the land. Under its rubric, the Congress enacts laws, the Executive carries them out, and the Judiciary adjudicates disputes and interprets the Constitution in the few places where its intent may not be crystal clear. Those roles are precise and unambiguous, and any attempt by one branch of government to usurp the function of another is a flagrant violation of the Constitution. In this vein she sees "legislating from the bench" as a grave threat to American life.

The third and final example is that of morality and religion. Our forefathers' writings are replete with the idea that the system they devised would only work for a moral people, and that those morals had to be grounded in religious faith. Our conservative gal subscribes to that notion. The people must strive to be good. Moreover, there is a well-determined standard for what it means to be good or moral. Those standards did not emerge haphazardly, and they are not changeable. They were established by God, or by an intelligent designer, or perhaps even by some very clever and wise group of people thousands of years ago. The rules are clear, well-known and we don't change them or make them up as the game evolves.

Our liberal guy, on the other hand, is the *relativist* here. He sees shades of grey where the lady sees black and white. When contemplating political, social and especially cultural phenomena, he believes it is unwise to see things in absolute terms. Many things are relative and have to be evaluated in light of the times in which they occur, the geographic locale at which they occur, the people who are affected, and the institutions they impact. He is definitely not a "one size fits all" kind of guy, and more seriously he believes that attempts to pigeon hole political ideas into neat categories based on absolute criteria will lead to unwise, unfair and indeed unjust outcomes.

Again we'll illustrate with three examples. The first is the matter of the culture that permeates a society. Legal precepts on which a society is built are critical. But culture is the glue that holds it together. Furthermore, a homogenized, static, rigid culture is completely inappropriate for a heterogeneous, immigrant-rich, dynamic country like the United States. For a long time we had such a culture, the WASP culture if you will. But with the increasing colorization of America, immigration from all corners of the globe, and increasing practice of numerous non-Protestant and/or non-Christian religions, it no longer makes sense to allow that culture to dominate the cultural scene of the country. It is vital that we make room for other cultural components. There is no basis on which to assert that WASP culture is superior to Latino culture, or Afro-American culture, or feminist culture, or perhaps even gay, atheistic or Wiccan culture. WASP culture was there at the onset. Now it's a different populace. There is no best culture. We must welcome and embrace all of them.

The next example revolves around the issue of family structure and sexual preference. We need to get out of the Ozzie and Harriett strait-jacket. Why do we accept as the ideal picture the image of man and woman and two children, house in the suburbs, dad commutes to the city, mom plays homemaker, children obedient and taciturn? It just does not accommodate the richness of numerous alternate possibilities—and why couldn't some or all of those alternates be as good if not better than Ozzie and Harriett? We should not constrain ourselves into one oversimplified view of the perfect family structure. There are many family and social structures that can provide happiness, dignity and stability to its members. We should welcome and encourage all of them.

And for our final example of relativism, let's go back to the Constitution that his conservative opponent is so fond of. He too reveres and respects the Constitution. He feels that its wisdom and clarity is matched by its purposeful vagueness and generality at points in order to allow the document to grow and evolve as the world it inhabits and governs changes over the decades. He rejects the biblical view as too rigid and not what the founders intended. He sees the Constitution less as a bible and more as a guide book—teaching us how to live in new times, how to reinterpret the law in terms of new scientific and moral knowledge. We tie ourselves down, constrain our society and perpetrate injustices if we try to live by an 18th century blueprint. The founders gave us a guide book that would grow as the decades and centuries pass. We should be thankful for that. And we should diligently set about adapting our living Constitution as the need arises.

D. Opportunist or Egalitarian

Batter up for the liberal fellow; his role in the dual terms of this framework is of course the *egalitarian*. He takes very seriously the middle exhortation of the cry of the French revolution: *liberte, egalite, fraternite*. His mindset, when contemplating the human condition is that, all things being equal, ... indeed all things ought to be equal. He sees no justification for any human having any more than any other, especially if the inequality is a result of accident, misfortune, malfeasance or duplicity. If indeed all men are created equal, then they ought to stay that way. Generally speaking, his ideal world is one in which we all have pretty much the same amount of stuff.

As usual, we'll give three examples—economic equality, cultural equality and political equality. In many ways, the first of these is the one that most animates his soul. Man enters the world bereft of possessions and what possessions he accumulates in life cannot accompany him upon his exit. During the intermediate journey, why should he amass any more than any other man? No human being has any greater intrinsic worth than any other; thus it is desirable that their material worth should also be equal. Yet, there is no denying the stark differences in income and assets between individuals, often between people who are alike in numerous ways. This grates on Mr. Liberal's value system. He observes that these distinctions often arise because of accidents of birth, misfortunes of health, geographical influence, or worse, greed, chicanery or gluttony. They represent a condition he calls "economic injustice"—unfair, unwarranted and unjust imbalances in the distribution of wealth among the population. He sees the cure resting squarely in the hands of the government and feels it should be empowered to correct economic injustice through legislation, regulation, taxation and judicial intervention. He favors corrective mechanisms like minimum wage laws (even better, living wage laws), steeply progressive income taxes, inheritance taxes and government welfare programs to aid the poor.

With almost as much passion, he advocates cultural equality. All societies have certain common cultural features: language, religions, ethnic or racial groupings, favored family structures, holidays, arts, legal precepts, etc. The development of a culture is infused by many elements: history, geography, climate, neighbors (who invaded whom), immigration, and more. There is absolutely no justification for asserting that any one is better than any other. If you have a multicultural society—or a multicultural world for that matter—in which one culture has a higher legal or moral status than another, then that almost certainly reflects the outcome of a power struggle between the two cultures' adherents, not of any fundamental higher worth that one culture enjoys over the other. No inherent rights or privileges should be granted to the adherents of one culture at the expense of devotees of another.

Finally, there is the matter of political or social equality, the lack of which is very dangerous to the individual or group on the short end of the stick. In fact, there should not be a short end of the stick. Social and political equality is one of the hallmarks of an enlightened society. This he believes deeply and is particularly peeved by the less than perfect history of America in this regard—to wit, slavery, the mistreatment of the Native American population, the incarceration of Japanese Americans during WWII, and the ongoing discrimination against African Americans and Hispanic Americans in the US today. These wrongs must be redressed. Palliative programs like affirmative action, racial set-asides and diversity initiatives are absolutely indispensable to correct historical and ongoing ills. It is inconceivable to him that this point is not appreciated by all Americans.

The conservative woman, whom we'll label an *opportunist* here, approaches the idea of life's outcomes completely differently. She sees utopian visions of equality of outcome as unrealistic, self-defeating, morally wrong, and, most importantly, potentially dangerous. The latter obtains because the only way to ensure equal outcomes is to coercively take from some and give to others. Such involuntary transfers inevitably lead to tyranny. The best we can do is to level the playing field before the contest, let the contestants play a fair game and accept the outcome as legitimate, recognizing that there will be winners and losers. That is how we approach sports, why not the rest of life?

Her examples will mirror the three given by her liberal friend. The first is economic opportunity. It is the job of government to provide a level playing field in the economic realm. Contracts must be honored, negotiations must be open and free of coercion, courts must be impartial, currency must be sound, private property must be respected and protected, and so on. Once fair rules and environments have been established, let the games begin. Those who are most creative, diligent and industrious, who read the tea leaves most accurately, produce the products that their fellow citizens most desire, acquire the most useful knowledge—they will prosper more than those who don't. As long as wealth is accumulated fairly and by the rules of the game, it is a good outcome. Wealth creation and accumulation is not a zero sum game. Free markets create wealth, they don't just shuffle it around. In the course of amassing his great fortune, Bill Gates has created tens of thousands of jobs, hundreds of products and real wealth for scores of people. To have stifled him early in the game in order to ensure that he would not "get ahead" of others would have been to deprive the world of all he created, and without a doubt made for a poorer world. That is always how it works—if you redistribute wealth so that in principle everyone has the same, as the history of socialism proves, the effect is that everyone is rendered poorer than they would have been if free markets were allowed to operate.

She also believes that not all cultures are equal. The only way that can be so is if there is no moral order, no notion of good and evil or right and wrong. To assert that the culture that reigned in Nazi Germany was no worse than that of Great Britain or the United States in mid twentieth century is to condone racism, aggression, torture and mass murder. In the same vein, there are societies on Earth today whose cultures foster sex slaves, religious intolerance, racial hatred and suicide bombers. Are they of equal stature with the cultures of the United States or Britain today? Obviously not. But the matter is perhaps more subtle. What of a culture that promotes or endorses sloth and indolence, promiscuity, unethical business practices, incohesive family structure or public lewdness? The egalitarian might say that some of that is present in our own culture, and besides if this hypothetical culture is not violent, then it is just another culture and we should not be judgmental. The conservative would, however, make subjective value judgments and evaluate that culture harshly. She is unlikely to accept all cultures as equally moral.

Finally, there is the issue of political, educational, and vocational opportunity. Again she sees this area as one where you level the playing field before the game and accept a fair outcome. We make available to all citizens the opportunity to stand for public office, to study at the best universities, to start and run a business, to secure the most lucrative jobs, etc. The openings are there for all to pursue, but only those who study the hardest, market themselves most effectively, create the best products, or acquire the appropriate skills will achieve success. That is the best and most moral way. Equality of opportunity, not equality of outcome, is the watch word of the conservative position on political/social equality/opportunity.

E. Pragmatist/Realist or Idealist/Utopian

In this last category the conservative lady assumes the role of *pragmatist* or *realist*. Her philosophy for dealing with the world she inhabits is to accept it for what it is and deal with it, rather than pining over how she dreams it might be and tilt at windmills trying to make it so. She accepts that human nature is not always as benign and benevolent as we wish it were, that there are certain immutable laws—of biology, chemistry and physics, and even of economics and sociology—that don't always work to the advantage of mankind, and that calamities occur, either through the fault of no human being, or indeed because of unwise or unjust human actions. This is Earth, not Oz. The best strategy for a happy existence, with a minimum of frustration and disappointment, is to deal with the vicissitudes of life realistically and pragmatically, not to get swept up in hopeless crusades to create idealized realities. She places great stock in the classic prayer, "Lord; grant me the strength to change the things I can change, the courage to accept the things that I cannot change, and the wisdom to recognize the difference."

The first example illustrating this mindset is in her attitude toward crime and punishment. The conservative accepts that some people are bad and that they break the law and injure their fellow citizens. She is not very interested in uncovering "root causes" for the criminal's anti-social behavior. She is much more interested in apprehending, prosecuting and punishing the criminal. God gave human beings free will. History is full of stories of people afflicted by disease, oppression, and misfortune who nevertheless chose to abide by the laws of society. She has little sympathy for those who choose otherwise.

The next illustration is found in her opinion of government regulation. She is deeply concerned by the proliferation of government agencies that regulate virtually every aspect of the life of American citizens. Through the alphabet soup of regulatory agencies, the bureaucrats in the U.S. Government tell her that: her young son must ride securely belted, facing backwards, in the back seat of her private vehicle, until he reaches some arbitrary weight, and she may not hold him while her spouse is driving, even if he has a fever or is in pain or discomfort; her toilet may expend no more than 1.6 gallons of water; and beginning in some future year, she may not buy a top loading washing machine, but must buy a front loading one, even if her aching back makes leaning over to fill it an awful chore. Undoubtedly, all this minutiae arose from liberal desires to correct perceived flaws and to create a more perfect American society. In fact, government regulations are usually self-contradictory, expensive, ineffective, and often prejudicial. But more important, she sees the vast majority of them as an encroachment on her freedom. In the name of some utopia toward which the alphabet soup is driving us, the government usurps the citizen's power to decide how to live her life.

The final conservative example is in the matter of judicial restraint—or lack thereof. Liberal judges have a keen sense of how they want America to be. They are not about to let a little thing like the law prevent them from implementing their vision. Thus, when faced with an opportunity to move society in the direction they wish it were heading, they issue rulings not based in law, but designed to make their vision a reality. The conservative sees judicial activism as a grave danger to the American republic. Judges usurp the power of legislators when they make law from the bench—usually in the service of some principle that is not found in the canons of American justice. For example, however one feels about abortion, it is undeniable that the Supreme Court invented a right, "privacy," that is not set forth in the U.S. Constitution. If we are to be a society under the rule of law, then the law cannot change at the whim of liberal, activist judges. Judges should be guided by the laws of the land, not by utopian visions.

The liberal man views the possibilities for human improvement very differently from his conservative colleague. He reasons that we are not unthinking animals or robots; we should use the free will that God gave us to improve the world. He is a staunch believer in the classic purpose that biblical Jews ascribed to themselves: Tikkun Ha'Olam. It is the job of mankind to fix the world. Why should we accept its imperfections? It is our duty to identify the faults in society (or the world) and to correct them. If that means being an *idealist*, then that is a label he wears proudly.

Now for the liberal's illustrative examples. The first is found in his stance on the environment. This is a perfect illustration, he asserts, for what is wrong with the environment is largely the fault of mankind. It is definitely our responsibility to repair the damage we've caused. Our obligation to maintain the health of the planet eclipses our desire for wealth, our need to pursue business opportunities and our leisure impulses. An environmentally healthy planet is a legacy that we owe to all humans in the future. Even if we have to sacrifice some of our present needs, it is mandatory that we fulfill the legacy. In this context, he sees the U.S. failure to endorse and adopt the Kyoto Protocols as an outrage and a disgrace.

The second example is his attitude toward the United Nations. The creation of the UN occurred as the world recovered from one of the greatest disasters it has ever inflicted upon itself—World War II. It represents the noblest aspiration of man and is a testament to our desire to live in peace and harmony with our fellow human beings. The UN must be given the resources, support and power it requires in order to help usher in an age when conflict resolution occurs peacefully, when disputes between nations are settled without bloodshed, and indeed when the borders between nations dissolve into a united brotherhood of man. The history of the nation-state is one of parochialism, chauvinism and aggression. He sees the UN (and other supra-national bodies like the European Union) as harbingers of a one-world future.

And finally, the last example—capital punishment. This one is simple. Thou shalt not kill. Especially if thou is a state. Nothing would signal the progress of mankind beyond its original bloody state better than the universal abolition of capital punishment. It is an abomination. No crime, however heinous, warrants state sanctioned murder. It must, and it will, stop!

Consistency and Predictability

Before concluding this chapter with the next personal recollection, I want, as promised, to address the issues of consistency and predictability. In fact the liberal/conservative stances in the five categories are quite consistent. Briefly summarizing, the liberal gentlemen is a strong government, multilateralist, relativistic, egalitarian idealist; whereas the conservative lady is a limited government, unilateralist, absolutist, opportunistic pragmatist. My point is that these multiple classifications are completely consistent.

If you favor broad government involvement in the lives of the people, then you will also favor the world's involvement in the affairs of your nation. Egalitarianism and idealism go hand-in-hand—a perfect state of equality between the components of a society is certainly an ideal state of affairs. And if you are a relativist who is unwilling to anoint "best" status, then you are also likely a multilateralist who seeks to encourage meaningful participation by many nations on a global issue. By the same token, if you believe in limited government because you distrust massive central bureaucracies, then you likely have strong pragmatic tendencies. Your unilateral inclinations for the United States march in step with your absolutist principles since you easily see as justified the morally good US acting on its own. And finally, opportunism and pragmatism go together—you are pragmatic enough to know that situations are always changing and your moment of opportunity will come if you are sufficiently patient.

One could go on at some length relating the stances in the separate categories in a consistent fashion. However, we shall see in the next chapter, when we fit the touchstone issues into the categories, that the consistency is not total. But for the most part, in the overall gestalt determined by the five compartments, whichever side you're on, the appropriate stances hang together in a consistent and logical way.

As for predictability, the point has already been made and in some sense is self-evident. If you locate an individual within the five compartments, then because of the aforementioned consistency, the person's stances are likely to line up in the already described neat alignment. Then you can predict with near certainty whether that person identifies with the liberal or conservative camp. Actually, predictability goes both ways. If an individual identifies himself as a strong liberal or, alternatively, an emphatic conservative, you can also predict with great success where he will land in the five compartments. This will also be reinforced in the next chapter.

Caveat. Despite the strong assertions in this section, I don't want to leave the impression that I believe the dicing up of humanity into liberal and conservative pieces is as neat as I might have suggested. There are always contradictions and counterexamples; human nature is never one hundred percent predictable and consistent. I already cited some instances in the very first paragraph of Chapter 1 (please refer back to them). Here are some more:

- Conservatives seek to limit the power of government, but they have supported restrictions on liberty entailed in some portions of of the Patriot Act.

- Liberals criticize their country when it acts without international backing, yet they certainly advocated and supported unilateral actions by the U.S. military in the Balkans in the 1990's.

- Conservatives see the "War against Terror" in absolute terms: regimes are either "with us or against us"; if a regime supports terrorist organizations, it is by definition against us. Yet many conservatives are ambiguous in their approach to the Israeli-Arab conflict—despite the fact that it is absolutely clear who is supporting and perpetrating terror and who is combating it.

- Despite their commitment to egalitarian principles, liberals routinely support policies that deprive white men of appointments, prizes, and college admissions in favor of females and peoples of color. I do not see how the purposeful denigration of one group in society in favor of another—regardless of whether there is any historical injustice in the other direction—can be classified as an action that will result in egalité. It will, and does result in anger, frustration and resentment.

- Conservatives engage in nostalgic, if not utopian dreams of returning America and its culture to a more pristine and innocent past. Not very realistic!

- Liberals will hold their noses and support Hillary Clinton's moves to the right, no matter how much it violates their, and her own liberal principles, if it increases the odds of her capturing the presidency. Not very idealistic!

These counterexamples not withstanding, I stand by my earlier claims of consistency and predictability. For the most part they hold. But not uniformly.

Despite my rude awakening to the ways of the world caused by the Eichmann affair, I still considered myself incredibly fortunate in the following sense. I had never, as I approached the age of twenty, experienced death personally. My grandparents were alive and healthy, no one—even in my extended family—had died since my last great grandparent passed away when I was eight. The closest I had come to a "death in the family" was of a high school classmate and fellow swim team member, with whom I was not particularly close. In fact, the first death that I remember engendering any sense of personal loss was that of Marilyn Monroe in August 1962. She was so beautiful and vibrant. And such a grotesque death, under questionable circumstances. But the emotions aroused by that death were nothing compared with those evoked by the violent death of President Kennedy 15 months later. Like many Americans, I was horrified, stupefied, and transfixed by the events that played out on American TV screens over that tragic weekend. I felt a deep sense of personal loss and bewilderment. I can still see the scene of students exiting and entering Shepard Hall on the campus of the City College of New York where I learned of the tragedy that Friday afternoon, and I can still feel the sickening, gut-wrenching mixture of sorrow and fury that enveloped me at the news. Another layer of innocence viciously ripped away.

Naturally, the lesson I took from John Kennedy's death was of the utter fragility of life. You just never know when some unexpected event is going to interfere with your life or the lives of those you care about, no matter how carefully you plan details or plot strategy. It is a lesson that one must use carefully as, on the one hand, you struggle to keep it from becoming crippling, and on the other, to keep it in mind so that the world will not perpetually surprise you. It propelled me eventually toward pragmatism. But it propelled others—and me also for a time—toward idealism. The reaction of my family, friends, acquaintances and indeed much of the nation was that the way to deal with Kennedy's grievous death was to embrace forcefully the liberal agenda that we thought he stood for, then advocate it and enact it. And under the heavy handed and misguided leadership of Lyndon Johnson, that is exactly what America did. Despite the prescient warnings of Barry Goldwater, America lurched sharply to the left and enacted collectivist programs: enhanced Social Security, Medicare, Medicaid, and a plethora of Welfare programs. (I'll discuss the ongoing leftward cascade, which continued until 1980, in Chapter 5.) I favored all of it. It was a fitting tribute to Kennedy—or so we thought—and it was the right thing to do. Of course, we would learn better later.

I think often about the early 1960s. One's late teen years are a wonderful time when you feel the infinite possibilities of life, the strength and agility of your body, budding new ideas for how you are going to remake the world. And to have a President and First Lady who seemed to embody and encourage it all. It was truly exhilarating. What a crash when it ended so abruptly. But of course it was largely a triumph of style over substance. John and Jackie certainly had style, wit, elegance and grace. But John Kennedy was a womanizer, who cavorted with mobsters, misrepresented his physical condition, exhibited incredible naïveté in matters of foreign affairs, and whose clan and/or coterie certainly had some role (if only peripheral) in the death of Marilyn Monroe. Ughh! I grew up some the weekend JFK died. I grew up a lot more as I learned the truth about his character and witnessed the harm caused by the policies that were enacted in his name.

4

Fitting the Issues into the Compartments

In this chapter we complete the organizational work (of the first part of the book) that will allow us to correlate age with political philosophy in the second part. In fact we have already done a lot of spade work and the ground is lying quite fallow before us. We began in Chapter 1 by identifying 24 key or touchstone issues that separate liberals from conservatives today. Then in Chapter 2, we formulated, on the basis of classic definitions of liberalism and conservatism, five "anchored" definitions, or world views, which codified in a somewhat more systematic way the distinctions between liberals and conservatives. We observed that, although these world views are quite useful for understanding the differences between the political beasts, they were not so helpful for the correlation effort we have in mind. Next, in Chapter 3, we reformulated the five world views into five new categories or compartments that also sharply highlighted the conservative/liberal divide, but which will serve us better in the forthcoming correlation investigation. In this chapter we come full circle and fit the touchstone issues into the compartments. When we are done we will have accomplished two things: (i) laid completely bare the very broad scope of the differences between liberals and conservatives; and (ii) set the cornerstone for the correlation work in the rest of the book.

So recall the table of touchstone issues in Chapter 1, and recall the five compartments of Chapter 3. Here's how we'll fit them together. We will list the compartments, and for each, we specify the issues that fit under its rubric. In fact, it is easy to put any particular issue into one or more compartments, where by doing so I mean to indicate that a person's stance on that issue will depend in a clear way on the person's mindset regarding that compartment. Nevertheless, although it is not hard to slot each issue into at least one of the compartments, the exercise is rather subjective. In fact, it is tempting, with many of the issues, to place it inside more than one compartment. I have resisted that temptation as far as possible. In most cases when the issue might fit in multiple compartments, I only listed the one that, to my thinking, most clearly would govern the stance on that particular issue. Whenever I could not make that distinction to my satisfaction—which happened in 7 of the 24 issues—I listed the issue in two compartments. However, for me there was enough clarity in the exercise so that no issue appears in more than two compartments.

It is possible that you, dear reader, might arrive at a somewhat different set of associations. It really does not matter. As we pursue the correlation in Part II, the various issues inside a compartment will play a role in the discussion. But some juggling in the assignment of issues to compartments would not really affect the overall conclusions that we will reach.

Below we shall present a table comprised of the five compartments (which recall are made up of a combination of two world views and three mental frameworks) inside each of which are the issues that it encompasses. For lack of a better phrase, I will call this structure the *Political Edifice*. Most of the associations of issues with compartments will be obvious, so I will avoid discussing them one-by-one. Instead, I will peer into the structure of the edifice by examining it in four ways. First, we will highlight the seven issues that are double slotted and explain briefly why that is appropriate in each instance. Next, we'll focus on a small number of issues that are especially important to the Jewish community. Then we'll consider a few that are of special significance to the academic community. In doing both of the preceding, we will be fulfilling a promise made in the Introduction. Finally, we'll examine several issues that are of historical significance in that if someone had drawn up a list of touchstone issues in the late nineteenth century, those issues would have been on the list.

The Political Edifice

The Role of the Government in the Country

- Government spending
- Taxes
- Government regulations
- Welfare
- Military spending

- Judicial activism
- Religion
- Constitution

The Role of the USA in the World

- Military spending
- International conflict resolution
- Sovereignty
- Immigration
- International trade

Absolutist or Relativist

- Abortion
- Homosexuality and marriage
- Religion
- Immigration
- Constitution
- Rights
- Culture

Opportunist or Egalitarian

- Taxes
- Welfare
- Diversity
- Wage regulations
- Leitmotif

Pragmatist/Realist or Idealist/Utopian

- Diversity
- Environment

- Animals
- Criminals
- Capital punishment
- Gun control

Double-Slotted Issues

There are seven and they are: taxes, welfare, military spending, religion, the Constitution, immigration and diversity. Taking them in that order, one can start by observing that it is obvious that one's position on the level of taxes must be decided in the context of how you see the role of government. But just as clearly, one's position on the nature of taxation is governed by how egalitarian-minded you are—the more you are so inclined, the more progressive you'll want taxes to be. Similarly with welfare, especially if taken in a broad sense—that is, to include Social Security, Medicare and Medicaid along with classic welfare programs like food stamps, aid to dependent children, head start, etc. In that broad context, your stance on welfare is governed equally by how you view the role of government as well as your egalitarian tendencies, or lack thereof.

Military spending is dual slotted because one's opinion on the level of military expenditures is likely tied up both with one's view of the role of government in the country as well as the role of the country in the world. I placed religion in two compartments because how high you build the wall between church and state is clearly determined both by your view of the role of government as well as how flexible you are in accommodating religious viewpoints. The same kind of duality applies to your opinion on whether the Constitution is a living document or not.

The last two double slotted issues appear further down the list. One's attitude toward immigration (primarily illegal) is governed by what role you see the US playing in the world and again by your relativistic nature, or lack thereof. And finally, your views on what has come to be known by the term diversity are determined by your place in both the opportunistic/egalitarian and pragmatist/utopian spectra.

Reiterating my earlier assertion, there may be other issues in the two dozen that you would list in two compartments, and there may be some among my double-slotted seven that you would restrict to a single compartment. But as I also said, that won't affect our final conclusions in Part II. Thus why build the edifice? Answer: because as we use the compartments to correlate with age, it will be useful to cite the specific issues in the compartment to corroborate, or refute any correlation claimed.

Jewish Issues

In this section dealing with Jewish issues, and in the next section on academic issues, you will be very hard pressed not to see my conservative tendencies. These issues, in the context of my two worlds (as explained in the Preface), hit too close to home for me to be totally objective.

The Jewish community in America can trace its roots to colonial times. The number of Jewish inhabitants of the country was small, but it was a vibrant community that, in an inhospitable world, had found a welcome haven. The welcome is illustrated beautifully in the famous letter from President George Washington to a Jewish congregation in Newport, Rhode Island. Those early Jewish Americans were almost exclusively "Sephardim," descendants of the fifteenth century Jewish communities in the Iberian Peninsula, North Africa, Turkey and the Near East. Virtually none of the descendants of these early American Jews was able to resist the call of assimilation over the ensuing two centuries, and so they married out, converted out, or simply drifted out of the Jewish community. However, the Jewish population of America was replenished, beginning in the early 1800s, by the arrival of Ashkenazi Jews, descendants of Jewish communities from central Europe (mainly Germany). Those immigrants also prospered, but like their predecessors from the "orient", they have mostly been absorbed into the great American melting pot—although not to the near total extent of their predecessors. A 40-year period beginning in the 1880s saw a tidal wave of immigration from Eastern Europe that brought millions of Jews to the United States, and from which the vast majority of today's American Jews trace their heritage. There were three further smaller migrations: from central Europe again in the 1930s, bringing those fortunate enough to escape the onslaught of the Nazi murder machine; an ongoing stream of Israeli Jews over the last 50 years; and another group from Eastern Europe fleeing Communism, especially in the 1980s and 1990s.

When I was a child it was universally acknowledged that there were 6 million Jews in America—roughly the same number that was murdered by the Nazis, and constituting after the Holocaust nearly one half the Jews in the world. This estimate was probably accurate because, although the method of counting was rather primitive—primarily, counting names in phones books—in mid twentieth century America it was a reliable method. Specifically, if an American was identified as Nathan Horowitz, the odds were overwhelming that Nathan was Jewish; but if a phone book entry read Frank O'Brien, then just as assuredly, Frank was not. Today, despite the three additional in migrations, the Jewish population of America is estimated at no more than 5.5, and perhaps as few as 5 million people. The uncertainty is because, like 50 years ago, Jews resist being counted in the United States Census. (This is a vestige of our paranoia about staying under the radar screen.) And because of rampant intermarriage and assimilation, the phone book survey method doesn't work so well any more. Anyway, the fact that 6 million Jews in 1950 are today fewer in number is astounding. Normal demographics would predict that any well-identified and strongly self-identifying group would have at least doubled and, taking into account the three additional migrations, perhaps trebled their number in 50 years. There should be 15-20 million Jews in the US today. Even more astounding, this population decline occurred in a period when the Jews in America were not persecuted, but rather welcomed and appreciated by the American people. So, my generation and its offspring have intermarried and assimilated at the same fantastic rate as our Sephardi and Ashkenazi predecessors did. We haven't vanished yet, but many think it's just a matter of time.

Juxtaposed against the explosion of Jewish population in Eastern Europe in the 18th and 19th centuries under repressive regimes, one might assert that Jews handle persecution better than open arms. By that remark I am not trying to plant any bad seeds in the minds of Gentile America. I prefer that the Goyim[1] marry my children rather than kill them. In fact, the central "blame" for assimilation lies not in the welcoming and accommodating atmosphere of American life, although it certainly plays a role. While there are small, nasty pockets of gentiles actively trying to convert Jews, mainstream gentile America does not wake up in the morning thinking how it can capture a Yid today. No, the vast majority of Jewish demographic losses are due to our own failure to inculcate our youth with sufficient pride in our people's accomplishments, knowledge of our people's history and devotion to our traditions and beliefs. Well, it may also have something to do with how hard it is to be a practicing Jew, but that is another story. Suffice it to say the phenomenon of Jewish assimilation is not new. At the time of Christ, there were several million Jews in the world. We are the only people who survive

---

1.   The Hebrew word *goy* (plural *goyim*) denotes a non-Jew or gentile. It is used both factually and pejoratively. My usage is in the former sense.

intact from that era. There ought to be hundreds of millions of us. That there aren't is not just—and maybe even not primarily—because the world has occasionally butchered us. I venture that more defections were voluntary than coerced. So America may be the sweetest home (outside of Israel) that we have ever encountered in our long journey in the Diaspora, but that hasn't exempted it from witnessing and perhaps abetting our historical attrition.

Well, all the preceding is very interesting—probably worthy of a separate book—but I am a little off track. Here I'm just trying to identify some issues that are particularly germane to Jewish America. Actually, the preceding short diversion will be helpful in understanding why the issues I've picked are indeed so germane. In fact, I've already pointed out that, politically, the Jewish community is overwhelmingly liberal. In the last 75 years, no Republican presidential candidate has received more than 40% of the Jewish vote, and the typical percentage is usually around 20%. (Only the black community votes more monolithically liberal.) Why is this so? The answer would comprise a large part of the aforementioned book. It's not my purpose to start it here. Instead, for now, let's identify the hot button issues (out of the 24) for the Jewish community. They are: religion, rights, culture, diversity, and leitmotif.

On the matter of religion and the wall between church and state, Jews have traditionally favored a very high wall. This is not surprising in light of our long history of persecution at the hands of rulers of states that had religious foundations, be they Christian or Muslim. We have long been enamored of the idea, born in the eighteenth century enlightenment, that the secularization of the state will afford the greatest protection for religious minorities in a nation-state. We see the United States as the embodiment of the ideal and the proof of the concept. The contrary idea that the US is a "Christian nation" is very troubling to many Jews. We acknowledge that the founders of our nation were almost exclusively followers of Christianity, and that the majority of our fellow citizens follow its faith. This is fine as long as we are free to follow our own faith—or not, if we wish—unfettered by restrictions imposed by the Christian majority. We see the total separation of religious practices and organizations from the organs and policies of the government as the best guarantee of the freedom of religion enshrined in the Bill of Rights. In this vein, the so-called Christian Right, which advocates policies (on many of the touchstone issues) that are religiously inspired, is seen as a threat. In order to forestall any such threat, many Jews and Jewish organizations take exceptionally strong positions in favor of total separation of church and state, and consequently they support the removal of religion completely from the public square.

I would like to point out some ironies in this position. First of all, the Holocaust, the greatest tragedy to befall the Jewish people since its expulsion from its homeland two millennia ago, was perpetrated by what was essentially a pagan regime, unchecked by any religious sensitivities or philosophy. Today, in the Christian world, anti-Semitism is much worse in the ardently secular states of Western Europe than it is in the United States or Latin America, where arguably the wall is much lower. In the Muslim world, a fear of state-sponsored oppression is more justified—Islamic-inspired regimes are more hostile to Jews than are secular ones like Turkey or ... is there another secular Muslim state? Well maybe Indonesia or Malaysia. But there are no Jews there. Incidentally, another bittersweet irony is that the staunchest supporters of Israel in the United States today are found among the Evangelical Christian Right. This is a particularly delicious irony as some of Israel's most virulent critics are people like Noam Chomsky and Norman Finkelstein—that is, Jews.

The issue of group rights versus individual rights is another particularly thorny one for American Jews. In 1950 Jews constituted approximately 4% of the total US population. Today that percentage has shrunk to less than 2%. Moreover, in the pall-mall rush to identify groups in America that are to be accorded special rights, "civil rights" advocates have settled on blacks, Hispanics, American Indians, occasionally Asians, but more frequently homosexuals and the disabled, and let us not forget females. The Jews rarely if ever make the cut. You would think that, constituting a shrinking percentage of the population, and not favored for any special status in the group rights game, Jews would be falling all over themselves to support the individual rights viewpoint. Not the case. Jews are amongst the biggest promoters of group rights.

This may be a case of political philosophy trumping ethnicity and self-interest. It is a well-known fact that in fields like education, business, science, literature and the arts, the millennia-old traditions of Jewish scholarship and study have produced a people who can compete extraordinarily well. Given a level playing field, we do indeed compete exceedingly well. The long roster of achievements by Jews in these areas: Nobel and Pulitzer prizes, selections for membership in the National Academy of Sciences, even Oscars, attest to that success. Why in heaven's name would we want to support rules that tilt the playing field to our disadvantage, impede our brethren from competing on even terms, and thereby diminish the chances of our continuing these stellar achievements? Why indeed! Because the lure of Leftist ideology blinds too many Jews to the folly and self-destructiveness of their devotion to group rights. Indeed, Jews and Jewish organizations are routinely found among the strongest advocates of group rights. For example, they fervently support diversity programs that have had the direct and documented effect of denying qualified Jewish applicants seats in medical and law schools. This is done in the name of atoning for sins committed by white Americans against black Americans—real though those sins were—at a time when the Jewish applicant's ancestors were peasants in Europe. Furthermore, the beneficiaries of those affirmative action programs often have no ethnic connection to those who suffered the outrage of slavery. So A is paying B to atone for sins committed by C against D. Is this wise? Is it just? Or even compassionate? I think not.

Moving on, it is also not surprising that many Jews support multiculturalism. They harbor a deep-seated suspicion of the classic WASP culture and its Christian origins and emphasis. The Jewish people have a very problematic relationship with Christianity and although things are pretty good now, one can never be too secure. Multiculturalism has the potential to loosen the grip that a Christian-oriented culture has had on America and this is a good thing for the Jews—or so the thinking goes. Of course a devotion to multiculturalism also fits nicely with both egalitarian and relativistic mindsets—two hallmarks of the Liberal gestalt and so a comfortable political cove for Jewish philosophical thinking. Thus you will find Jews lined up squarely in the multicultural ranks.

But as with other aspects of the Jewish political agenda, the commitment to multiculturalism might be short-sighted. The overwhelming majority of the Jews of America, those alive today and those who have lived in the republic since its birth, would categorize the US, as I have, as the warmest haven the Jewish people have encountered outside Israel in the last three thousand years. Well, things were pretty comfy in Persia 2500 years ago, and in Babylon about 1500 years ago, and in Spain some 600 years ago, but it is understandably hard to compare the levels of comfort in those societies to life in America during its existence. In any event, I note that the environment in America that offered the Jews such great comfort was dominated, for most of that existence, by the WASP culture that we are so anxious to denigrate. Is there some kind of disconnect here? Yes, I had to sing a few Christmas carols when I was in public school. That does not change the fact that from the arrival of my grandparents in this country about a century ago through the arrival of my grandchildren less than a decade ago, my family has lived a good life, free to pursue our Jewish religion, culture and traditions as much or as little as we wished. The non-WASP cultures that the multiculturalists are so keen to graft onto the American scene emanate from countries and regions where my fellow Jews have not had such a cozy existence. Again, I question whether a commitment to multiculturalism by Jews is not self-defeating. It's worth noting that the good gentile people of America in the last generation began to refer to the religious component of Western Civilization as the Judeo-Christian heritage. And we are going to turn our backs on that!

A discussion of the Jewish approach to diversity would mirror rather closely the above discussion of group rights vs. individual rights. The salient points, and the ironies, are pretty much the same, so we'll jump ahead directly to the last Jewish issue: leitmotif. Let us ask: Which motto better describes a fundamental concept to which your "average" American Jew is committed: rugged individualism or social justice? This is not a hard question to answer. Where does your average Jew find himself in his free time—climbing a mountain or writing a letter to the editor on why government should do more to redress this or that societal ill? There have not been too many Jewish decathlon winners, but there are lots of Jewish lawyers active in the ACLU. Social justice defeats rugged individualism hands down.

In this regard, the Jews of Israel are somewhat different from those in America. This may reflect the different psychological programming experienced by Jews in the Galut[2] versus those b'aretz.[3] Life for Jews has been precarious in exile. Centuries of dealing with oppressors have caused us to develop defensive mechanisms. Clearly a society committed to social justice—which in truth is nothing more than a euphemism for a socialist society, but which to many Jews connotes a fair and equitable society—would provide a safer environment, and it makes sense to work for that rather than grandstanding about the rights of the individual, rights which most societies have not accorded him. Well, despite the freedom the US grants to exercise these rights, the Galut mentality dies hard.

---

2.   Another Hebrew term. *Galut* means exile and is a much more pejorative term than Diaspora for Jews who live outside of Israel.
3.   And another one. *B'aretz* means literally "in the land" and colloquially means "in Israel" as if no sane Jew would live anywhere else.

The ironies connected with this last issue are as poignant as the previous. The Jewish people of America have a remarkable record of individual success. Through hard work, dedication and perseverance, Jews have climbed to the top in many professions, in business, science and the arts. Moreover they did it without affirmative action or other artificial governmental mechanisms to prop up their efforts. They constitute a true testament to rugged individualism—even if more of the cerebral than physical kind. Yet they remain committed to social justice in the form of government set asides, group preferences in college admissions, special loans for minority businesses and the whole plethora of welfare-like programs which scream out that this or that individual from certain groups cannot succeed on his own without special assistance. The Jewish experience in America is proof of the fallacy of that thesis. But why should Jews deal in reality when their dreams of social justice are so much more enticing.

Academic Issues

I entered first grade at the age of five and I have not left school yet. I have been fortunate in that my early interest in and aptitude for mathematics blossomed into a lifetime career. After high school, I went directly to college, then immediately to graduate school, followed by a postdoctoral position and then up the professorial ladder, leading to my current stint as an academic administrator. No military service, no peace corps, no "real world" jobs (other than several summers at national research laboratories). Just school.

Actually, my story is not unfamiliar to my colleagues on campus. Many have traveled the same exclusively academic career path. It is a fulfilling life for those with the temperament to take advantage of its benefits and the wherewithal to ignore its drawbacks. You pretty much get to set your own hours. To a large extent you decide which problems to work on and areas to study. You have easy access to the best computer systems, libraries, and world class cultural and sporting events. There are ample opportunities for professional travel. You meet very intelligent people from all over the world. The benefits and job security are excellent. And you are forever surrounded by attractive young people. It's wonderful—except for a few things. The pay is so-so, especially compared to what one could conceivably earn in the corporate world, or by starting one's own business. There is a certain amount of drudgery—for example, preparing and grading exams and reports, dealing with student complaints about grades, going to too many pointless meetings, and serving on committees that waste time and achieve nothing. The university's bureaucracy, like that of any large non-profit organization, is chaotic, inefficient, over-priced, intrusive, and unresponsive. And finally, if you happen to be a conservative, you find yourself in a milieu whose mindset, accepted wisdom, political philosophy and de facto rules are largely hostile to your beliefs.

Nevertheless, it is a good life and I have been privileged to live and enjoy it. At its best, it is a community of scholars engaged in the pursuit of knowledge: theoretical and experimental scientists striving to unlock the mysteries of the universe; historians, poets and artists helping mankind to understand the past, appreciate the present and anticipate the future; economists and psychologists delving into the complexities of the market and of the human mind.

Any university president will tell you that the preoccupation of the faculty is its pursuit of truth, beauty and knowledge. It's an honorable pursuit, many faculty really do it, and occasionally they succeed. Furthermore, at its best, the university educates the youth of America about the accumulated knowledge of the past and the exciting challenges of the future; trains the future leaders of the nation; develops ideas and inventions, which lead directly to new products that improve the health and prosperity of the community; and counsels government and corporate partners on science and social policy. I think of the professoriate as a noble calling and in its better moments, it lives up to the nobility of that calling.

On the other hand, at its worst, the university is: marginal scholars and pseudo-scholars pursuing academic trails that are uninteresting, harmful or wasteful; timid administrators, unwilling to prioritize—bullied by their faculty, students and boards of advisors; bloated budgets supporting programs of no merit; tax dollars and endowment dollars wasted on unnecessary buildings, academic programs of little value, and extra-curricular activities that belong in the local political club, rather than the Student Union; students who pay more heed to dimwits who can put the ball in the hoop rather than to professors who could challenge their imaginations; skyrocketing tuition that buys a product very different from the one students' parents think they are purchasing; and worst of all, a mind-numbing conformity of thought that belies the stated purpose of seeking truth.

On balance I think (hope) that the best outweighs the worst. When I look back on my career, I remember: the gratification I experienced when I was able to inspire a student; those glorious moments when a mathematical problem I was trying to crack suddenly surrendered to my weary intellect; the excitement, rare though it might be, I felt when a programmatic idea I conceived actually came to a successful fruition; and the camaraderie and sense of accomplishment when my colleagues and I completed work on a book. By and large the colleagues I have worked with over the years have been hard-working, honest and intelligent. But I will temper my praise with a qualifying observation—namely, my colleagues, like virtually all university faculty across the nation, suffer from three significant experiential holes that render them different from other segments of the population.

First, because of the cradle to grave academic experience, and in part because of the tenure system, way too many of them have no sense of how the world of work works outside their university cocoon. They haven't a clue what it means to meet a payroll, balance the books, control an inventory, market anything, or live in fear that you may go out of business because the services you provide or products you produce may suddenly be obsolete. Despite my similarly insular background, I have a better appreciation for the business world than most of my colleagues for the following accidental reason. With the exception of a single first cousin (out of a total of eight), no person in my family has ever held an academic position. Not my spouse, my children, my parents, grandparents, aunts, uncles, or cousins (except for the one). This comment even applies to my extended in-laws. Instead my relatives were/are businessmen, laborers, contractors, office workers, professionals and artists. (Incidentally, no one worked in a government office, lab or agency either.) The talk at my family's gatherings is never about curricula and research, but always of layoffs, construction costs, interest rates, supply chains, and the market. It does not make me an expert, but it does provide me with a different, non-academic perspective. This perspective is often missing among faculty—who not uncommonly have multiple academics in their family tree. In fact the "two-body problem," where husband and wife, or individual and significant other, hunt for academic jobs at a single institution, happens with great regularity these days.

The second lack is that of military experience. Over my career, among the thousands of faculty I have encountered, not more than a handful—and I mean *one* handful—have admitted to me that they served in the US military. Can this be a good thing? I maintain that it is indeed not—neither for the military, nor for our country in general. This is obvious regarding the military. If a group of people who potentially have the skills and talent to be among the leaders of our armed forces is removed from the pool of recruits, then the overall level of the military must be diminished. But it is also detrimental to our country, aside from the fact that the military is not as fine an institution as it could be. In fact, it creates an unnatural division in society—into those for whom the military is, or has been, a significant part of their lives (as personnel or as their family or close friends) and those for whom it is not, nor ever will be. This has many unfortunate consequences. First, the military has traditionally played a homogenizing role in affording like experiences for the many components of our multicultural populace. If a significant portion of that populace is not subjected to a key feature of the "melting pot," then less melting takes place. Second, a famous phrase asserts that "the price of liberty is eternal vigilance." It is not healthy if the price is not paid by all segments of our society. Next, communication, understanding, and trust between groups with different constituents and frames of reference are often lacking. If our civilian and military populations cannot understand and trust each other—as happened tragically during the Vietnam War—then we have a recipe for disaster. Finally, and perhaps most importantly, one of the fundamental principles of our society is civilian control of the military. If the civilians who are supposed to guide the military have no experience in it, nor any understanding of it, how can they wisely set policy, allocate funding, or direct warfare?

Twice in the last century our country's destiny was to confront, and fortunately defeat, the evil of totalitarianism—first fascism, then communism. Of course, the military played a critical role in both struggles. Today a new battle with a third totalitarian enemy—radical Islam, or Islamofascism—is enjoined and once again the military's role is crucial. The elite of America, in particular faculty, were well-represented in the armed forces during the first struggle. They were engaged in the second struggle as well, but more commonly in civilian roles as researchers and strategists. Thus far they seem loath to play any salutary role in the third struggle. That does not augur well—for the struggle or for the faculty.[4]

The third hole in the faculty profile is that of religious experience. There is no question that faculty life correlates negatively with religious practice. Not entirely, but certainly noticeably. Polls routinely show that substantial majorities of Americans believe in God, pray regularly and attend and affiliate with houses of worship. These percentages drop precipitously among faculty. I don't want to

---

4.   There are exceptions—again in the R&D role. Still, not many in our volunteer army have faculty positions in their resumes and history suggests they won't add any when their enlistment is up.

get into a long discussion about why—presuming I even knew for sure. I just want to point out that your average faculty member doesn't spend a lot of time in church and has a difficult time relating to his fellow citizens that do.

I don't intend as criticism the previous observations, which indicated significant differences between faculty experience and attitudes (on business, the military and religious practice) and "lay people." All of us, in whatever milieus we land, are products and reflections of those milieus (and to some extent, we probably gravitate toward them because of predispositions). As I've said, I have great admiration and respect for many of my colleagues and their achievements. But I would never, nor should anyone else, confuse them with businessmen, soldiers or priests.

As you just saw, I am nearly as passionate about academic issues as I am about Jewish ones. And I am equally out of step politically in both worlds. The academic vote is harder to quantify than the Jewish vote—it's not easy to identify residential neighborhoods that contain a lot of academic types. But numerous polls and surveys of faculty political preferences have been done and, as a bloc, faculty may actually be more liberal than Jews—at least in the humanities, social sciences, and media/communications/journalism schools. So I'm knocking my head against another stone wall, and the history of my attempts to break through on campus might fill yet another book. But I have no more intention to start that book here than I did the Jewish book. Instead, let's turn to the issues that resonate most loudly among faculty: government spending, government regulations, diversity and the Constitution.

Prior to World War II, private universities got their funding from two sources: student tuitions and donor-funded endowments. For the most part, public universities that is, state universities, also received their funding from two sources: student tuitions and state budget allocations. A few public universities had significant endowments, but most—like mine, the University of Maryland—had almost none. This situation changed dramatically at mid century as the federal government began a massive build up of its support of higher education. Actually, it started modestly but it grew and expanded quickly and today it exceeds a hundred billion dollars[5]. Moreover, it takes many forms. Much of the public is familiar with so-called Pell grants—direct aid from the federal government to pay tuition and expenses for "needy" students. But in fact there are numerous programs that channel federal money to institutions of higher education and the people who populate them: student loans, programmatic grants, diversity grants, equipment grants and all manner of grants and programs designed to support teaching and learning in the halls of higher education. But that is not where the bulk of the money goes. In fact, it goes to support the research enterprise at several thousand campuses and research institutes throughout the country. Through federal agencies like the National Science Foundation (NSF), the National Aeronautics and Space Administration (NASA), the National Oceanic and Atmospheric Administration (NOAA), the National Institutes of Health (NIH), the National Institute for Standards and Technology (NIST), the National Endowment for the Humanities (NEH), the National Endowment for the Arts (NEA), and also through cabinet level departments, mainly the Department of Defense (DoD), the Department of Homeland Security (DHS), the Department of Energy (DoE), the Department of Commerce (DoC), the Department of Education (DoED), the Department of Housing (DoH), and probably a few others, a king's fortune is funneled from the taxpayers (that's where the feds get the dough after all) to universities, colleges and research institutes. My campus gets about $350 million. Not chump change, but others get quite a bit more. These moneys go to support scientific and other forms of research at the country's august institutions of higher learning. Some of the types of expenditures that are supported include: salaries, equipment, conference expenses, building renovations, power and HVAC, computer systems and software licenses, professional travel, fringe benefits, and—let us not forget—indirect costs (IDC). To the uninitiated, roughly speaking, IDC is a surcharge, usually equal to around 50% of the total of everything else, which the campuses hit up the feds for. The rationale is as follows. All these researchers working on projects on campus that are funded by federal grants use: light, heat, air conditioning, parking lots, toilets, computers, libraries, etc, beyond what they would if they were not working on the grant projects. This costs the university serious money. The claim is: the research is in the national interest and serves the public good—the feds ought to pay and so the IDC is passed on to them.

You can bet your boots that on campuses all over the nation, presidents, provosts and faculty senates pay very close attention to the federal budget—especially those portions from which come the appropriations to pay for the campus

---

5.   According to the American Association for the Advancement of Science, the administration's FY06 budget request was a *measly* increase in R&D spending of $732million bringing the total to $132billion.

research enterprise. Any chill in the process causes university presidents to catch cold. Campuses hire lobbyists who cultivate federal agency program directors, sub-cabinet level administrators, and congressional staffers on behalf of the university's interest in the continued flow of money. It may be that pigs at the trough in not an apt metaphor, but there is no question that universities have learned very well how to suck at the federal teat.

Now don't get me wrong. A lot of fabulous stuff results from this process. I have been administering science and scientists from the Deans Office of the Physical Sciences College at my university for nine years. I have learned a great deal about the scientific research done by mathematicians, physicists, computer scientists, astronomers, geologists and meteorologists, and to a lesser extent by chemists, biologists and engineers. A lot of it is truly fascinating and innovative. And also often practical, yielding applications that are vital to the interests of the State of Maryland and the nation. To cite a few examples: the notion of ensemble weather forecasting, which has led to dramatically improved long range weather forecasts, was pioneered by meteorologists at Maryland; a physicist is building a working model of the Earth's magnetic field by rotating molten sodium inside a sphere with the expectation of learning things that could help protect our planet from the suns radioactive emissions; and work in computer security is pursued with the support of DHS that has implications for the nation's war against terrorists. One cannot help but be impressed and awed by the scientific projects.

But there is a price. It is a truism of life that the one who foots the bill also calls the tune. We (that is, faculty) don't like to admit it, but the research agenda of the nation's universities is set—even if only subtly and not completely—by the feds. We chase their money wherever they dangle it. If they stop funding research in A and start funding research in B, you can be sure that faculty researchers will switch their research programs from A to B. In this way bureaucrats and politicians in Washington influence the choices of research areas and problems that faculty pursue. It is not supposed to be that way. Academic freedom gives faculty the opportunity to pursue avenues of thought wherever their intellectual curiosity sends them. Well, the feds' dollars often trump curiosity.

In truth, I believe the federal intrusion on the academic community has been relatively mild thus far. But that doesn't mean that it always will be. Here's one area of concern that exists at the moment. Because of heightened security as a consequence of September 11, many more restrictions are being placed on grants funded by the Department of Defense, the Department of Homeland Security and other federal agencies. These restrictions include: various kinds of export controls on equipment and software, restrictions on foreign nationals (which many graduate students and some faculty are) participating on projects; and the requirement of clearing scholarly publications with federal "censors." All of this is anathema to the university's faculty and academic administrators who take pride in the open, free, and inclusive atmosphere in which university research takes place. So are they refusing the money? Not on your life! They are setting up phony shell organizations "off campus" to administer the grants. Power may corrupt, but so does money.

In a related vein, government regulation is also a large academic issue. Since we take all that money from the feds, we have to abide by their rules when administering it. So we on campus have become experts at the Americans with Disabilities Act (ADA), the Family Leave Act, minimum wage laws, and federal safety regulations. For a long time, a physics colleague had a sign on his door reading, "If you think OSHA is a small town in Wisconsin, then you are in big trouble." In fact, the university has a small army of staff required to cope with a legion of federal laws, regulations and bureaucratic clap-trap that impinges on virtually every aspect of university life: salaries, student admissions, tuition and fees, retirement, budgets, capital plant, inventory, lab equipment and safety, research grants, labor relations, work visas, and on and on. This issue does not play out as well with the faculty as the last one does. While they are generally pleased with high government spending, since it correlates very nicely with vast government support of higher education, they are not so thrilled with the massive government regulation that accompanies it. Faculty like to administer their affairs in an independent, seat of the pants fashion. They feel perfectly competent to design a curriculum, conduct a course or seminar, plan a research agenda, devise theories and carry out experiments without interference from senior university administrators, much less from federal bureaucrats. They see the numerous federal regulations that govern their operations as a very unwelcome intrusion.

The amazing thing is that they often fail to make the connection between the two—that is, government as teat and government as nuisance. They see their work as critical to the welfare of the community and the nation—and often it is—and therefore eminently worthy of government support. But they also feel perfectly capable of administering the projects, budgets and equipment the government support affords them on their own; they see the government's intrusion as meddlesome. They forget the maxim cited earlier: he who foots the bill calls the tune. Of course, much of this is highly ironic. For the faculty, with their liberal bent, are totally in favor of government regulations—as long as they don't interfere with their world. For example, the government regulation that keeps your kid in the back seat of the car facing away from you is fine. Government regulations on gasoline usage that drive up the price of cars and drive down their size (rendering them less safe naturally) are also fine. As are regulations mandating HOV lanes, which sit empty while you creep along in traffic right next to them. Government regulations on the amount of water your toilet can flush; on the number of smoke detectors in your new house; even on whether you can develop your own property (heaven forbid a snail darter, or a small pool of water lies nearby); these are all fine. The government assault on smokers is certainly fine. But if any government regulations impinge on faculty research, then it's not so fine. Well, you can't have it both ways. If you want a huge government driving the national academic research enterprise, then it is inevitable that the huge government will step on the toes of those pursuing the enterprise.

Let's move on. Sometimes I think the most oft used word on campus is *diversity*. The university seems to be positively obsessed with the concept. It enacts policies and pursues programs designed to "enhance diversity," motivated on the one hand by its faith that special dispensations for anyone who is not a white male will make up for past ills that the ancestors of said white males perpetrated on just about everyone else, and which today's white males would surely repeat if not held in check by diversity policies, and on the other hand by its fervent belief that "making the university look like America" is the right thing to do. Our campus' strategic plan asserts that we shall achieve "excellence through diversity"; all of our search committees must be diverse; our campus publications are over-stuffed with articles about the wonders of diversity and our commitment to diversity; we give awards to people who pursue research in diversity—whatever that is; we have councils, committees and task forces that study diversity, implement diversity, enforce diversity and shake a stick at the corners of campus that are not sufficiently diverse. Of course, the one kind of diversity to which a university should be truly committed—diversity of thought and opinion—well, on certain matters such diversity is definitely verboten.

The diversity mania is not restricted to the university. It runs rampant in the government, media, foundations and other segments of society that have succumbed to Leftist thought control. I am thinking of the legal profession, the courts, parts of the religious community, and surprisingly—although to a lesser extent—big corporations. But the university has it perfected. It is enshrined now in our by-laws, paid homage to in our strategic plans, enmeshed in our operating procedures, accepted as a wise principle by virtually all administrators and those of us who have doubts are silent before the juggernaut it has become.

Well, I'm in big trouble now, so I might as well keep going.

At its most benign, diversity—as it is practiced on campus—is a harmless feel good exercise that has little effect. In its original incarnation, namely in the form of affirmative action, it asserted that *all other things being equal*, the minority or female candidate would prevail over the white or male. But of course all other things are almost never equal. While affirmative action might have made sense 40 years ago as a means to redress prior wrongs and allow for a period of catch up, diversity today—at its least benign—is nothing more than reverse discrimination. It is invoked to legitimize the practice of passing over white or male candidates who may be better qualified than the selected minority or female candidate. Two wrongs do not make a right.

The previous three issues—government spending, government regulation and diversity—are the main ones (of our 24) intimately connected with academic life. But I have included a fourth, Constitution. In truth, it is no more a purely academic issue than is culture or rights, but I listed it here for three reasons. First, I think the argument about whether the Constitution is a living document or not takes on a particularly intense flavor in political science departments and law schools inside universities. Second, university faculty, who tend to be iconoclastic, with egalitarian and utopian tendencies, are particularly receptive to the idea of a living Constitution. Third—and now I am going to really be in deep trouble with my colleagues—because virtually everything that is done in the name of diversity on campus is in violation of the Fourteenth Amendment to the Constitution, universities have a vested interest in an evolving interpretation of the Constitution.

In this regard, I would like to point out the following delicious irony. University faculty and administrators, folks who are deeply committed to the idea that the Constitution was meant to be updated and reinterpreted in the light of modern times, are the same folk who often are intractably wedded to university structures and strictures laid down generations ago, and which they consider sacrosanct and untouchable. Thus faculty members will argue that academic freedom and tenure are inviolate, and subject to no loose interpretations that could jeopardize faculty independence or job security. These are the same people who will argue that the Constitution: grants a right to privacy that permits partial birth abortions and countenances homosexual marriage; mandates a one-man/one-vote principle that is incompatible with non-direct election of Senators and the President as originally specified in the Constitution; provides for rights of criminals way beyond the Fifth Amendment; and endorses judicial supremacy over the executive and legislative branches despite Hamilton's assertion in the Federalist Papers that the judiciary would be the weakest branch of the government. Tenure is sacrosanct, but the Constitution is fair game.

Historical Issues

Before we turn to the personal recollections that conclude the chapter, let's briefly comment on the staying power of the touchstone issues. In say 1875, quite a few of those issues would simply not have arisen in the political debate of the day—either because they would have had no meaning or because there was such a strong consensus on the issue that no dispute ever occurred. I am thinking of: abortion, welfare, homosexuality, diversity, wage regulations, gun control, capital punishment, the UN, the environment, animal rights and social justice. Today's fireworks over any of those issues are inconceivable a century and a quarter ago. But at that time, the following issues resonated just as loudly as they do today: spending—both government and military, international trade (tariffs), rights (slavery and Reconstruction), and if you fast forward 15-20 years, both immigration and culture would join the mix, as would the environment if you move forward into the early twentieth century. In analogy with today's battle over judicial activism, there was a tug of war between the executive and legislative branches of government—not that that conflict doesn't exist today, but it is increasingly overshadowed by the struggle between those two branches and the judiciary.

The point I want to make begins with the self-evident observation that issues come and go. If you look at the issues in the nation's past, some will look similar to those of today, some won't. But, at whatever period in American history, I believe it likely that the issues will spread out, as do today's issues, across the compartments set up at the beginning of this chapter. For example, the first two compartments have embraced hot issues throughout the history of the republic. But so have the final three. To cite some examples, the absolutist vs. relativist dichotomy shows up in the battles over Prohibition, the suffragette movement and many states rights disputes. Similarly the opportunist vs. egalitarian choice is present in battles over the gold standard and the birth of the labor movement. Finally, one can see the pragmatist vs. idealist duality clearly in the struggle to end slavery, settlement of the western frontier, and the infant nation's relations with the great powers in Europe. Thus, although issues come and go, there is some permanence to the compartments—yet another reason to feature them in our work in Part II.

I can still feel the knot in my stomach that I endured throughout the closing days of May and the first few days in June 1967. Like virtually all Jews outside Israel, I was terrified that a second Holocaust was about to be perpetrated. In retrospect, in light of Israel's lightning and stunning victory, those fears seem almost ridiculous now. But if you consult the Bible—er, that is, the New York Times—from those weeks, you will see that it was widely thought that the Jews of Israel were going to be in for a very rough time. The Soviets had armed the surrounding Arabs states to the teeth, Lyndon Johnson and the US State Department were making noises about remaining neutral in the forthcoming conflict (they were preoccupied after all with another little conflagration in Southeast Asia), Europe, led by France, had abandoned any support of the Jewish State, the Straits of Tiran were blockaded—an eventuality that the US had promised Israel would not be permitted to occur, and Arab armies were massing on Israel's borders to deliver a crushing, decisive and, according to Nasser, fatal blow to the 19-year old Jewish nation.

I remember thinking: How could God permit this to happen again—the slaughter of millions of Jews while the world does nothing to prevent it. I repeat that in retrospect those fears were groundless—but we didn't know that at the time. With the first reports that war had erupted on the morning of Monday, June 5, the knot and fear became unbearable. But the fear was dispelled when, within two days, it became clear that no second Holocaust was in the offing, but rather a tremendous Israeli victory.

In fact I should have known all along what was going to happen. For I had visited Israel in the summer of 1965 with my wife, Shelly. Shelly was the child of parents who had emigrated from Palestine to the US just before the Second World War. Shelly's father's entire family, who had moved from Estonia to Palestine in the 1920's, still lived in Israel, and it was to visit them that we traveled to Israel in 1965. Among the relatives, I met the husband of my wife's first cousin, an amazing fellow named Arieh Rigevsky. Arieh was without doubt the most dynamic person I have met in my entire life and during the ensuing 30 year relationship we enjoyed,[6] he had a tremendous influence on my thinking on a host of topics. In 1965 he predicted that there would be another war soon and that Israel would devastate the armies of Egypt, Syria and Jordan. Over the years I came to have great faith in Arieh's prognostications, but in 1967 I had not yet built up the confidence that I would later have in his opinions.

Here are some of the things that Arieh taught me:

- *After a two thousand year hiatus, the spirit of the Macabees was alive and well in the Jews of Israel, and Masada would not fall again.*

- *The poison of anti-Semitism is endemic in certain regions and among certain populations and the only way to deal with it is for the Jews to be strong, prepared and willing to fight—offensively preferably to defensively, and for generations if necessary.*

- *The war between the Jews and the Arabs—and indeed it is an ongoing war dating to the early part of the twentieth century, its inception being no later than the establishment of the British Mandate after World War I, continuing constantly since, with regular major outbursts (1929, 1936-1939, 1947-1949, 1956, 1967, 1970, 1973, 1982, 1987-1990, 2000-20??)—was bizarre in that, although, at least since 1956, the Jews are stronger militarily, the Arabs hold all the other cards. They have a tremendous population advantage, the oil, the political support of 95% of the countries of the world (or so it seems at the UN), the time and patience to fight for centuries if need be (as they did in order to defeat the Crusaders), and the deep religious conviction that their cause is just. They have something else that is rare in the annals of world history—the unwillingness or the inability to ever admit defeat. No matter how many times the Israelis clobber them, they never cry uncle; they just start preparations for the next round. At the end of WWII, the Germans said to the Allies, "OK, you win, we lose. What do we do next?" Ditto for the Japanese. Fortunately they both took our advice. But as the aftermath of the swift American military victory in Iraq demonstrates, the Arab mind seems incapable of admitting defeat and moving on. It's a strategy that usually insures great misery for their people, but one has to admit it may be a winning one over the very long haul. (See e.g. the aforementioned Crusaders.) Incidentally, they're still itching to win back Spain and to*

---

6.   Tragically, Arieh died at the age of 60 in 1995 from pancreatic cancer.

conquer Europe as their fellow Muslim Turks failed to do in 1683. They may actually be succeeding.

Arieh understood all this, and like the loyal Likkudnik that he was, he endorsed the policy that his party followed from its birth until sometime within the last decade or so. Namely, the only conceivable era in which the Arabs will reconcile themselves to a sovereign Jewish State in the Middle East is when their societies become liberal democracies. This will not happen soon, if ever. Therefore, Israel's only strategy for survival is to accept a state of perpetual war with the Arabs as the normal course of events, keep the guns oiled, and beat the crap out of them every time they forget the last beating. It is a very difficult atmosphere in which to lead a normal, peaceful, productive life, and it is absolutely unimaginable to the American mind. It worked for the Israelis for a long time, but it is proving difficult to sustain. A warrior like Yitzchak Rabin succumbed to the delusion that the arch terrorist Arafat was ready to make peace. It would appear that Ariel Sharon was similarly deluded about Arafat's successor.

I took virtually the same sage lessons on power, weakness and evil from the 6-Day war that I had taken from the Eichmann affair (see the end of Chapter 2). And I began to see more clearly the mistaken lessons from the latter exercise. It was impossible not to discern the impotence of the United Nations, the antagonism of Western Europe and the ambivalence in certain quarters of the United States. These new lessons, along with Arieh's encouragement, started me off on my long trek from Left to Right. Nevertheless, I was still quite naïve. I figured, as did most of my fellow Americans, that the great Israeli victory would bring about an end to the conflict. The Arabs would finally understand that they couldn't defeat Israel militarily, that they were doing more harm to their own people than to the Jews by continuing the struggle, that Israel would willingly yield all the lands they gained during the war in exchange for peace, and so the Arabs would surely, finally agree to a true peace. How foolish! It is now 40 years later, more than twice the time from the birth of Israel to the 6-Day War, and the Arab world is no closer to peace with Israel today than it has been at any time in the last six decades.

If you take the Israeli side of the Jewish-Arab conflict and give any credence to what Arieh has taught, then your position is irreconcilable with the liberal side in four of the five compartments in this chapter. Yet, the Jews of America, many of whom are rabidly pro-Israel, are deep in the liberal camp. How can they ignore the evidence? Well, they can because they are still stuck in 1967, believing that if Israel offers just the right set of concessions, the Arabs will extend the hand of peace. The only concession the Arabs will accept is Israel's bare neck before an Arab sword.

5

The Liberal/Conservative Divide in the USA; The Past

Now that we have a firm grasp of the key issues that divide liberal from conservative opinion, as well as the global world views and mental frameworks that account for those opinions, it behooves us to consider how we got here, how these issues have evolved over time. I will do that in this chapter, and then pick up the thread in Chapters 8 and 12. More precisely, in this chapter I will trace the history of the liberal/conservative divide over the last century, then in Chapter 8, I will assess the status and relative strengths of the two camps today, and finally in Chapter 12, I will offer some predictions about those relative strengths over the next few decades. Moreover, in all three chapters I will purposefully adopt the vantage point of the present. Of course, as historians will point out, nineteenth century Americans would approach the issues of separation of church and state, role of the military and international relations very differently than we do. Nevertheless, I shall interpret the stances and attitudes of nineteenth century Americans on those issues in the context of how we understand them today.

I intend to focus my attention primarily on the last century for the following reason. At the risk of some oversimplification, I will argue that, viewed from today's vantage point with an early twenty first century mindset, there was a fairly broad political/cultural consensus in the land from the early 1700s until roughly 1900, which would be characterized in today's lexicon as conservative. The early settlers of America, right up to the American Revolution, took their political cues from John Locke, Edmund Burke and Adam Smith, unlike the French and Germans of that era, who were animated more by the radical philosophes of the French school like Jean-Jacques Rousseau. From the early part of the eighteenth century until the later part of the nineteenth—and again I emphasize, from the vantage point of today—the overriding political philosophy of the United States of America was basically conservative. What is the evidence?

The founders were extraordinarily mindful of the harm that governments historically inflicted on their subjects. They were well-schooled in European history, as well as the history of the ancients. Therefore, they knew well that the unchecked powers of monarchies, oligarchies, military dictatorships and religiously-inspired sovereigns were prescriptions for loss of freedom, liberty and tranquility. But they were not idealists—they also knew that America could not consist of a series of bucolic villages, mercantile towns and seafaring ports, each pursuing prosperity while having little to do with one another. There had to be a central government, but it had to be designed wisely so as to avoid all the drawbacks associated with non-democratic forms of government. Actually, it took them two rounds to get it right—the failed Articles of Confederation preceded the successful Constitution. That said, I believe it is undeniable that our founding documents (the Declaration of Independence, the Bill of Rights, the Federalist Papers, and of course the Constitution) are a pragmatic, yet clearly and forcefully stated set of guidelines for a very conservative—by today's standards—form of government.

The federal government was small, limited in scope and proscribed—explicitly and implicitly—from meddling in the affairs of individual citizens. Its powers of taxation were very limited, therefore it did not have a lot of money to spend, and of course it regulated little beside interstate commerce. Its primary roles were to keep the currency sound, see that the laws were enforced, and protect the nation from foreign adversaries—testified to eloquently by the existence of only four cabinet level departments in George Washington's administration: Treasury, Justice, State and War. While today the activities of the federal government are sufficiently extensive and pervasive to fill the front page of any American newspaper, I venture the average American citizen in the 1700s and 1800s thought little about the federal government on a daily basis.

While the principle of separation of church and state was enshrined in the nation's lore—and law—at its birth, it was nevertheless true that religion played a huge role in society. Every city, town and village in the country had many churches, and within the latter a church was usually the focal point of the village green. Church attendance was very high. Religious references appeared often in public documents—as they do in the founding documents. Church officials commanded great respect among the populace. And without a doubt, the morals, principles and practices of the various Christian denominations held great sway in the minds, mores and homes of the American people. The percentage of the population to which these sentences would apply today is debatable, but in eighteenth and nineteenth century America, it was overwhelming.

Having stated the case in some detail for two of the key components of the conservative milieu in pre-twentieth century America (i.e., role of government and role of religion), let us pass more quickly through several others. The vast oceans separating America from Europe and the Orient, combined with the slow pace of communication, allowed most Americans to be blissfully unaware of world affairs. In fact the Yankees of that time—although they admired many of the cultural achievements of European civilization—were definitely chauvinistic about what they viewed as their evidently superior political system compared to those of Europe. While not homogeneous like Sweden or Japan, the country was overwhelmingly White, Anglo-Saxon (meaning of British and, to a somewhat lesser extent, central European descent) and Protestant—thus WASP. (Of course, this ignores the substantial number of black slaves, but we'll deal with that elsewhere.) Issues like animal rights, gun control, abortion, the environment or diversity simply had no context or meaning to pre-twentieth century Americans. In 1800, America was an agrarian society, the economy was firmly in laissez-faire mode, local affairs dominated everyone's attention, and religion was public and pronounced. I don't mean to paint an idyllic picture, yet life was simple, generally without copious choices and there was a common ethic. People looked to family, neighborhood, church and especially to themselves, to solve their problems. While life generally did not match Hobbes' classic description, that is, "solitary, poor, nasty, brutish and short," there were few safety nets and fewer creature comforts in comparison to the relative nirvana that we enjoy today. There was little time or inclination to ponder one's disadvantages, or to hatch schemes for others to fix them. There was even less opportunity to contemplate the general ills of society, nor any thought of asking the government to address them. Like I said, in the context of today, a very conservative society.

Well you might object that this description is apt for 1800, but much less so for 1900. Indeed, the United States went through major, convulsive transformations during the nineteenth century that resulted in enormous changes to the country: civil war and the abolition of slavery, industrialization, massive immigration, and the settling of the west and eventual closing of the frontier. Certainly

America looked very different at the end of the nineteenth century than it did at the beginning. Its population increased fifteen times, from roughly 5 million to 76 million souls. The land mass of the United States increased more than four-fold, from 865 thousand square miles to 3.5 million square miles (the latter includes a few territories that would eventually become states). The South's cotton-based economy was destroyed. Large numbers of freed slaves were not properly assimilated, but instead were segregated and confined to a poor rural life in the South and increasingly a poor urban life in the North. A rural America in 1800 was looking increasingly urban in 1900. Massive immigration from Western Europe in the early and mid part of the century yielded new citizens who were readily digested, but an even larger wave of immigration from Eastern Europe at the end of century produced more new Americans who—although they were largely assimilated—began to sow the seeds of great social, political and cultural change. The country remained overwhelmingly Christian, but it was no longer exclusively Protestant; there was now a substantial Catholic population. The number of Jews increased dramatically and although they constituted a small percentage of the population, they had a disproportionate effect in several critical areas, for example, business and the arts, and later in science, journalism, law and politics. The destiny of the country was no longer played out exclusively east of the Mississippi River. The vast scientific and technological advances of the nineteenth century created prosperity and opportunity. Those advances may seem primitive to us more than a century later, but railroads, electricity, telephone and telegraph, typewriters and adding machines, new methods of production (cotton gins, steam engines, coal-fired furnaces and sewing machines), and soon automobiles and airplanes, had a transforming effect on the everyday lives of American workers, consumers and producers. Instead of farmers and ranchers living and working in predominately rural areas, there were steadily more factory workers living and working in urban areas. And finally America was increasingly engaged in world affairs. This new engagement was highlighted at the fin de siècle by what many characterized as an aggressive role in the Spanish-American War.

These changes were reflected in some of the new issues that were coming on the table at century's end. These issues, which had no meaning or context a century earlier, included: the environment, the nature of the culture, the treatment of animals, and perhaps most importantly, "social justice" or the vast disparities in income and assets between the richest and poorest Americans. Some of the ideas of central and eastern European social and economic reformers were finding their way across the Atlantic in the books and minds of the new immigrants. It was only a matter of time until some of those seeds would bear fruit.

But not quite yet. It is my contention that at the end of the nineteenth century, despite the enormous changes wrought by the convulsive events described above, the fundamentally conservative political/cultural philosophy of the eighteenth century still reigned. Why do I say that? For the following reasons:

- The government is still small. It is true that Chief Justice John Marshall radically expanded the power of the judicial branch of government—contrary to Hamilton's assurances—when he created the concept of judicial review. And it is true that during the Civil War Abraham Lincoln accreted more power to the Federal Government than it had ever exercised in the country's first 85 years. Nevertheless, at the end of the nineteenth century, the national government is still accurately described as limited. There is no income tax, no federal involvement in education, health care, pensions or housing, and no alphabet soup of federal agencies actively regulating countless aspects of American life.

- The focus is still local. The life and interests of most citizens are still dominated by local events, organizations and people. Americans don't pay too much attention to what is going on in Washington, much less Paris or London.

- Religion is still important. Liberal Protestantism may no longer hold a monopoly on the people's religious affiliations, but religiously affiliate they still do. America remains a church-going, God-fearing people who define their morals primarily in terms of the teachings of their spiritual leaders and their holy books.

- WASP culture is still intact. Even though no longer monolithic, the percentage of the citizenry that is WASP is still very high. Moreover, the newcomers who are not, and especially their children, buy into the WASP culture quite avidly. The Protestant work ethic, the Calvinist tradition of modesty, respect for private property, spirit of rugged individualism, ideal of the traditional family—these are alive and well.

- The country is still insulated from the European continent. The telegraph and faster ships improve communication with Europe, but America remains largely uninvolved in the affairs of the Great Powers of Europe. The influence of European culture on America is still mainly confined to the upper crust.

- The predominant landscape is still rural rather than urban. Although this was changing rapidly, the breakdown between rural and urban land mass is still 60-40 in 1900. (It was 94-6 in 1800 and 19-81 in 2000.)

- There is still no mass media. People get their news from books, periodicals and newspapers. Radio, movies with audio and television are still decades away.

- Life expectancy is improved, but the concept of retirement for other than the very wealthy does not really exist yet. People just don't live long enough. Those who do are cared for by their children.

- Technological advance has been stunning, but not enough to fundamentally alter the roles of men and women as they would be altered in the twentieth century. Earning a living and managing a family are just too time-consuming and labor intensive; therefore, the division of those labors with men and women in the traditional roles remains engraved in stone and unchallenged.

- And finally, there is still a sense of the founders. In that vein, I recall when I was young, in the middle of the twentieth century, reading stories about people—admittedly very old people—who were alive during the Civil War, or even about a women who was only in her fifties but widowed from a much older man who fought in that conflict. It had the following effect on me when I studied the Civil War. I felt a sense of closeness to that epoch, not so unlike what I felt about World War II, during which I was born, or World War I, in which people from my grandfather's generation participated and spoke about. I had a completely different feeling when I studied the Revolutionary War—it might as well have been the Peloponnesian Wars. Well, in 1900 there were people alive who were also alive when Thomas Jefferson was alive. I imagine it created the same sense of pseudo-closeness to Revolutionary times that I felt to the Civil War era. Today of course both the Revolutionary War and the Civil War are just too long ago to be in anyone's personal frame of reference. But, speaking of the American Revolution, those in 1800 lived it, and those in 1900 could still relate to it in a personal way that we can no longer do today.

As I said, the core conservative political/cultural milieu of our forefathers was essentially intact at the end of the nineteenth century. But not for long.

It is difficult to pinpoint exactly when the liberal ascendancy began. But certainly the conservative dominance that marked the political/cultural philosophy of the American people for two centuries began to crumble somewhere in the neighborhood of the turn of the twentieth century. That dissolution was propelled by many events, ideas and movements. Let's list some key ones:

- The triumph of John Dewey's ideas about "free" public education, including how the government should mold pupils' beliefs;

- The growth of a powerful domestic labor movement;

- Increased environmental concerns, sparked by President Teddy Roosevelt;

- Wilsonian ideals of world peace and international cooperation;

- An infusion of socialist ideas that accompanied central and eastern European immigrants;

- The ratification in 1913 of the 16th amendment to the Constitution authorizing an income tax;

- The anti-trust movement;

- The suffragette movement;

- The advent of muckrakers who exposed excesses of American business;

- Adverse public reaction to the lives of robber barons and the extravagance of the Gilded Age;

- The Russian Revolution.

All of these events/developments occurred essentially during the first twenty years of the twentieth century—a period known to historians as the Progressive Era. I will now summarize what followed that era in a breathtaking recapitulation, by decades, of the seesaw nature of the liberal/conservative battle throughout the twentieth century. In fact, the last gasp of the conservatives occurred in the 1920s, the liberals took control in the 1930s, cemented their gains in the 1940s, enjoyed smooth sailing as their dominance was uncontested in the 1950s, then overreached in the 1960s, generating the beginnings of a backlash in the 1970s, that erupted into a full fledged counter-revolution in the 1980s, which, depending on your perspective, in the 1990s, achieved supremacy over, reached parity with, or still trails significantly behind the fifty-year liberal hegemony. Now let's flesh that out a little bit.

I will consider separately the nine periods: 1900-1920 and then each of the succeeding eight decades. The key events of course don't always fit neatly into separate decades, but it will be a handy device for outlining the progression of the liberal/conservative struggle during the century just concluded. For each period, I will do three things. First, I will supply a short bulleted list of the major events, ideas and movements that shaped the struggle in that period. Second, I elaborate on some of the bullets in a more discursive description of the crucial moments and distinguishing features of the decade that determined which way the liberal/conservative vectors were aligning. Third, I will highlight some of the touchstone issues that played key roles—those that came on the table and those that changed their position on the table. My treatment of the last period, the 1990s, will be a little skimpy, as I don't want to steal any thunder from Chapter 8. That is, I prefer to leave any assessment of recent events to the point when I am outlining where the liberal/conservative divide stands today. Anyway, when you reach the end of the discussion of the nine periods, you will have experienced, in about 20 pages, my quick political tour of the twentieth century. I confess that it reads a little like a description of an exciting, see-saw nine inning baseball game, so I hope you will enjoy the "reporting."

1900-1920. The Progressive Era

The bulleted list for the Progressive Era is found above. Viewed in the context in which I have described conservative America in the eighteenth and nineteenth centuries, the changes of the Progressive Era were actually rather radical. Government power expanded markedly, the market became less free, collectivist ideas gained currency and were implemented, notions of group rights were ascendant and a laboratory model for testing these ideas more concretely and vigorously was born in Soviet Russia. The alterations in society wrought by these changes were dramatic, although in truth not nearly as substantial as those that occurred in the century's other two major liberal outbursts—namely, during the 1930s and 1960s. Furthermore, the changes came along a very broad front as indicated by the variety of areas touched upon in the bulleted list. One remarkable feature of this story is that much of the impetus for the progressive program came from a Republican—Teddy Roosevelt. But I think more of the impetus derived from the real and perceived excesses of the business community as the full flower of the Industrial Revolution took hold. It would have been difficult to ignore the great fortunes amassed—and flaunted, the poor working conditions under which many laborers suffered, the industrial pollution, the denial of voting rights to women, and the exploitation of immigrants. There is no question that these and other abuses occurred. Guided by the statist philosophy sweeping Europe, America also looked to the government to solve these problems—as it would increasingly throughout the century, and still does today. The great unanswered question is: what if we hadn't done that? Would the market have corrected the abuses on its own? Would the drive for profits unearthed more effective entrepreneurs who would have built better, cleaner, cheaper widgets, under more palatable working conditions, thereby eventually curing the ills I described? We'll never know. We cannot run a controlled experiment on an alternate time line as they do in Star Trek. Adherents can argue forcefully from both sides. Yes, the market would have corrected the abuses and spared us the soft government tyranny that burdens us today. No, the market failed us and we were headed for industrial tyranny; only the benevolent intervention of government saved us from that horrible fate.

During the Progressive Era our schmorgasbord of touchstone issues underwent the following changes. Of course government regulations and government taxes became major issues, with the more liberal stance in favor of increasing each gaining acceptance. International affairs also became more prominent as America, starting in the Spanish-American War and proceeding to World War I, began to play a major role in world affairs. For example, although the US never joined, it played a crucial role in setting up the failed League of Nations. Not only did America increasingly intervene in world affairs with the goal of affecting the behavior of other nations, but also Americans, especially new Americans, were more receptive to the idea that political and economic structures deployed by European governments might provide models worth emulating. This increased internationalism was advocated primarily by those on the Left. The Right tended toward isolationism and insularity from world engagement—quite the opposite of today's relative positions. We'll discuss this more fully later. Continuing with the changes in the issues schmorgasbord, liberal thought on many social issues was also gaining the upper hand. One consequence of mass immigration and the industrial revolution was an increase in crime. But now the country responded with more emphasis on rehabilitation and less on punishment. Environmental concerns jumped onto the radar screen in a big way. People became conscious of pollution and they wanted the government to fix it. One response: national parks were carved out of huge government land holdings. Next, the culture was called into question for the first time. America was no longer exclusively WASP—why should the WASP culture be paramount? Irish and Italian Catholics sought a place at the table. One of their number, Al Smith, even secured the Democratic nomination for President, although he did not win. Finally, the greatest issue change was the arrival of social justice on the agenda. The inequalities in wealth among the populace are stark and the people start to expect the government to do something about it.

1920-1930. The Roaring Twenties and a 'Return to Normalcy'

The phrases I would use to highlight this decade are:

- The roaring twenties;
- A "return to normalcy";
- Protectionist fever;
- The "business of America is business";
- The end of mass immigration;
- Media superheroes.

The decade of the 1920s, commonly called the Roaring Twenties, represented on the one hand a strong reaction to the Progressive Era and on the other—although it was not evident at the time—the last gasp of the classic American conservative age. Sentiment in the country moved against big government and in favor of big business. The end of the Great War (as World War I was known then), reductions in taxes, the increasingly favorable business climate in the States—especially in comparison to the devastated economies of Europe, and a growing confidence in the destiny of America, all these led to a resurgence of the private market and an economic roar of the kind that had not been seen in the United States for some time. The times were summed up in the chief campaign slogan of Warren Harding, elected President in 1920, calling America to a "return to normalcy." A similar clarion call by his successor, Calvin Coolidge, namely "the business of America is business" also captured the spirit of the period. The decade also saw the emergence of what we would today call *media superheroes*. America never lacked for superheroes (George Washington, Benjamin Franklin and Thomas Jefferson at the outset, Andrew Jackson and Abraham Lincoln at mid 19th century, and later Thomas Edison, Mark Twain and Teddy Roosevelt), but in the 1920s, the advent of the mass media (large circulation newspapers, radio and talking movies) elevated the concept to that of media superhero—a concept that has only grown with the passing decades. The two that stand out for me are Babe Ruth and Charles Lindberg. Both captured the imagination of the public in a way that former heroes, in an age of much more limited media, were not able. I think this phenomenon was representative of the boom times, the roaring twenties. Indeed, the number of cars that Henry Ford put outside American homes was staggering; America exhibited a newfound confidence on the world stage; and fortunes were made on Wall Street.

But there was a dark side to the story. Harding's was one of the most corrupt administrations in the nation's history. The fever of protectionism swept the land as both business and labor—for different reasons—mistakenly advocated high tariffs. America's international confidence unfortunately manifested itself in a trend toward extreme insularity and isolationism (that would grow more intense in the next decade). This was highlighted by America's refusal to participate in the League of Nations—despite the fact that it was Woodrow Wilson's idea. And the country, when bringing mass immigration to a close, did not adopt a measured policy, but instead slammed the door shut. Finally, the folly of prohibition resulted in crime, contempt for government edicts, and a cynicism that would soon be reinforced by the events of the next decade.

During the roaring twenties, the changes in the touchstone issues were few in comparison to what transpired in the Progressive Era. People put a brake on the rapid pace of change experienced in the first two decades of the century. The chief observation is that the needle on the international meter continued to read high as free trade was impeded by high tariffs, mass immigration was halted by the severely restrictive new immigration laws passed at mid-decade, and fitful attempts to create an international legal system proved futile. What of this was conservative and what liberal is hard to pinpoint here as the liberals were becoming increasingly internationalist, while the conservatives were moving in the opposite direction. We'll explore that development in greater depth later. Two other issues did register to some extent: (i) the culture, as the backlash to massive immigration was reflective of WASPs trying to reassert control; and (ii) religion, highlighted by Smith's candidacy, although it is still the case that the conservative hold on the religious constituency in the nation remains intact.

1930-1940. The Depression and the New Deal

Here's the list of the main events and movements:

- The Great Depression;
- Fascism in Europe;
- The rising sun in the Orient;
- The New Deal;

- Nazi aggression;
- The triumph of liberalism.

Of course the decade began in some sense a couple months early when the Stock Market crashed on October 29, 1929. That event, traditionally viewed as the beginning of the Great Depression, is one of the signature calamities of the American experience. The economic and social difficulties that followed cast doubt on the viability of our nation. It caused millions of Americans to decide that the country needed to be structured and governed differently from how it traditionally had, and thereby heralded the triumphant ascendancy of a liberal philosophy. Franklin Roosevelt and the liberal democrats who accompanied him to Washington seized the opportunity to expand the power, influence and reach of the federal government on society in a fashion completely unknown in the preceding century and one half of US history. Income taxes were increased and the idea of withholding it from paychecks was conceived.[1] Social Security and its attendant payroll tax were enacted. A slew of new government agencies were created to regulate American agriculture, transportation, energy and the environment. And even though these intrusions would pale in comparison with government interventions in these and other areas 30 years later, they were still monumental in comparison with past practice. As usual, there are two schools of thought. The New Deal was at best "socialism light" and its collectivist policies were and remain an albatross that restricts freedom and limits economic growth. The New Deal saved America from a fascist destiny, which was the fate that Germany—suffering from similar economic conditions—endured, and which, without the New Deal, we might very likely have replicated. You take your pick!

Having invoked Nazi Germany, I will mention the self-evident fact that fascism is the other great story of the 1930s. In Germany, in Italy and in Japan, fascist regimes took control and initiated policies that would lead in the next decade to the greatest conflagration in the history of the world. Why did these racist, aggressive and intolerant regimes come to power? There is no quick and easy answer, but here are two that match the spirit of my presentation. They arose because the unscrupulous business class, unconstrained by moral concerns for the people's welfare, sought to control the means of production and concentrate power in a limited number of hands. Au contraire, each regime was a grotesque manifestation of collectivist government in which socialist ideas of government

---

1.   but not implemented until 1943.

control of means of production and ownership of all property were carried to their logical extremes—namely, tyranny, which, as predicted by Hayek, is the inevitable outcome of collectivism. Your choice again!

In America, evolution in attitudes on the touchstone issues picked up speed. Being a decade of great upheaval, the evolution actually was more like a revolution as the pendulum swung sharply to the Left. The biggest change of course was in the area of social justice as the Roosevelt administration's big government solutions to the economic calamity found favor in the eyes of large portions of the population. Opinion swung in favor of drastically increased government spending, regulations and taxes, also in favor of wage and welfare laws, and against military spending. The liberal position was also gaining popularity in other areas, like a living Constitution, high tariffs, environmental activism and in the broadening of the cultural base. At the risk of beating the same drum, I would remark that, drastic as these changes in attitude were, opinion would move even more sharply to the Left in the 60s and 70s.

1940-1950. World War II

The main events are easy to recognize:

- War in Europe and the Pacific;
- Atomic weapons;
- The division of Europe at Yalta;
- The emergence of communism as a world force: start of Word War III;
- A new attempt at world government—the UN;
- Economic reconstruction: the Marshall Plan;
- Occupation: converting Germany and Japan into democracies;
- The end of colonialism and dismantling of empires.

Once again the decade began months earlier, this time when Germany touched off the Second World War by invading Poland on September 1, 1939. The calamity that befell Europe, and the world for that matter, is without parallel in the annals of history. Tens of millions brutally slaughtered, the heavy boot of Nazi occupation across much of the continent for more than 5 years, disruption in the lives and economies of virtually all countries around the globe, and of course the destruction of European Jewry through the purposeful, methodically planned and systematic murder of six million people. That America rose up to defeat the German and Japanese racist, fascist regimes is one of the great rescue stories of history. Had fascism triumphed, it is horrific to imagine the fate of the world and its peoples. It is important to remember that America's struggle was not associated with the Left or the Right. Aside from some crazies on the extreme Right, who doubted the evil of the Nazi regime, and some equally loony Leftists, who only cared about the health of the Soviet Union, the country was remarkably united in the fight. The victory was not complete, however, in that an equally totalitarian and evil Soviet empire emerged victorious, and thereby ensued four and one half decades of continued conflict—to be touched upon in the description of later decades in this recitation. Another caveat is that the nuclear genie escaped from the bottle. But the foreign policy unity in America continued with the Marshall Plan, the rebuilding of Europe, the establishment of the United Nations, a sustained and eventually successful effort to convert our defeated foes into liberal democracies, and finally our support and encouragement of the divestment of their colonial possessions by our European allies.

The foreign policy consensus was, in a perverse way, replicated in domestic affairs. For while the international affairs consensus was one among equals, that of domestic affairs reflected the fact that one side had thoroughly trounced the other. Indeed, the radical growth of government instituted in the 1930s was solidified in the 1940s—first because it seemed necessary to prosecute the war, and second because the conservative forces in America offered only the most token opposition. The country coasted toward mid century (1950) with gargantuan income tax rates, the regulatory agencies purring along on overdrive, and a consensus throughout the land that this was for the best—a well-regulated business community with massive government programs was the way to ensure continued prosperity and no return to the economic disaster of the Depression.

It was a remarkably quiet decade regarding changes in the issues—very little in the way of evolution was going on. There were these consensuses after all. The upheavals of the 1930s were consolidated and institutionalized. No substantial change in attitudes on the touchstone issues was occurring. But it would be less so in the following decades as the pendulum would lurch again, further to the Left.

1950-1960. The Liberal Hegemony

The major events:

- The Korean War—a surrogate battle of WWIII;

- Nuclear arsenals;

- Suburbanization of America;

- Ike—normalcy means something different from 30 years earlier;

- Desegregation and the civil rights movement;

- The Warren Court.

The 1950s are almost always misrepresented in schools and the media as a decade of conservatism and calm. This is false in both respects. First, the conservative America of 1800 or 1900 was by 1950 dead and buried. The key point is that the Republican administration of Dwight Eisenhower made no effort whatsoever to roll back or undo the New Deal. It could not if it wanted to, which it did not. Liberal political philosophy reigned unchallenged in the land. To cite just three examples: federal marginal income tax rates topped 90%; the Warren Court rode roughshod over the other branches of government; and the massive federal bureaucracy created to fight the Depression and prosecute the War against Fascism was not trimmed, but instead continued its steady growth. People may have felt after the world-wide conflict of the preceding period that things were back to normal—but that "normal" was the welfare state created by the changes of the Progressive Era and the New Deal, not the normalcy of the roaring twenties and certainly not 1880s normalcy. More importantly, the liberal consensus is so firmly entrenched and unquestioned that people do not realize it. The New York Times can blithely castigate the reactionary alliance of big business and conservative southern politicians who supposedly control America, whereas in fact every time the Times identifies a new national crisis, the people support its clamor for new government programs and agencies designed to deal with the urgent situation.

The second assertion, that of "calm," is also without merit. A little perspective is in order. America enjoyed 30 years of peace between the end of the Revolutionary War and the War of 1812, then another 45 peaceful years between that conflict and the Civil War (the Mexican-American War does not count as a truly major conflagration), and another 50 years of peace between the end of the Civil War and the start of World War I (the Spanish-American War also does not count), and then a 20 years interval until World War II erupted. The point is that World War III began immediately as WWII ended (perhaps even earlier).

Incidentally, this wretched phenomenon has been repeated as WWIV commenced as WWIII concluded—and again, perhaps even before. During the decade of the 1950s we saw the drive to build nuclear arsenals, the battle for the allegiance of non-aligned countries and of course the Korean War (which was, like the Vietnam War, a great battle in WWIII). One could argue that the Marshall Plan and the rebuilding of Europe were also battles in WWIII and that, although they commenced in the 40s, they are properly associated with the post-war 50s era. America was not enjoying a postwar calm in the 1950s; it was in fact, despite its wishes, gearing up to fight WWIII. The fact that the war was more "cold" than "hot" masked its intensity, and often even camouflaged the fact that we were at war at all. (Of course we can be grateful that we never had to meet Soviet troops on the battle field and no nuclear exchanges occurred.) But it is important to reiterate that, like domestic policy, there was a consensus on foreign policy. The former was overwhelmingly liberal, but the latter could still qualify as conservative as the nation was fairly united in identifying the ultra Leftist Soviet Union as an enemy of American freedom that had to be combated. That unity would come unhinged in the next decade.

One could argue that it was in the 1950s that America became the nation that we know today: vast military strength, prosperous, technologically advanced, suburbanized, motorized, materialistic, truly pluralistic, and confident that the moderate welfare state it had established would ensure continued prosperity. All of these attributes remain valid a half-century later except the last. The consensus on the welfare state has been challenged and shaken from both sides: in the immediately ensuing decades in the furious assault by the Left to enhance collectivism, followed by the Right's counter-revolution to limit government scope.

Befitting the two consensuses I've described, the needle on the issues meter stayed relatively calm throughout the decade—with one enormous exception. The country attempted to come to grips with, and reach a benevolent resolution of, the most egregious stain on its record—slavery and its successor, segregation. The shame of slavery had ended formally nine decades earlier. Now the country confronted segregation—the dreadful system that succeeded slavery, less evil perhaps, but still woefully immoral. Speaking as a conservative here, I would acknowledge that this is an arena in which "privatization" was less than a booming success and that government intervention seems to have been required in order to resolve the problem. The achievements of the Civil Rights movement—a moral and political coalition of clergymen, politicians and social leaders—were stupendous. Arguing and cajoling with great moral clarity, the movement—with Martin Luther King in the lead—effected a great change in the attitude of the majority of Americans, and the system of *legal* discrimination was finally laid to rest in a process that was completed in the next decade.

1960-1970. Woodstock

The major events:

- The assassination of JFK;
- Annihilation of Goldwater;
- Vietnam War;
- The Great Society;
- Woodstock;
- Urban riots;
- A trip to the moon.

The decade of the 1960s, unlike its two predecessors, "began late." The election of John Kennedy in 1960 seemed, at the time, to herald great change. But in fact, in the grand scheme of the liberal/conservative divide, it changed little. His death in 1963, on the other hand, was a catalyst for major changes. It was the spark that triggered events, which in some ways we are still trying to cope with four decades later. The Johnson administration that came to power after Kennedy's assassination proved to be the conveyor of the third great leap to the Left—following the Progressive Era and the New Deal. It brought us the Great Society. We saw an even more extensive intervention by the federal government into the affairs of the American people—in areas that had escaped its attention heretofore (health care, housing, the arts, and more).

The Left interpreted the rout of Barry Goldwater in 1964 as a total repudiation of conservatism by the people of the US, and it felt free to steer the ship of state sharply to port into uncharted waters of collectivism. For example, the administration declared War on Poverty—a "war" we are subsequently winning, but primarily by decommissioning the "weapons" deployed by the Great Society, which worsened the problems in many areas and created numerous new ones in others. Monetary policy was pursued that drove inflation and interest rates sky high—in line with liberal policy that such practices will, so they believe, increase government revenues. As already mentioned, the legal civil rights battle was brought to a successful conclusion, but policies, principles, programs and practices were put in place that several decades later would result in the perversion of Dr. King's expressed goals, and in many ways prolong the suffering of a significant portion of those formerly deprived of their civil rights.

In foreign affairs, the Johnson administration would emit the last gasp of aggressive liberal internationalism. It attempted to prosecute the surrogate World War III battle in Vietnam by pretending the struggle was less serious than the great leap to the Left that it was pursuing domestically. In the end, neither effort succeeded. We fought in Vietnam with one hand tied behind our back, and we got our fannies kicked.[2] The liberal response to their own debacle in Vietnam was basically, "I'm never doing that again," an oath they have adhered to faithfully ever since.

But the domestic Great Leap Forward continued unabated. The assault was not only political and economic, it was also, and perhaps more importantly, cultural. The liberals emptied the prisons and the mental hospitals, paid poor women to boot out their husbands and have babies with multiple partners, built urban ghettos replete with Soviet style housing and gave the residents free reign to trash them, coarsened the culture by removing all moral checks on what could be depicted in the media, celebrated depravity in orgies like Woodstock, and excused—perhaps even encouraged—urban riots as a legitimate means to express displeasure with society's injustices—or, as in the case of Mayor Lindsay, paid protection money to social extortionists to forestall the riots that were threatened if said payments were not forthcoming. Near chaos reigned. Was America viable? Where would the turmoil end? The Soviets watched, took note and struck out on the offensive in the next decade.

Two events occurred at the end of the decade to suggest that perhaps the liberal dominance was not quite so total. But, as we shall see, these were false signals. The first was the election of Richard Nixon as President in 1968. Many interpreted this as a sign of fatigue among the people from the convulsions spawned by the liberal (mis)governance of society. But in fact Nixon's election represented

---

2.   Or so it is perceived. In truth we fought the Communists to a draw and left South Vietnam in a position to defend itself—until we cut off their aid and stopped delivering weapons.

no more of a turn around than Eisenhower's did sixteen years earlier. The liberals hated Nixon—they still do. But a close examination of his record reveals little that is conservative, and no attempt at a rollback of the Great Society. For heaven's sake, Nixon instituted wage and price controls! He also dramatically expanded the number and power of federal regulatory agencies. In fact, Nixon represented no threat to the liberal hegemony—people just didn't want to go quite as far left as the Democratic Party sought to lead it.

The second "false" sign was the moon landing in the summer of 1969. The fulfillment of President Kennedy's dare, stated at the outset of the decade, was unquestionably a great achievement for America, and showed that working together with dedication and perseverance, the nation could still aspire to and accomplish monumental feats. Such a feat ran counter to the increasingly bleak picture that the liberals were painting of American society—one characterized by racism, nationalism, colonialism, and economic injustice. How could a society afflicted with those defects achieve something so spectacular and noble? Well, their answer was that the achievement was in fact a great accomplishment of the federal government, not corporate America, and so space exploration was institutionalized as the sole province of the federal government. Like all the other federal government programs of the 1960s, today it is evident that NASA is no more accomplished than any other inept, mismanaged and often misguided federal department or agency. So if the second sign was not false, it was at least misleading.

The continued liberal dominance is reflected in the country's attitudes on the issues. The needle screeches unceasingly to the left. The liberal stance is victorious on government spending, government regulations, welfare, wage laws, judicial activism, social justice, criminal rights and almost every other barometer in the touchstone issues. Although the NY Times is still railing against the conservative forces that are blocking progress, it is in fact true that the liberal position on the key issues is accepted wisdom, the liberals control all branches of government, and they are increasingly dominant in the media, university, legal profession, foundations and virtually every other elite corner of American life.

Will the new liberal philosophy reign for 200 years the way the conservative philosophy did? It has a firm grip. But the grip will become a vise, and a serious backlash would ensue.

1970-1980. Stagflation

The major events:

- More Vietnam;
- Nixon and Watergate;
- Roe vs. Wade;
- Soviets on the march;
- Malaise in America;
- Fall of the Shah and rise of the Ayatollah;
- Emergence of Pope John Paul II, Margaret Thatcher and Ronald Reagan.

In the history of our beloved republic, the 1970s will not be remembered as one of its more glorious decades. The Vietnam War dragged on through half the decade, ending only after we negotiated a strategic retreat and then cut our South Vietnamese allies off at the knees. In the record books it went down as our first defeat in war, although (as previously mentioned) it should be more accurately described as a draw. The final defeat was suffered by the ally we betrayed; if we insist on categorizing it as a defeat for the US, then it should be remembered that we were not defeated militarily on the battlefield, rather our defeat was political in the court of domestic public opinion. Incredibly, the loss was compounded by our disgraceful treatment of the war's veterans.

Aside from the Vietnam battle, the overall Cold War was not going well. The Soviets and their surrogates were on the march in Africa, Asia and Latin America. Our European allies were increasingly nervous about our ability to protect them and were reverting more and more toward their natural inclination—appeasement. The Soviets spent wildly on conventional and nuclear weapons, despite—as we now know—the fact that little was left for domestic needs. They spawned vicious little clones of themselves all around the globe; probed our weaknesses at every opportunity; violated every arms agreement we made with them; tried to cajole us into unilateral disarmament (a course of action that many "peace-loving" liberals endorsed); kept a heavy boot on the enslaved countries of eastern Europe; and at the end of the decade brazenly invaded a neighboring country.

The difficulty of our international position and our military weakness were reflected in a declining ability to control world events. This was highlighted by the gasoline embargo imposed upon us in 1973-74 by various oil-producing countries—a group that included many so-called friends. Some of those friends are still our friends and behave as duplicitously and treacherously toward us as they did 30 years ago. That a bunch of two-bit countries could inflict economic hardship and political embarrassment upon us revealed how weak our position had become in the international arena. We had lost the will to punish our enemies and discipline our friends. I believe these calamities were a natural consequence of virtually unopposed liberal policies that were increasingly marked by isolationism, pacifism, third world worship and an inclination toward unilateral disarmament. But matters would get worse.

Indeed, following the caretaker government of Gerald Ford, the dominant liberal milieu coughed up the naïve, inexperienced and manifestly inept Jimmy Carter—unquestionably the most incompetent president of the 20th century. His failures were both domestic and international. His economic policies literally drove the economy into the ground: high unemployment, astronomical interest rates, explosive inflation, and stagnant economic growth. The pejorative coined to describe his accomplishments was "stagflation." By the end of the decade, the economic mess was so bad that articles were written predicting that Japan, Western Europe and even the Soviet Union would surpass the US economically. Carter was equally adept at foreign affairs. The strongest move he ever made against the Soviets was to deprive hard working American athletes of the chance to compete in the 1980 Moscow Olympics. In retrospect, the gravest mistake he made was to apply his misguided notions of international justice to Iran. He aided the overthrow of the Shah and opened the door to the mullah thugocracy that still governs there and spreads its poison throughout the world. So in summary, while Carter was guiding us to defeat in World War III, he was simultaneously wrecking the economy and helping to launch the careers of the barbarians who would eventually initiate World War IV. Carter's horrendous presidency was summed up poignantly by two events at the end of the decade: his pathetic speech in July 1979 that blamed the "malaise"[3] of the American people for the dour state of affairs, and the utter humiliation of the hostage crisis in Tehran.

---

3.   The word is never invoked in the speech, but the intention is clear and the appellation was immediately affixed.

Like I said, not our finest decade. But I cannot leave it without mentioning two more points. The first concerns the Supreme Court. In our country's first century and one-half, the Supreme Court largely lived up to Hamilton's prediction that it would be the least powerful of the three branches of government. Certainly the Court, led by Chief Justice John Marshall, invented its own power of judicial review in Marbury vs. Madison (1803). But, with the exception of several monumental—and for the most part, wrong-headed—decisions like Dred Scott vs. Sanford (1857) and Plessy vs. Ferguson (1896), the Court mostly fulfilled its role of judicial referee assigned to it by our founders. This began to change drastically in mid twentieth century with Brown vs. Board of Education (1954), Engel vs. Vitale (1962), Griswold vs. Connecticut (1965) and Miranda vs. Arizona (1966). In the reigning liberal hegemony, what could not be legislated in legislatures was legislated in the courts. Some would say this movement reached its zenith in 1973 in Roe vs. Wade, the ruling that mandated legal abortion nationwide.[4] Surely this has proved to be one of the most contentious rulings ever issued by the Supreme Court. More than 30 years later the country remains badly divided about its legitimacy and no consensus is in sight. Whether one believes that Roe vs. Wade was a blow for human freedom in that it legitimized a women's control over her own body or that it was a huge step toward a culture of death, there are several points that are incontrovertible:

- At the time, many States had already legalized abortion and it was clearly going to be legal in the vast majority of the country's jurisdictions rather soon; there was no compelling need for the federal intrusion on the prerogatives of State legislatures.

- In fact, this was a classic case of "legislating from the bench." The Supreme Court rendered legal abortion the law of the land.

- Moreover, there were absolutely no grounds for its decision to be found in the US Constitution. The justices invented a right to privacy that is neither present nor implied in the Constitution, but according to the eminent justices, was hiding in the penumbra of certain clauses[5]. The justices wanted a certain outcome, so they made up the justification. Even many proponents of legalized abortion admit that Roe vs. Wade (and Griswold vs. Connecticut for that matter) was very bad Constitutional law. The

4.   But maybe not; others would cite Regents of the University of California vs. Bakke (1978), Bush vs. Gore (2000), or even New London, Conn. vs. Kelo (2005) as equally controversial "power grabs."

Constitution was never more *alive* than in these two cases. Since Roe, the Court has not hesitated in its pursuit of *judicial activism*—by which I mean discovering new rights in the Constitution, legislating from the bench, and exceeding its Constitutional authority, *not* overturning or reversing rulings that liberals happen to favor and/or are constitutionally not viable.

The second point I want to make is that despite the setbacks of the 1970s, there was a silver lining to the cloudy forecast. In fact, there were three silver linings that appeared toward the decade's end, and they were Karol Wojtyla, Margaret Thatcher and Ronald Reagan. Of course, it would not be until the 1980s that these three great heroes of freedom would roll back the tide.

Regarding attitudes on the issues, the needle continues to drift Left. Little would change regarding pro-liberal positions on government spending and taxation, military affairs, social justice and the living Constitution. The biggest changes are in the cultural issues wherein abortion is legalized, homosexuality is increasingly accepted as a lifestyle choice (whether voluntary or not) instead of an aberration, criminal rights are expanded, environmental and animal rights activism is encouraged (the first Earth Day was in 1970), and religion is progressively banished from the public square. A virtual clean sweep for the liberal agenda. But the counter-revolution is poised to begin.

1980-1990. Ronald Reagan

The major events:

- Ronald Reagan;
- Defeat of communism and fall of the Soviet Union;
- Emergence of Islamic fundamentalism;
- Robert Bork and Clarence Thomas;
- Tiananmen Square;
- An Economic Boom.

---

5.   More precisely, according to Justice Douglas in Griswold vs. Connecticut (1965), the right arises because "specific guarantees in the Bill of Rights have penumbras, formed by emanations from those guarantees that help to give them life and substance." Roe was based directly on Griswold.

The liberals will choke on this sentence, but "The two politicians of the twentieth century who achieved the greatest good were Winston Churchill and Ronald Reagan." Without Churchill, Britain falls and the Nazi menace might still be with us. Without Reagan, the evil Soviet empire is still at our throats. The number of human beings who live in freedom today, thanks to those two gentlemen, is counted in the hundreds of millions. Ah, but a liberal might counter with "What about Woodrow Wilson or Franklin Roosevelt? I might begrudgingly acknowledge that Reagan played a role in the West's victory in WWIII, but Roosevelt and Churchill won WWII together and Wilson won WWI." (Actually a case for Mahatma Gandhi might be made since India is the largest democracy on earth.)

Well, there is a recent book[6], which asserts that the US entry into WWI, which Wilson engineered, tipped a balance that might have led to a genuine stalemate, a stalemate that could have prevented the rise of both Nazi Germany and Communist Russia. Maybe! But there is no question that Wilson's "war to make the world safe for democracy" did not achieve its objective; nor did the League of Nations or the Treaty of Versailles—both closely associated with Wilson—lead to any "great good." On the other hand, Franklin Roosevelt certainly deserves enormous credit for understanding clearly the ominous consequences of not opposing fascism and for leading the free world in combating it. But conversely, I see him, since he is the author of the New Deal, as the instigator of much that is harmful in our economic and social systems. Moreover, he is legitimately criticized for underestimating Stalin and thereby acquiescing to agreements that resulted in the enslavement of Eastern Europe for two generations. But those criticisms aside, his candidacy is disqualified by one inescapable fact: his tangential complicity—intended or not—in the Nazi final solution to the Jewish problem. By not opening the door to Jewish immigration before the war, by seeming to turn a blind eye to Jewish pleas for help[7] and thereby giving at least an inadvertent green light to Hitler when the screws were tightening, by refusing to acknowledge the slaughter even when it was known to be happening, and by ordering American bombers to avoid the crematoria as they flew over Auschwitz/Birkenau, Roosevelt's reputation is forever sullied. Had he appeared in front of a camera in 1943 or even 1944 and said, "Herr Hitler, I

---

6.   Jim Powell, Wilson's War: How Woodrow Wilson's Great Blunder Led to Hitler, Lenin, Stalin, and World War II."

7.   Consult, e.g. the well known stories of the Conference at Evians-les-Bains in 1938 or the voyage of the refugee ship St. Louis in 1939.

know what you are doing and I will see to it that you and your cronies are punished appropriately as soon as I get my hands on you," the Nazis—who attempted to cover up their atrocities when the tide of war turned against them—might well have tempered, or even ceased their genocidal campaign, thereby sparing hundreds of thousands, if not millions of lives.

But I digress. The election of Ronald Reagan in 1980 marked a sharp turning point in American political history. The confused, inept and liberal Jimmy Carter was replaced by the bold, clear-thinking and conservative Ronald Reagan. Reagan had three prime objectives: bring down the Evil Empire; restore the American economy by implementing lower taxes and deregulation of government-regulated industries; and dramatically reduce the scope of government. He succeeded in the first two. Through a combination of a serious military build up, the Strategic Defense Initiative (SDI or Star Wars), economic dynamism (see below), support of local armed resistance to Soviet clients, and moral clarity, he brought the Soviet Union to its knees. Eastern Europe was unshackled and the USSR dissolved in less than a dozen years from his inauguration—with almost no bloodshed! Surely this ranks as one of the great accomplishments of mankind. That we don't annually celebrate the fall of the Berlin Wall or the day the Soviet Union disbanded—as say we celebrate VE Day or VJ day—is a sorry testament to the liberals continued control of the opinion making organs in the country. But in fact, our victory over communism in the Cold War, or WWIII, was as great, as important, and as liberating as our victory over fascism.

Reagan's program to restore the economy also succeeded brilliantly. After a relatively brief, albeit painful recession, the economy responded to the stimuli he fed it with one of the longest economic expansions the country has ever experienced. Aside from an exceedingly mild and transitory recession in George H.W. Bush's term (grossly exaggerated by the liberal pundits), the economy roared ahead at a record pace for nearly 20 years. During that time, the US put to rest the notion that Japan or the European Union would eclipse us economically. Today, our growth far succeeds theirs, our unemployment is way below theirs and our economic engine makes their look paltry. The only countries that matched us in that period were several East Asian nations (and perhaps Ireland), whose economies also enjoyed open markets, low taxes, deregulation and curtailed welfare state entitlements. Today, new challenges arise in India and China, but these occur long past the Reagan era of the 1980s.

Reagan's triumph was not complete. He failed to reign in the size of government and the leviathan has continued to expand ever since. Also, his triumph over Soviet Communism did not extend to a defeat of Chinese Communism. For a brief period in the spring of 1989 in Beijing's Tiananmen Square, it looked like that victory might be within reach. But the protests of the Chinese students were brutally crushed by the Chinese Army and the Chinese Communist nightmare goes on. Their version of perestroika seems to be working: economic liberalism coupled with social and political repression. Those of us who believe in the power of the idea of liberty cannot fathom how this fundamental contradiction can persevere—but it has for more than 15 years. History and Ronald Reagan would teach that their economic liberty will ultimately either be revoked or will inevitably sweep away the political tyranny. All of us in the free world pray for the latter.

Another area in which Reagan failed was his inability to recognize the face of the war that would follow the one that he was on the verge of winning. He paid some attention to Qaddafi, and when he entered office he made clear to the thugs running the show in Tehran that he, unlike Jimmy Carter, was not to be toyed with. But he retreated ignominiously when the Iranian surrogates in Hezbollah killed over 200 Marines outside of Beirut. This remains a serious blemish on his record, but I just don't think the rise of Islamofascism and Islamic terror was high on his radar screen. He was too busy with his three objectives. But there is no question that a new virulent form of radical Islam was emerging in the 1980s. (It would erupt more violently in the 1990s.) It was perhaps unclear to East and West that the global conflicts of the twentieth century had conspired to keep Islamic passions in check. But once fascism and communism were defeated, and the US was the only major player strutting on the world's stage (benignly at that), radical Islam emerged from its hibernation with a vengeance.

The last major scene from the 1980s that I wish to cite is in the Supreme Court. The liberals, sensing that the tide was turning against them, faced a grave danger. Yes, their control of the media, foundations, universities and law schools was still fundamentally unchallenged. (They would be seriously challenged—at least the first of these—in the 1990s.) But they were getting clobbered in the executive and legislative branches of government—both federal and state. The people were changing their minds and there wasn't much the liberals could do about it. So they identified their red line—the courts. The judges of America had been selected from left leaning lawyers who were produced by the country's similarly inclined law schools. With conservatives increasingly in control of the executive and legislative branches of government, it would just be a matter of time until "progressive" judges were replaced by "right-wing judicial activists." This had to be stopped. Enter Robert Bork—and later Clarence Thomas (whose story, although his lynching was in the early 1990s, is appropriately placed here). Bork was the liberal's nightmare. Two or three appointments like him and all of the Supreme Court's judicial progressivism dating back to the Warren Court would be in jeopardy, perhaps even undone. Unacceptable! Thus began a scorched earth, fight-to-the-death, no-holds-barred, Marquis of Queensbury rules be damned, campaign to deny Bork a seat on the Court. And it succeeded. Probably because its depth and ferocity was unanticipated by the Right. Similar campaigns were not waged by conservatives against President Clinton's two nominees, at least one of whom was as far to the left of center as Bork was to the right. Whether this proves that Republicans are more polite than their opponents, or that they really are "the stupid party" as John Stuart Mill characterized all conservative parties, is unclear. What is clear is that the Courts remain largely in liberal hands. Will that last?

Regarding touchstone issues, the needle shook like that of a seismometer. All of the liberal hegemony is suddenly in question—many issues are, for the first time in decades, open to serious discussion. The conservatives were questioning current attitudes on the touchstone items, and people were paying attention and rethinking their positions. This applied to almost all of the issues: but especially to taxes, government regulation, abortion, military spending, gun control, welfare (although in this case more so in the 1990s), and judicial activism. Conservative manifestations of this changed thinking appeared in new organs like the Washington Times, the Heritage Foundation, Paul Weyrich's direct mail organization, and many more. Conservative talk radio would explode into view somewhat later.

1990-2000. The End of World War III; Beginning of World War IV

The major events:

- The Gingrich revolution;
- America as sole superpower;
- Eruption of Islamic fundamentalism (while America sleeps);
- Kyoto protocol; third way;
- Moral rot.

As announced earlier, I will be purposefully brief and sketchy in this section. Some of the issues mentioned quickly here will be developed more fully in Chapter 8. So, having associated the fall of the Soviet Union and the Clarence Thomas affair with the previous decade, then clearly the 1990s is a decade that "began late." Some would assert that Bill Clinton's election in 1992 should count as a turning point. But in fact Clinton governed from a point in the political spectrum not nearly as distant from George H. W. Bush as was the political chasm between Ronald Reagan and Bush I—although of course that chasm would only become readily apparent after the latter's election. There really was no liberal backlash to Reagan—many in Reagan's regiments simply chose not to join the Bush brigades when they saw that Bush I was cut from the same cloth as Eisenhower, Nixon, Ford and Rockefeller rather than the staunch conservative mantle of Ronald Reagan. Clinton's election was the replacement of "liberal light" by the real thing. There was really nothing very dramatic going on. No, the decade began, from a domestic political point of view, in the earthquake called the 1994 congressional elections. The stunning capture of the Senate and House by the Republicans for the first time in more than 40 years, and their subsequent ability to hold onto a Congressional majority through several succeeding elections, which had not happened since the 1920s, was truly a watershed event—the repercussions of which are still with us.

The record of the Republican congress over the last decade will be examined later. Certainly, as the decade progressed, as HillaryCare was defeated, as true welfare reform was rammed down Clinton's throat, one might conclude that indeed America was becoming more conservative. That may or may not be true, but it clearly wasn't true of our allies. Leftists won elections all over Europe and Latin America. These elections further entrenched the "non-confrontational and non-judgmental" mood and posture of our allies and reinforced the position of the US as the sole superpower on Earth. Although, in comparison with the behavior of other sole superpowers in history, we did precious, little "throwing of our weight around" in the 1990s (a stance that would change in the next decade/ century/millennium), and our behavior caused neither greater trust among our fiends, nor greater fear and respect among our enemies. Regarding the former, their misgivings about our unchallenged power led them to create leveling mechanisms like the Kyoto Protocol, the International Court of Justice, the International Criminal Court, a more robust European Union—replete with its own currency, and even a rather pathetic attempt to initiate a European military counterforce. I do not mean to imply that the Western Alliance was torn asunder, but unquestionably our allies were uncomfortable with our military supremacy and what they saw as the potential for unchecked military aggressiveness on our part. The following is a drastic oversimplification, but I see this attitude also as a manifestation of the "third way" movement that swept the continent. The idea is as follows: recognizing that "pure" socialism had failed miserably, but believing that the laissez-faire, aggressively free market approach of America was likely to lead to gross inequities among individuals and nations, the enlightened sought a third way somewhere in between. This middle way approach was applied to international politics as well as to domestic economics by the quest for accommodation and conciliation between totalitarian regimes like Communist China and Saddam Hussein's Iraq and free wheeling cowboy America. Personally, I fail to see the distinction (economically) between third way ideas and those of the modern welfare state, and more egregiously the distinction between third way ideas internationally and the tried and false method of appeasement, but Europe's voters apparently did. Many saw Tony Blair as the epitome of a third way politician, but developments in the next decade would lead them to question that assessment. Clinton also tried to latch onto the third way label, but I don't think it ever really fit.

Regarding the lack of fear among our enemies, it is now clear in retrospect that our benign neglect helped the emerging Islamic radicalism of the 1980s erupt into a full blown epidemic in the 1990s—although, as I implied, we did our best to ignore the explosion. The pre 9-11 atrocities perpetrated by Muslims are well-known: Mogadishu, World Trade Center I, bombings of the Israeli embassy and cultural center in Latin America, bombing of two American embassies in Africa, the fiendish practice of Palestinian suicide bombers causing carnage and mayhem on Israeli streets, the sneak attack on the USS Cole. We treated these events as if they were criminal activities instead of the opening salvos in WWIV. We were perhaps confused by the horrific bombing perpetrated by Timothy McVeigh, thinking that terrorism might be a ubiquitous affair, not the almost exclusive province of Muslim fanatics. After September 11, such naiveté was no longer possible—although the Left has not given up on it.

I will make one last point before drawing this grand tour to a close. Despite, and maybe independent of, the apparent move to the Right, the US is afflicted by moral rot: rampant pornography on the Internet, violence and promiscuity celebrated in the media, a vicious assault on traditional marriage, schools that teach multicultural drivel instead of pride in America, more than a million abortions per year—including the particularly heinous practice of "partial birth" abortion, pervasive gambling, an unwillingness to protect our borders, the banishment of religion from our schools and the public square, and the lack of concern at the behavior of an amoral president who compromises the morals of a naïve young lady. What is going on? Keep on reading in Parts II and III to find out.

Surely one of the most misrepresented stories in the history of American journalism must be the North Vietnamese Tet offensive in January, 1968. The American newspapers, led by the New York Times of course, portrayed it as an enormously successful surprise attack that dealt a huge blow to American forces and their South Vietnamese allies. Today we know it was nothing of the sort. In fact, it was a calamitous military defeat for the North Vietnamese and their Vietcong agents—one that could have propelled us to a conclusive victory over the communist forces that were attempting to invade and conquer South Vietnam. But it took many years for the truth to emerge conclusively as the liberal media and liberal politicians who ruled the roost propagated the fiction that we had been surprised and defeated.

I remember being skeptical at the time. Despite the reports of defeat, the numbers seemed to tell a different story; as did the military commanders in the field and a tiny cadre of reporters and politicians who bucked the trend. But I also recall vividly the congealing sentiment around me among my family, friends and colleagues: Vietnam was an unwinnable war; it wasn't a war in which we should have intervened because it was not really an invasion of the South by communist forces from the North supported by the Soviets and Chinese, but rather a civil war between the indigenous Vietcong and the right-wing reactionary forces of General Nguyen van Thieu; it was immoral of us to fight this war and in fact our troops were regularly perpetrating atrocities against innocent Vietnamese villagers. Moreover, the opponents of the war were so certain of the justice of their cause that they saw no harm in engaging in the most egregiously bad conduct: burning American flags, trashing recruitment centers, stealing military records, vilifying our troops, demeaning and maltreating returning veterans, and ascribing to war supporters malevolent intentions and unscrupulous motives.

It was the first time in my life that I began to feel noticeably out of step with my circle of comrades—especially in my two special milieus, my Jewish world and at the university. Indeed my attitude, which did not mesh with the above sentiments at all, could be described essentially as: Vietnam is clearly a hot battle in the Cold War against the Soviets and their proxies; even though the strategic parameters of the struggle might not be in our favor, we must find a way to over-

come those disadvantages—*for we will suffer dire consequences if we don't prevail in the struggle; therefore, we should fight to win, not in the self-limiting fashion the Johnson administration (and later the Nixon administration) adopted; there is no question who the bad guys are, and we are not among them; the treasonous behavior of Jane Fonda and others of her ilk should not be excused, but instead punished; and finally, why is it that I have the impression that the war's opponents are actually rooting for the enemy?*

Clearly I was moving to the right—at least on this issue. On other issues as well—as later installments in my story will reveal. In fact, I probably would have completed my journey to the Right much sooner than I did, but for one person: Richard Nixon. The loathing for him in my family was so intense (tracing back 20 years), and the resultant programming on my head so effective, that my visceral dislike of the man did not permit me dispassionate thought. I am ashamed to say that in 1972 I voted for George McGovern. I recall nearly choking in the polling booth when I pulled the lever (no touch screens or hanging chads in those days). I instinctively knew that the vote was misguided and contrary to inner feelings and growing beliefs, but I just wasn't ready to cast off the liberal yoke.

More powerful motivating forces were about to come my way—as you will see in future installments at the end of succeeding chapters. Still, as the 1970s unfolded and the war gradually began to recede from the front page, I knew I was out of sync with my liberal brethren when I compiled my summary of what we should have learned from the Vietnam fiasco:

- *The Vietnam War was a great battle in WWIII, not some isolated conflagration unrelated to the 45-year war between the free world and Soviet communism. It was a battle that we lost.*

- *We did not lose it militarily, but politically. Our troops held their own and defeated the enemy in open engagements. The political support for the war was killed at home, dooming the effort.*

- *The disrespect and calumny that we heaped on our Vietnam soldiers and vets is a scandalous shame that we as a nation must bear. It was disgusting and historically out of character for the American people.*

- *There was nothing to celebrate in our defeat. Because of that defeat:*

  ❥ *WWIII was prolonged needlessly, lengthening the period of enslavement for peoples behind the iron curtain.*

  ❥ *Death and misery was the lot of millions of people in Southeast Asia. Once the communists got the upper hand, the result was boat people, killing fields, re-education camps and genocidal slaughter (in Cambodia).*

  ❥ *Too many of our own people were crippled by the experience. I speak not so much of the veterans who suffered debilitating injuries or struggled with drug addiction, but more of the young anti-war zealots, who have aged into curmudgeons that cannot see the truth to this day. They maintain beliefs about and profess policies for America that are warped by the tragically wrong conclusions they took away from the conflict. While completely evident today, this last assertion was already clear in the late 70s as the leadership of this group took America down the path of unilateral disarmament and appeasement of our foes.*

Holding these opinions in the mid/late 1970s put me out of the mainstream in my two milieus. It still does. Said otherwise, by the age of 35 I had already gone over to the dark side. However, as you will see, the Vietnam War was only the first of four events, my instinctive reactions to which—together with my self-examination of those reactions—pushed me to alter my political thinking and philosophy from liberal to conservative. The other events were: court-ordered school bussing, Watergate, and a sabbatical year spent in Jerusalem. Those episodes in my life will be described at the conclusion of future chapters.

PART II

Correlation between Age
and
Political Philosophy

6

Liberal Hearts and Conservative Brains

If you are young and not liberal, then you have no heart; but if you are old and not conservative, then you have no brain. Measuring the accuracy of that famous quote against reality is the prime objective of this book. In Part I, we examined various methods for splitting up the residents of the American political universe into liberal and conservative camps. Those methods included: pigeon-holing the people's attitudes on two dozen touchstone issues; investigating which of five anchored definitions most accurately encapsulate their world views; and designing five categories or compartments that characterize one's position in the political spectrum. It was clear in Part I that we could use any of these methods to easily and accurately distinguish between liberals and conservatives. But we also pointed out that the first two methods do not lend themselves readily to our task of associating or correlating a political philosophy with the age of its adherents. In Part II we shall focus on the third method as a means to achieve that correlation.

In this chapter we will examine each of the five compartments established in Chapter 3 and, in each case, try to argue that there is a correlation between age and the position one occupies in the compartment. Recall the compartments:

How you view   A. The Role of the Government in the Country,
                          B. The Role of the USA in the World;
Whether your mental framework is more accurately described as
                          C. Absolutist or Relativist,
                          D. Opportunist or Egalitarian,
                          E. Pragmatist/Realist or Idealist/Utopian.

Actually, we will consider them in a different order, arranged so that the correlation is easy to make for the first compartments we consider, but harder to make as we go through the revised order. For example, for the first compartment we will look at, Pragmatist/Realist vs. Idealist/Utopian, wherein we established that the former tends to be associated with conservatives and the latter with liberals, we shall argue without difficulty that young people are more likely to be idealistic than their more pragmatically inclined elders. We'll develop similar arguments for the other four compartments, but with decreasing effect as we proceed through the compartments. Nevertheless, taken together, I will eventually assert that a case has been made, to wit: if you're young, you should be inclined toward liberalism, while if you are old, your propensity ought to be conservative—and therefore, it is reasonable to expect that as most people age, their political philosophy will become less liberal and more conservative.

Now please note: not being a historian did not stop me from taking you (in Chapter 5) on a historical tour of the liberal/conservative divide in the United States during the twentieth century. Well, I am also neither a psychologist nor a sociologist. But that won't stop me from offering psychological and sociological justifications for why it is "normal" to migrate from the Left to the Right as you make the trek from cradle to grave. Indeed, you should recall the spirit of the book I outlined in the Style subsection of the Preface—namely, it is not an academic tome with elaborate cross references and bibliographical citations, but rather a "long op-ed piece" detailing one man's opinion on the distinctions between liberals and conservatives and whether the number of candles on their birthday cakes has anything to do with those distinctions.

So to summarize, in this chapter, using the five compartments and how they characterize the liberal/conservative divide, I will present my opinions on how the positions in the compartments correlate with chronological age. I will do this by identifying groups of "typical" young people, old people, and those in between. Then I will proceed by associating generally acknowledged characteristics and preferences of those groups with the possible positions in a compartment, and from that try to make the correlation between age and political philosophy. It's not particularly scientific, and the correlations are not uniformly strong across the compartments, but—as I said—the overall conclusion is that there is a lot of truth in the old saw.

In the next chapter, I will test the strength of that conclusion by returning to the touchstone issues. We already observed earlier in the book that there were issues on which there is no discernible reason for there to be a difference of opinion according to age. Indeed, that was one of the reasons for developing the five compartments. But that is not true of all the issues, and perhaps of fewer than I lead you to believe earlier. Anyway, we shall see in Chapter 7 whether a *reexamination of the touchstone issues* strengthens or weakens the assessment of the correlation we shall arrive at by the end of this chapter, following our investigation *using the compartments*, of the influence of age on political philosophy. Next, in Chapter 8, we pick up the thread of the story left off at the end of Chapter 5. We examine in some depth the liberal/conservative divide today, and we will again be struck by the rather stark differences on the issues between modern liberals and conservatives. It's not a pretty picture, so we shall try to keep in mind the commonality issues laid out in Chapter 2 as we offer up some conjectures in Chapter 9 for why the divide seems to be so deep and rancorous now.

So let's get to work arguing the merits of our famous quote. Let's start by identifying some typical groups inside three age cohorts. Instead of dividing our adult population into young, middle–aged and old (which might correspond to say under 35, 35-55 and over 55, we shall use the appellations *young people, people in transition* and *mature people*, which I shall think of roughly as less than 30, 30-45 and over 45. I have skewed the groupings in this way because if your political philosophy is not settled by age 45, then either you don't have a political philosophy or you are so confused that you are likely to remain so forever.

When you think of people whose age is between late teens and 30, what groups come to mind? There is of course no correct answer to that question, but there are some obvious candidates. Each of the following groups has a membership that is large, easily recognizable and—although not monolithic—exhibits characteristics and tendencies that are very representative of

> Young People
> students
> soldiers
> entry-level white collar workers
> entry-level blue collar workers
> newlyweds
> athletes.

Next, let's develop similar lists for the transition and mature groups. As with many of my lists, I imagine a corresponding list that you might compose would mention some groups that I have not and omit some that I have included. That is not of great concern as I only use the lists for illustrative purposes in describing the political proclivities of people from these groups. Here are the other two lists.

People in Transition
parents of school children
middle-level managers
small business owners
shop stewards
first-time homeowners;

Mature People
retirees
captains of industry
grandparents
long-time homeowners
investors with substantial portfolios
persons in positions of high leadership (whether it be in government, foundations, media, military, religious organizations, education, or elsewhere).

Now, for each compartment, we'll start with an assertion as to how strong the correlation should be, and then we'll test that assertion against the age cohorts we have identified.

Pragmatist/Realist vs. Idealist/Utopian. We have already asserted that young people are more likely to be idealistic or follow utopian visions than their elders who are more likely to take a pragmatic approach to life. Why is that? Well, how could it be otherwise? When we are young and have no appreciation of our mortality, all things seem possible. Our imaginations run unfettered through the myriad changes that need to be effected in order to perfect the world, and we lay plans for our role in bringing about those changes. Our dreams know no boundaries as we envision a society that is free of crime, devoid of poverty, not despoiled by pollution and congestion, laden with excellent job opportunities for all its members, at peace with its neighbors on earth, and which provides unparalleled health care for all its citizens.

We are anxious to get to work bringing it all about. The dreamers include: students who worship the humanistic and social science professors that encourage them to complete the tasks the scholars haven't quite finished yet; soldiers who imagine that their fight against an evil enemy might usher in a golden age of peace and prosperity; callow office workers who see themselves at the top of a well-run and enlightened corporation; young construction workers who dream of owning the company; newlyweds who envision a future filled only with children, homes, travel and family joy; and of course athletes who can taste the championship that surely lies in their future. They are young and the (often harsh) realities of life have not yet pressed down upon them. The future for these young people is a wonderful place that will accommodate their dreams, eliminate injustice and inequality, and repudiate a past full of societal imperfections that their plans will render obsolete. The tag idealist, even utopian, fits them like a glove.

But waiting to greet them in that rosy future is the sobering image of a mature person who has been kicked in the teeth a few times by the journey that we call life. Recalling similar dreams, and emitting a knowing sigh, she acknowledges reality—namely that, not only is the world not perfect, neither will the plans of any budding young idealist render it so. The best we can do is to accept the imperfectability of the world, learn from the hard knocks it dishes out, and make wise and sensible choices as we navigate the inevitable roadblocks that life tosses in our way. Utopian plans are foolish; we should just try to fix the things that we can, get out of the way of the ones we can't, and use our acquired knowledge from experience to differentiate between the two.[1] Thus the retiree looks back on her career with some satisfaction, even if her efforts did not remake the industry; the captain of that industry is content if she can keep the company profitable and please her stockholders, again even if the company's product has not revolutionized the industry; grandma is more thrilled and fulfilled by the children that her offspring have produced than by any manifesto she ever wrote; Henrietta Homeowner takes great pleasure in her home, more pleasure that she derived when she neglected it in order to pursue causes of social justice; the experienced investor is satisfied if the value of her portfolio is rising, and that satisfaction easily outstrips any gratification she got from knowing that some of the companies she owned built green buildings for their corporate headquarters; and the leader knows that

---

1.   A little play on the famous prayer, "Lord grant me the strength to change the things I can change, the courage to accept the things that I cannot change, and the wisdom to recognize the difference."

if she can convince 51% of her flock of the worthiness of the direction she wants to lead them, that is more important and achievable than unanimity of opinion on hypothetical visions. It all sounds quite pragmatic to me.

Now what about the folks in transition? In fact, the term is really very appropriate as the people in these groups are at a point in their lives where the unbridled idealism of youth is beginning to yield to a temperance borne of experience, but the realism, or perhaps cynicism, of full-fledged maturity has not quite arrived yet. The parents of young school children enjoy the fervent enthusiasm of their offspring, but they know that life will eventually bring their feet back to ground. The middle-level manager and shop steward have been through enough tribulations to wear down the naïveté of their callow youth, but they are still striving to climb the ladder of success. The small business owner is further along in this process as accumulated experiences pile up faster for her. And finally, the relatively new homeowner is beginning to realize that she's not living in paradise, but she hasn't quite given up on her dream of a perfectly harmonious, yet multicultural neighborhood.

In summary, this compartment speaks loudly for a positive correlation. Namely, youth nurtures idealism, which leads to liberalism; while maturity fosters pragmatism, which favors conservatism. That said, we move on to the next compartment. As we do, you'll notice our customary alternating pattern in both the use of personal pronouns and the order of application of the groups.

Absolutist vs. Relativist. Our assertion here is that young people are more likely to have a relativistic approach to life, while older people are equally likely to follow more rigid rules and principles. Evoking Chapter 3 again, we recall that the relativistic choice was associated with liberals and the absolutist with conservatives. Well, our examples will show that again the assertion has substantial merit, although perhaps not quite as much as the assertion in the previous compartment. As our lives progress and our experiences pile up, we begin to sort out what works from what doesn't. Our opinions harden and our approaches become more rigid. We assess rules, systems, organizations, philosophies and we decide which to keep and which to jettison. And then we proceed through the rest of our lives largely convinced that we've picked the best philosophy to live by. Even if not convinced, we're still pretty set in our ways of doing things, and our axioms of life are well established—even if the amount of self-examination that we've devoted to them is minimal.

This observation applies particularly well to our retiree, and to grandpa too. Indeed, which group in our society can compare with retirees in inflexibility and obstinacy? I don't mean that in a pejorative way—it's just that after a lifetime of accumulated habits and beliefs, retirees tend to be fairly dogmatic about the rules and philosophies that govern their lives. Similarly, grandpa has played all the standard child-rearing scenes numerous times. He has definitive ideas on all the aspects of raising children, ideas which he wishes his children would adopt in raising the grandchildren—but of course, being young, they don't follow the script. Similar adherence to time-tested methods and beliefs are exhibited by our other mature groups. For example, long-time homeowners have allegiance to the financial and practical methods to manage their home that have sustained them over a long period of ownership. And, while it's true that captains of industry often display great flexibility in adapting to changing circumstances, they also usually have strong core beliefs and well thought out strategies that have been successful in propelling them and their companies forward, as well as keeping them at the helm. Similar comments apply to long-time investors. Regarding great leaders, I would say that the applicability of the previous sentences is less clear. People display different styles of leadership and it can be argued that relativists are as prevalent as absolutists in the halls of leadership. Nevertheless, if we speak of someone who is "set in his ways," it is usually an older person that we are describing. And so the tag absolutist goes well with mature people. But were they always like that?

Probably not when they were younger. At that time, they wanted the freedom to test different approaches to a vocation, to families, to religion, to life in general. When we are young, we don't want to be bound by the strictures of others—especially our elders; we want to find our own path, our own value systems. Thus we are more likely to entertain the possible validity of multiple cultural, political, religious (and other) philosophies so that we can retain the freedom to adopt those that are most appealing to us. Indeed the student is virtually a blank slate, waiting to be written upon so that he can choose what to erase and what to preserve. Such is also the case for entry-level workers as they seek the methods and strategies that will best propel them and the company forward. The athlete too prizes flexibility—the freedom to adopt a different batting stance, to alter a golf swing, or to adjust weight training methods. He does not want to be locked into the training techniques employed in the last generation. Similar freedom of choice is not generally available to the soldier or the newlywed. The soldier is simply not permitted the latitude to consider military practices other than what his superiors deem proper. And the newlywed, well if he experiments too much, it is likely to be fatal to his marriage.

The trajectory of the transition people is somewhat less clearly demarcated than it was in the last compartment. But generally, these people are at a point where they are beginning to select from life's smorgasbord of value systems which they want to take as their own and their philosophical arteries are beginning to harden. Thus parents of schoolchildren are observing which theories of education are applicable to them and their children and increasingly they are doing battle with school boards to get them to adopt like views. The middle-level manager and shop steward have seen what works in advancing their departments and meeting their production quotas; their opinions are hardening on strategies to follow. If the small business owner has no absolutes yet, then he is certainly going to be out of business very soon. And finally, I will make no claim regarding the new homeowner in this part of the discussion. Still overall, this compartment does support the positive correlation that I have posited, although perhaps not quite as strongly as did the previous compartment.

The Role of Government. I would like to again assert that there is a correlation between one's age and one's position in this compartment. In fact I believe that younger people are more naturally inclined than older people to look to the government to solve society's problems—and so once again, the younger folk are aligned with the liberal position. However, I recognize that, in light of Social Security and Medicare, my assertion sounds a bit far-fetched. So let me try to make the case via the following simple observation. There's barely an adult mouth in America that hasn't uttered the following sentence, "They ought to fix that!" The 'that' is almost always some societal problem that the speaker, or someone with whom she is conversing, has identified. The problem may be grave or minor, but the utterance usually suggests that the problem has festered for a long time and/or has resisted prior inadequate attempts at a repair and/or surely could be resolved if the right resources were brought to bear. The 'they' is typically not specified. But over the decades it has increasingly, if not overtly, come to mean *the government*—federal, state and local. At least it does for liberals, who take the utterance literally and strive to have it implemented by surrendering power to, transferring money to, deferring to the expertise of, and deploying the resources of THE GOVERNMENT. In the liberal mode of thought, any clearly identifiable societal problem that has gone unremedied falls under the purvey of government—usually, the federal government.

A conservative would agree if the problem were: a pothole in a busy thoroughfare; the sudden appearance of counterfeit bills in the local grocery store; illegal immigration; a jurisdictional dispute between two states on exactly where, in the river that separates them, the border lies; or an attack on the nation by foreign enemies. But the vast majority of problems that 'they ought to fix' are not, like the ones just cited, clearly proscribed to the government by the US Constitution. Thus, although the stated problem may indeed need to be fixed, the repair is more properly left to—and likely better handled by—the private sector in the hands of business, civic associations, religious organizations, charitable foundations, and all the other truly non-governmental organizations (NGOs) that used to solve the country's problems prior to the advent of the age of liberalism. NGOs would certainly do a better job, she thinks, than the government that has 'fixed' education, housing, space travel, disaster relief, illegal immigration, homeland security, passenger rail travel and the postal service—not to mention retirement, health care, taxes and deficit spending.

The point that requires justification is the assertion that the youth of America indeed look to the government to fix things, more so than do their elders. So let us forget for a moment the massive social changes engineered in the 1930s and 1960s, which converted the elderly of America into, if not wards of the State, then at least a group that has come to rely, in a very critical way, on the federal government to help take care of their needs. Then we can reason as follows. When a young person insists that 'they ought to fix that,' it is a reflex reaction not infused with deep thought or copious personal experience. She sees something broken, wants it fixed, and if Daddy can't or won't do it, then she is more than willing to assign the job to Uncle Sam. Thus a student is quite comfortable with her federal Uncle picking up the tab for her higher education. A soldier quite naturally depends heavily on the federal government—not only is it her boss, but it equips her with the tools designed to keep her safe. Young workers may be less inclined to rely on the government, but I don't see them refusing workman's compensation, unemployment insurance or affirmative action assists when it suits their purposes. Newlyweds are searching for help wherever they can find it—e.g., low interest federal home loans, access to federal worker training programs, and of course they are incensed that the marriage penalty (which, after all, is the work of the government) acts against their interests. Finally, there is nothing to say about athletes.

On the other side of the coin, a retiree or grandparent has made her way in the world and is wise enough to know that if you want something fixed, you have a better chance of success if you do it yourself. That's the key point for everyone in any of the mature groups. She knows that "remote" solutions don't work. No federal bureaucrat in Washington is going to help her with her issues more effectively than she herself, her family, friends, colleagues or business associates. She knows this—instinctively and from experience. But the rules of the game are so skewed that she can't keep it in focus (see below).

The transition people highlight the point I am trying to make. They are past the point of thinking the government can fix all the "broken windows" in their neighborhood, but not yet totally jaded on the government's ability to deliver on its promises. For example, parents of school children may have lost their faith in public education, but they still seek to fix it rather than abandon it. Similarly, small business owners may be fed up with OSHA, EPA and the FDA, but that won't prevent them from applying for a loan from the SBA. And so on.

These arguments suggest a correlation in this compartment analogous to the previous two. Nevertheless, I cannot ignore the elephant in the room—Social Security and Medicare. It is impossible to be on the rolls of those programs or to be in close anticipation of that status and not to have your view on the proper role of government altered toward the liberal position. Utterly impossible! So my final conclusion regarding this compartment is decidedly mixed. Philosophically, the correlation should be there. But practically, the politics of the last 70 years has reversed the polarity. There is just no getting around that fact.

The USA in the World. This is anther dicey compartment. We shall see that the verdict on the correlation is inconclusive here also—but for very different reasons from the last compartment. In fact, this compartment manifests two "anomalies" that are not present in any of the other compartments. The first unusual aspect of this compartment is that, generally, younger people have little presence in it. By that I mean the following. Three of our compartments are defined by personality traits or mental frameworks. These traits are manifested by young as well as old, so all age groups are represented in the compartment. This is also true of the last compartment we considered, "the role of the government in the USA." It is not a topic that anyone—young, middle age, or elderly—who is not politically brain dead can ignore. You simply cannot consider yourself a political animal unless you have contemplated what you see as the proper role of government in the affairs of the nation's people. But that is not true of this compartment. I claim that, with a few exceptions, "the role of the USA in the world," is not on the radar screen of many young people—even those who are otherwise politically aware. The main exception is of course soldiers. But aside from them, and from the relatively small number of students who participate in overseas programs, most young people pay little mind to this topic. This is especially the case at a time when the country is not at war—e.g., most of the 1990s. So this feature—namely, that one of our age cohorts is largely absent from those taking a position in the compartment—a feature which is not present in the other four compartments, interferes with our ability to justify any correlation here.

The other anomaly is that this is the unique compartment where the attitudes of liberals and conservatives have switched positions in the last half-century. We discussed in Chapter 3 how, 65 years ago, it was liberals who were internationalists, advocating a major role for the USA in world affairs, while conservatives were isolationists. The role reversal began as the Cold War progressed, crescendoed during the Vietnam War, and was virtually complete as World War IV erupted. The result is that, today, liberals are isolationists while conservatives are increasingly adopting a more aggressive and unilateralist position regarding the role of the USA in world affairs—even to the tune of nation building in the Middle East.

Well, there are two caveats to that last statement. First, we should acknowledge that conservatives are actually split on this issue. The previous description is more aptly applied to the so-called neoconservative wing of the conservative movement than it is to the other so-called realistic wing—which, while not isolationist, is quite skeptical of the probable success of US intervention in the affairs of non-Western nations. Both groups are strongly unilateralist, but the neocons are much more messianic than the realists on the possibility of converting the heathens into democrats who will create a rule of law, free market, tolerant society. The schism on the liberal side is much less dramatic. Most liberals seem to have decided that America has lost its moral authority to lead the world, that our intervention causes more harm than good, and that we should mostly mind our own business. A small number admit the desirability of our involvement in the affairs of our adversaries and competitors abroad—but only if given the stamp of approval by our allies. That is, they may not be isolationists, but they are strong multilateralists. In any event, the role reversal between liberals and conservatives, like the first anomaly, makes a definitive assertion on a correlation difficult to justify.

So what finally is our assertion here? Is it that younger people are more averse to the USA taking a robust, unilateralist stance in world affairs than their elders who would eschew a quiescent, multilateral posture? This is what a positive correlation would predict. Is the correlation the other way? Or is there no such correlative assertion to be made at all? Indeed, my position here is that there is no definitive correlation in this compartment between age and political philosophy. I will try to justify that claim by a series of statements that reflect substantial inconsistency on attitudes in this compartment. Those statements will involve older rather than younger people since, as I pointed out, the latter often don't take a stance on international issues.

In fact, I think it likely that people in transition or mature people will pay close attention in this arena—the involvement of the US in world affairs, whether in unilateral or multilateral fashion—primarily in two contexts: their pocketbook and their safety. The small business owner will take a position that least adversely affects his business. If he thinks that US intervention generally opens markets for him, then he will be in favor of such intervention. But if thinks that it would curtail his business, he is likely to take the contrary stance. Similarly with a retiree or investor. If US intervention will benefit the economy or improve his portfolio, then he is a gung ho internationalist. But if aggressive action by the US overseas is likely to diminish his economic status, then he is happy to have Uncle Sam stay on the sidelines. The lack of underlying principle is apparent in the safety context also. Grandma and grandpa are willing to support aggressive foreign policy if it will help keep them, their children and their grandchildren safe. But if they believe that such a policy increases the danger, then see how fast they become multilateral isolationists. Ditto for your homeowners and captains of industry.

So what I'm saying is that one's position in this compartment does not derive from underlying political philosophy as much as from opinions on core issues. That is, it's not so much that your fundamental philosophy on the role of the USA in the world determines your attitude on the relevant touchstone issues—but rather vice versa. And since we have already observed the general lack of correlation between age and many touchstone issues[2], we are not in a position to assert any correlation in the context of this compartment.

Opportunist vs. Egalitarian. We now consider the final compartment and we recall that liberals occupy the egalitarian side of the compartment, while conservatives identify more with the opportunists. A positive correlation would assert that young people tend towards an egalitarian stance more frequently than their elders who would be more inclined toward opportunism. In fact I assert that the vectors point in the reverse directions. It's not an exceedingly strong correlation, but I will argue that it is the older person who has a natural tendency to favor equality of status whereas the younger person is more interested in opportunities than outcomes.

The rationale for this claim is as follows. When we are young, idealistic and forward-looking, the future offers great opportunities for us—what kind of career to pursue, whom we shall marry, the friends we will make, the places we'll visit, etc. We have no objection to others pursuing the same objectives, but when we're young we tend to focus on ourselves and our own dreams. We do not want to be denied any opportunity. For example, we would not want to be prevented from visiting the Great Wall of China just because the average Jane can't afford to get there. Even if we have utopian visions of an egalitarian future, in our youth we prize the opportunities that are and should be available to us.

Later on, when we're older, wiser and more experienced, the Great Wall doesn't look so compelling any more. Whether we've seen it or not—well, it's just a wall. As the sands of time begin to run out on our lives, the Great Wall is not nearly as important as ensuring that we get a healthy dose of our basic American pie—a decent home, good neighborhood, healthy family, secure job. Our pragmatic and absolutist tendencies not withstanding, we feel it would be nice if life would or had spread around its wealth a little more.

So let's check in with our representatives from the three age cohorts to see if they agree. Indeed, our student does not want her ability to study new subjects that interest her thwarted by some uniform university curricula requirements. That kind of one size fits all higher education was swept away more than a gener-

---

2.   This point will be reinforced for the issues associated to this compartment (see the Political Edifice in Chapter 4) in the next chapter.

ation ago. She wants the opportunity to sample a buffet of subjects, not to cram down the same academic courses as all her classmates. The soldier agrees—she wants an opportunity to advance in rank by exhibiting her own special talents, not be judged by some egalitarian decrees that apply to all her comrades. A similar comment applies to our entry-level workers. If they have any self-confidence, they want their shot at the brass ring, the opportunity to advance up the "corporate ladder," without being held back by global rules that apply to all employees. The same is true of our young athlete—in spades. She's not looking to be treated exactly the same as her teammates—she wants the opportunity to shine. Finally, there is no relevant comment that I can make for newlyweds relative to this compartment.

Are the older folks as opportunity-driven? Well, they're a little tired and they have in some sense played most of the cards they were dealt. That is, they have already availed themselves of the opportunities life presented. At this point they might be willing to settle for a little artificial leveling. Social Security guarantees and predictable COLAs are welcome security for our retirees and grandparents. Veteran homeowners and investors are running low on energy. They may be willing to compromise on possibilities for big changes in return for guarantees of safety. This sentiment is much less evident in captains of industry and prominent leaders as they're still deeply engaged and need freedom of movement and opportunity if they are to continue to function at a very high level.

The transition folk also tend to support the argument. The middle-level workers don't see as many opportunities ahead—they are beginning to think about guarantees. Experienced parents and homeowners have rolled their die—now they wouldn't mind cashing in their winnings and solidifying their positions. As usual, the small business owner is in her own place, still seeking opportunities, expecting no guaranteed security. These observations do not overwhelmingly support the assertion of a negative correlation, but rather lend it general support.

So let us summarize the discussion. We have seen that, in the five compartments, when we search for a positive correlation between age and political philosophy—meaning specifically that the older folks line up with those parts of the compartments that signal conservatism and younger folks align with components that indicate liberalism—we find a strong positive correlation in two compartments, an uncertain or mixed situation in two other compartments, and indeed a moderately negative correlation in the fifth. I wouldn't call that an overwhelming endorsement, but the general trend is clear. Reasoning like a mathematician, I see two plusses, two zeroes, and one minus. The algebraic sum therefore is a net plus, which leads me to conclude that, overall, the percentage of young people who veer from liberal to conservative as they age should be greater than the percentage who move in the other direction. Of course, many are going to stay right where they started. But when there is movement, the conclusion from our consideration of the five components of political philosophy suggests that: as you march along with Father Time, more people should be marching from Left to Right than from Right to Left.

My wife and I bought our first home in the spring of 1972. It was new, afford-able, much nicer than any apartment either of us had ever lived in, within walk-ing distance of the university, and—very importantly—in a neighborhood (in Prince Georges County, Maryland) where the local elementary school had a ter-rific reputation. Our eldest son was about to enter kindergarten and, reflecting the importance my wife and I attached to education, we had investigated the school and its personnel thoroughly when mulling various factors that affected our decision on a home purchase.

We moved into the house in June 1972, during the same week that Hurri-cane Agnes converted my new basement into a wading pool—but that is another story. A few weeks later I noticed a small article deep in the pages of the Washing-ton Post describing a suit brought by the NAACP against Prince Georges County, charging its school system with a legacy of segregation and demanding redress. Over the ensuing months I watched the story grow larger until it dominated the front page. In the late fall, after my son had begun his kindergarten career, a judge in a Baltimore Federal Court ruled in favor of the NAACP and then, in an act of breathtaking arrogance, ordered the initiation of a massive school bus-sing scheme involving over a hundred thousand school children. My son was bussed to a manifestly inferior school in a neighborhood down county, abutting the District of Columbia. So were all his new friends in our neighbor-hood—quite a few of whom were black, Asian and Hispanic. For, you see, my neighborhood was well integrated racially.

But that inconvenient fact didn't stop this myopic judge from stealing my right to choose a school for my son. His actions were nothing short of judicial tyr-anny. I cannot convey the depth of feeling of betrayal that I experienced and can still feel vividly more than three decades later. My family was being punished, arbitrarily and capriciously, to atone for sins committed by people with whom I had no present or historical connection—as were the families of the neighbor-

hood's black children who were presumably connected to the <u>victims</u> of the past discrimination.

I have previously claimed that the liberal hegemony, which dominated the country's political atmosphere in the 1960s, overreached in the 1970s. Forced school bussing was one of the most egregious manifestations of that political over-reach. It was a prime example of government interference in the lives of private citizens, an interference for which the federal government had absolutely no authority, and which was implemented by judicial tyrants answerable to no one but their own misguided notions that social tinkering would cure real and imag-ined ills, regardless of the injustice, the inappropriateness, and the horrible conse-quences of their decisions. For me, the forced bussing of my precious son was an epiphany. As you saw from previous installments, I was already questioning the liberal regime and pondering whether it merited my support. Forced school bus-sing greatly accelerated my trek from political Left to Right.

Here are some more concrete thoughts I had at the time and also over the next few years, as my wife and I summoned the financial resources and strength of will to abandon Prince Georges County.

- *Government fulfills its assigned roles by coercion. It collects taxes, prose-cutes and incarcerates law-breakers, imposes zoning ordinances, con-scripts its citizens into the military, enforces various restrictions on interstate and overseas commerce, etc. We the people recognize the neces-sity of government authority, without which our society might degenerate into anarchy. But the founders, recognizing the danger of unchecked gov-ernment power, imposed severe constraints on it through various checks and balances, a republican form of government, designated limits to the jurisdictions of federal and state government, separation of responsibili-ties between distinct branches of government, and more. Their intention was to limit the government's ability to usurp the freedom of the nation's citizens by setting boundaries beyond which the government could not transgress. That judge in Baltimore, who shall live forever in infamy in my mind, overstepped those boundaries.*

- *One way he overstepped was by acting as an executive rather than as a judge. We hear much—and legitimately so—of judges legislating from the bench, i.e., circumventing the legislature by essentially creating law with their rulings. Well, our infamous judge "executed from the bench." He assumed control of the County's public school system and proceeded to set up rules and regulations that had to be followed in the execution of the school system's mission. He usurped the power of the County Executive and the Superintendent of Schools. There is nothing in our legal system that gave him the right to do so—but he did it anyway and he got away with it.*

- *In fact, we had a total failure of government in this affair. No legislator, from either the Maryland legislature or the US Congress, nor any executive (of the County, State or Federal government) made any attempt to impede the lawless actions of this out-of-control judge. The Constitution gives the national legislature the right to regulate the judiciary. But in the long, sorry history of judicial tyranny over the last 50 years, virtually no effort has been made by any legislative branch of government to reign in the imperial judiciary.*

- *Mr. Jefferson said that, "… all men … are endowed by their Creator with certain unalienable Rights, that among these are Life, Liberty and the pursuit of Happiness." I viewed the judge's actions as an assault on my rights in two of those categories. Thank God no US judge has yet assaulted the third—although Terry Schiavo's parents might disagree with that assessment.*

- *The best face I could put on the bussing ordeal was that it resulted from the mistakes of a well-intentioned individual. Indeed the actions of an activist, meddling and overreaching government are often justified on the grounds of good intentions. However, good intentions are no substitute for good judgment. The history of the last 75 years is replete with colossal blunders by our well-intentioned government. These include but are not limited to: implementing poorly-considered monetary, tax and tariff policies that exacerbated and prolonged the Depression; unilaterally disarming after World War I, thereby encouraging the warlike tendencies of Nazi Germany and Imperial Japan; ceding control of Eastern Europe to the Soviets when we had the power to prevent it; imposing price controls during the gas crises of the 1970s, causing shortages and misallocations; designing a welfare system that rewarded deviancy and then being surprised when deviancy was what it produced; eviscerating our intelligence services (beginning in the 1970s of course, but especially) in the 1990s, exactly at the time when we needed to be fortifying them to confront the Islamo-fascists who would exploit their weakened status; deciding that it wasn't enough to expel the tyrant Saddam Hussein but that we would also graft democracy onto a people who are completely unprepared to adopt it[3]. Of course these failures of government pale by comparison to the atrocities perpetrated by the governments of Nazi Germany, Soviet Russia, Pol Pot's Cambodia, Castro's Cuba, Khomeni's Iran and of course the aforementioned S. Hussein. Perhaps this last observation merely illustrates Churchill's quip, "Democracy is the worst form of government, except for all the others that have been tried."*

So how did the bussing story end? We left the County. So did thousands of other middle class families who did not want some foolish judge deciding where their kids would go to school. Naturally, Prince Georges County was devastated. The loss of economic resources was severe, and the County continues to wrestle with the consequences today. The bussing went on for 25 years and when it finally ended the schools were much more segregated than when it started. A perhaps well-intentioned judge, who was totally lacking in foresight, caused grievous harm. Hey, but he helped me to see the light.

---

3.   Well, the book might still be out on the last one; there is no question though that the others cited were monumental blunders.

7

Where the Correlation is Strong;
Where it is Weak

We continue to examine our assertion that there is a correlation between age and political philosophy. More precisely, we argued in the last chapter that there is—or should be—a modest tendency for older people to advocate a more conservative political agenda and for younger people to favor a more liberal stance. We arrived at the claim by considering the five compartments according to which we classified the liberal/conservative divide in Chapter 3. It turned out that there was a decent likelihood of such a correlation in two of the compartments, little or contradictory evidence for the correlation in two other compartments, and actually a tilt toward a negative correlation in the fifth compartment. Reasoning like a mathematician, I added $(+1) + (+1) + (0) + (0) + (-1) = +1$ and took that as evidence for a modest correlation in the direction asserted. In other words, the reasoning suggests that it ought to be the case that as people age, if their political views and allegiances change, then more people should be moving from the Left to the Right than the other way around.

How might one test that assertion? Well, the temptation is to test it like we test any other well-formulated political hypothesis—take a poll. And at one point—when I was laying out the plan for this book—I originally thought I would fill up this chapter with data from a slew of polls documenting the difference in political attitudes of young and old people. Of course, the data would not track the compartments, which do not lend themselves easily to polling; but rather the 24 touchstone issues, whose concrete nature make them readily amenable to polling techniques. However, I decided ultimately not to do that for the following reasons. Such a report would be exceedingly voluminous, shot through with inconsistencies, and ultimately inconclusive.

- **Voluminous**. In order to be convincing on any issue, I would have to cite multiple polls. Given that there are 24 issues, the amount of data and interpretation to be reported would more than double the size of the book.

- **Inconsistent**. In fact the existence of multiple longitudinal polls on every issue is problematic. There are some issues on which repeated polling has been done over a period of years, and other issues on which polls may not be repeated for 5-10 years or more. More seriously, even in instances where there are numerous polls on a specific issue, they vary greatly on the parameters measured. Many polls do not go beyond a simple yes-no or favorable-unfavorable kind of statistic. Some compile data according to race, gender, geography, political party and numerous other categories—which may or may not include age. The observed inconsistency in this regard is extensive.

- **Inconclusive**. Then there is the famous quote, attributed by Mark Twain to Disraeli, that "there are three kinds of lies: lies, damned lies and statistics." It is well-known that polling data can easily be skewed to suit a political agenda. How you phrase the questions; how you ask them; how you report the answers—all can influence the data. There are well-established polling techniques to minimize the chances of biased data—but these are not always adhered to. And in fact, in my examination of polling data, I saw contradictory results on many issues. Well, given that the correlation is not overwhelming, contradictory data is not so surprising. Still, I had little faith that I could compile objective and unbiased data for many of the issues.

So I decided that, instead of trying to offer justification for my assertion of a positive correlation based on polling data, I would continue in the same vein already established—namely, present my opinion. Remember: "long op/ed piece"; not academic tome. So taking the issues one-by-one—albeit in an order determined by the Political Edifice (see Chapter 4) rather than the original (random) order of Chapter 1—I will continue to play amateur psychologist/sociologist and offer up my take on where the people stand on the touchstone issues in relation to age. When I am done, I will compare the conclusions with the compartment-oriented review in Chapter 6 to see whether the new assessment argues on balance for or against the correlation, and whether in strong or weak terms.

Let's get started. We have 24 issues to consider. For each, we are trying to decide how opinion on the issue tracks with the age-philosophy correlation that we asserted in Chapter 6—namely, that older people tend toward conservatism while younger people lean toward liberalism. For each issue, I shall state the outcome of that decision in one of four ways:

a. *Positive*—meaning that opinion on that issue supports the correlation;

b. *Negative*—meaning that opinion on that issue refutes the correlation;

c. *Inconclusive*—meaning that opinion on that issue manifests evidence for the correlation as well as its opposite;

d. *Neutral*—meaning that opinion on that issue bears little if any relation to the age of its adherents.

Following the statement of the status in each case, I will then briefly provide observations and/or arguments that support the stated conclusion.

- **Abortion.** *Positive*: This one is straightforward. The people availing themselves of the procedure are overwhelmingly young (or at most of transition age). They are often less concerned with the moral or philosophical underpinnings of the "right to an abortion" than they are with their access to one. Older people, unconstrained by the need to relate to the procedure in a personal way, are free to mold their stance to match general underlying political philosophy. That is not to say that there are not young pro-lifers or older pro-abortion folks who are guided by religious or philosophical principles. However, absent deep moral convictions, practicality dictates an opinion curve in line with the one we are positing—that is, more of a propensity for younger people to adopt the pro-abortion, or liberal position, while the older generation is more receptive to the pro-life, or conservative stance.

- **Homosexuality and Marriage.** *Positive*: The rationale for this rating is not dissimilar from the previous issue. Once again the choice (voluntary or not) of a homosexual lifestyle is typically the action of a young person. The freedom to make that choice and not be stigmatized by it is liable to be more precious to a younger person than an older one. I am arguing once again that, if not motivated by strong philosophical convictions and/ or moral scruples, practicality is likely to steer a younger person more than an older one, toward acceptance—and perhaps even promotion—of a homosexual lifestyle and/or same-sex marriage. The older person—whether married or divorced—is aware, from copious experience, of how important traditional marriage is to the preservation of society and the safety of children. So again we have an issue where opinions are likely to conform to the correlation we have posited. But for clarification, let me state: I am not claiming that if you are young, you are definitely pro-gay. All I am claiming is that if you stack up a whole bunch of people (millions of them), then the percentage that is pro-gay will be greater among young people than among older people—even if both percentages are well below 50%.

- **Religion.** *Positive*: This one is a little trickier. Recall the issue is not whether you are religious or not, but rather the role religion plays in society and its relation to government. In fact, I think there is little intrinsic correlation with age on this issue—the philosophical question is not influenced by the longevity of those pondering it. However, it is the case that the propensity to put organized religion high on one's list of life's priorities is significantly greater among older people than among the younger population. Thus the percentages are skewed by the size of the sample pools and once again it is likely that the percentage of those taking the conservative position (welcoming religion in the public square) is higher among the elderly than among the youth of America.

- **Immigration.** *Inconclusive*: Well, you didn't think all the topics would continue to fall in the "positive" category, did you? Let's see why opinion on this issue is inconclusive regarding our correlation. If you are young, idealistic and multiculturally-inclined, then you are likely to be in favor of massive immigration. You welcome the influx of new cultures and potentially liberal voters. On the other hand, you may also see the arrival of huge numbers of immigrants as a threat to your entry level job, to your entry level neighborhood and even as a source of potential crime. Older folks are also ambivalent but for slightly different reasons. On the one hand, they are proud of our nation's history of successfully absorbing immigrants from all over the world and recognize the tremendous contributions that immigrants and their descendants have made to American society. Heck, the vast majority of us don't have to go back very far to locate an immigrant ancestor. But older folks are also deeply troubled by *illegal* immigration and the country's inability or unwillingness to do anything about it. Thus, this issue falls in the inconclusive category regarding support or refutation of our correlation.

- **The Constitution.** *Neutral*: I quote from the first paragraph of Chapter 2, "What does your opinion on interpreting the Constitution have to do with how old you are?" Indeed, not much. This is an issue—specifically whether the Constitution is a living document that needs to be reinterpreted in every generation, or whether it is a "biblical" document, for which the jurists who interpret it are only empowered to divine the original intent of its authors—on which one's opinion is generally not influenced by one's age.

- **The Origin and Nature of Rights.** *Positive*: For this and the next issue (Culture), I find it hard to divorce the issue from the unique compartment in which it resides—Absolutist vs. Relativist. Referring back to the formulation of the issue in Chapter 1, we see that your opinion on it amounts to which rights you see as paramount, to whom they are granted, and by whom. The relativist is likely to emphasize rights such as free speech, freedom from unreasonable searches, freedom from cruel and unusual punishment, and freedom of (or is it from) religion; and these rights are conferred on groups by the Constitution as interpreted by the current Supreme Court. The absolutist on the other hand focuses on the right to bear arms, the right to due process, and the right not to be set upon by a government that is engaged in activities proscribed to it by the Constitution; and these rights are conferred on individuals by the Constitution, which respects the Creator as the ultimate authority. Since the young are more likely to be relativists than the elderly, and in parallel fashion, the latter are more inclined toward absolutism, opinions on the Rights issue will tend to conform to the age-philosophy correlation that I have postulated.

- **American Culture.** *Positive*: The justification is virtually the same as in the last issue. Multiculturalists are relativists and those who promote traditional American culture are absolutists. The final sentence of the Rights paragraph continues to apply.

- **Diversity.** *Inconclusive*: This issue leads to inconclusive data regarding our correlation for a simple reason—too many people's attitude on the matter is governed by their perception of whose ox is being gored. The heart of the issue is whether preference should be granted—in job placements, university admissions, awards of small business contracts, etc.—to individuals in groups that have suffered discrimination in the past, or perhaps are only underrepresented in the category under consideration. The practice is widespread and has "benefited" virtually every segment of American society, with the glaring exception of white males. And even within that besieged group, various subcategories, for example, disabled, gay, certain religious denominations, and also the aged, have managed to glom onto the diversity machine. Given the broad, scattershot and chaotic application of diversity programs, it is not surprising that one's stance on the matter would be governed largely by self-interest. It is clear then that there can be no meaningful correlation between age and attitude on this issue.

- **The Environment.** *Positive*: Here and in the next issue (Animals), the situation is very analogous to what we encountered with the Rights and Culture issues. Namely, one's opinion on the issue is likely to be governed to a great extent by one's place in the unique compartment inside which this issue sits—Pragmatist vs. Idealist. Once again, referring back to the formulation of the issue in Chapter 1, we see that your opinion on the environment is determined by whether you place the needs of humanity above those of Mother Earth, or vice versa. The pragmatist is likely to focus on the need to feed and clothe mankind, and to provide him with sufficient energy, transportation, employment, recreation, safety and public order. The idealist insists that these goals, while eminently worthy, must be superseded by the need to care for and nurture the environment in which all these pursuits occur. Without a healthy Earth, which it is our absolute obligation to protect and preserve, the attainment of the prior worthy objectives will be at worst unachievable and at best ephemeral. Since the young are more likely to be idealists than the elderly, and analogously, the latter are more inclined toward pragmatism, attitudes on the environment will tend to conform to the age-philosophy correlation I have stated.

- **Animals.** *Positive*: The justification is essentially identical to that of the last issue. Animal Rights activists are idealists, while those who place human life over animal welfare are pragmatists. Thus the concluding sentence of the Environment paragraph continues to apply.

- **Treatment of Criminals.** *Positive*: Yet again we have two issues that are closely paired—this one and the next (Capital Punishment). If we summarize this issue as one primarily of retribution versus rehabilitation, then it is natural that the elderly will take a harder line on the punishment of criminals than will the young. There are several reasons. First, the elderly have far more to protect (materially) than do the young and so want lawbreakers removed from society. Seniors don't believe that society should experiment with rehabilitation programs that place their interests at risk. Second, the elderly have the experience and wisdom to recognize that recidivism rates are discouraging—rehabilitation is at best a long shot. Idealistic youth have more faith in the possibility of redemption. Next, the elderly are more likely to be victimized by crime—except perhaps in urban ghettos, where people are generally not pondering sophisticated political issues like rehabilitation versus retribution. And finally, the young are statistically more likely to be criminals. It's not unnatural for them to look after their own interests. For all these reasons, the elderly adopt a harder stance toward criminals, and so we have another issue in the positive column regarding the correlation.

- **Capital Punishment.** *Positive*: Attitudes on this issue parallel those on the last one. The elderly see capital punishment as *punishment*, not as a *deterrent*. Indeed they consider the media focus on whether capital punishment acts as a deterrent as a red herring. They are more into an eye-for-eye kind of protocol, unlike younger people—for whom the loss of life means forfeiting more years—who may be swayed more by the deterrence argument. At this juncture, I would like to highlight a point often made by those opposed to capital punishment. They accuse proponents of hypocrisy. Namely, how can you be both in favor of capital punishment and simultaneously against abortion? Both are a form of killing—by medical professionals in one instance and by state correction officials in the other. Isn't the stand for capital punishment and against abortion inconsistent? Yup, it is! But so is the liberal stance—i.e., in favor of abortion and opposed to capital punishment. You are willing to kill babies but not murderers. Many conservative folks take refuge in the Bible for justification of their inconsistent stand. Namely, capital punishment is clearly sanctioned in the Old Testament: if you criminally take a life, then you forfeit your own. But abortion is the taking of an innocent life, purely for the convenience of the parents. If the life of the mother is at take, that is another matter; but that is rarely the case. Nevertheless, I recognize the legitimacy of the inconsistency argument, but I have no resolution of it, other than the biblical one. So I will merely observe that this is another issue that supports the correlation.

- **Gun Control.** *Neutral*: This is the last of the issues that fall in the two compartments, Absolutist vs. Relativist and Pragmatist vs. Idealist, which we decided in the last chapter track positively with the purported correlation. And not surprisingly, on many of those issues we have also described attitudes in this chapter that support the correlation. That will change for other issues below; and incidentally, the previous ones that were not characterized as positive were all double slotted issues. That is not the case here. Although you might expect attitudes on gun control to mirror those on the treatment of criminals and capital punishment, the verdict on this non-double slotted issue is otherwise. The reason is as follows. Basically, the media hysteria on the evils of guns, rivaled perhaps only by the equally hysterical treatment of smoking, has confused many people and forestalled rational thinking. The facts that the cities with the strongest gun control laws rank among the most dangerous in America, while the communities that have concealed weapons laws are among the safest, these facts just do not register on the public meter. In an emotionally-charged atmosphere, philosophical thinking, e.g., about the Second Amendment, is confined to policy wonks. And for that reason I have placed this issue in the neutral, rather than inconclusive category. To summarize, it is not that people of the same age reach different conclusions as much as they are not thinking clearly about the issue at all.

- **Government spending.** *Negative*: Here is the first instance of a negative correlation. In fact this issue is the first of a group of three wherein the correlation is refuted—all three for very similar reasons. The issue is the size and expenditures of the federal government, and to a lesser extent, state and local governments. Does one favor a large, powerful and activist government, which is involved in all facets of society? Or does one believe that the current government is a bloated behemoth, mucking around in aspects of US citizens' lives where it is not wanted and in which it has no Constitutional authority? When we ponder these questions in the context of the age of a hypothetical responder, we come smack up against that nasty old elephant in the room—a three-legged pachyderm whose legs are labeled Social Security, Medicare, and Medicaid. The pervasive influence of these government programs on the American elderly cannot be over-stated. The old folks are hooked, willingly or not, on these federal pro-grams, and because of that, it is almost impossible for them to come down on the conservative side of the issue. So, the correlation we seek is contra-dicted by opinion on this issue. But, at the risk of belaboring the obvious: this does not mean that there are no elderly opponents of massive govern-ment spending, nor an absence of young people who yearn for more fed-eral programs; it only means that if you compute the percentages in each age group that support big government, the number in the elderly group will be higher than it will be for the young folks.

- **Welfare.** *Negative*: The same dynamic is at work here, although perhaps not as intensely. Not all of the government's welfare programs are tar-geted at the elderly, but more than enough are so as to exert a significant influence on opinions on welfare. One only need think of Medicaid, food stamps, housing assistance, and various aspects of the tax laws. Admit-tedly, Aid to Dependent Children is not targeted at the elderly; so as I said, the effect here is only significant, not pervasive. But the influence is enough to once again cause the elderly to be more in favor of aggressive government welfare programs than are their younger peers. And therefore, we have another negative correlation.

- **Government Regulations.** *Negative*: The story line is similar. Colored by their outlook on the previous two issues, older people are less inclined than their younger comrades to question the validity and effectiveness of the alphabet soup of federal regulatory agencies. They rely—some would say too heavily—on the federal government for their health care, their retirement funds, their last housing arrangements, and perversely, to confiscate what's left of their nest egg after all the other needs are taken care of. It is therefore not unnatural for them to be receptive to the government regulating the rest of their lives. They view the FDA, SSA, EPA, HUD, etc. as, if not their friends, than lat least their protectors. While it may be a little surprising, I think the young are more suspicious of these agencies than the seniors. Thus we have yet another negative correlation.

- **Taxes.** *Neutral:* Well, that's a surprise—wouldn't you think that opinions on the tax issue would parallel those on government spending, government regulation, and welfare? Certainly you can't have a high level of the latter three without high taxes to support them. Yet, although the elderly are wise enough to make that connection, they cannot resist a tug that affects *all* citizens. Namely, no one likes to pay taxes. Regardless of your level of support for the nanny state and government largesse, you would prefer that some one else pay for it. Everyone despises the tax man—young and old, male and female, married and single, rich and poor, cowboys and Indians. Because of that, I have placed this issue in the neutral category, signifying that attitudes on taxation are not really influenced by age. Incidentally, there is a second aspect to this issue—namely, aside from the level of taxation, there is the progressive nature of our tax system. However, I think that people don't focus on the nature of the taxes they pay nearly as much as they do on whether they see their own tax bill as high or not. This further reinforces the choice of neutral for this issue.

- **The Role of the Judiciary.** *Neutral:* This issue plays out in a similar fashion to the Constitution issue. To quote Chapter 2 again, "How does your opinion on the role of the judiciary correlate with the number of birthdays you have celebrated?" Indeed it does not. This issue—whether the judiciary should restrict itself to strictly interpreting the Constitution and the laws passed by legislators or on the other hand redesign those statutes to suit their reinterpretation of the legislators' original intent—is another on which one's opinion is largely independent of one's age.

- **Military Spending, International Conflict Resolution, Multilateralism vs. Unilateralism (Sovereignty), International Trade.** *Inconclusive:* By combining these four issues, I have deviated from the presentation style adhered to thus far. I have done this for two reasons. First of all, opinions on them tend to run in lock step. Second, these are issues that appear in the "USA in the World" compartment and as explained in Chapter 6, younger people tend not to pay them much attention. Most of the thinking about these issues is done by middle-age and older people.

And what is their thinking? In fact I will argue that they are of decidedly mixed mind, and so no clear cut tendency emerges in regards to age. Why is that? For example, consider military spending. One's opinion on this matter is liable to be governed by one's assessment on whether an aggressive US military presence overseas contributes to or detracts from the safety of the American people. There is evidence in both directions and people of all ages legitimately arrive at contradictory conclusions. Some say: the projection of American power overseas has disrupted the networks of the Islamofascists, resulted in the death or capture of most of the senior leadership of Al Qaeda, and prevented these new enemies from attacking us at home again. Others argue: America's overseas adventures have resulted in increased hatred of the USA in the Muslim world, led to the death of more than three thousand American soldiers and countless innocent Iraqi civilians, and exposed our country to much greater risks of terrorist attacks by heightening the motivation of those who seek to harm us. Both positions are strongly held, by seniors, indeed by all people who think about these matters. The inconclusive characterization is the obvious choice for this issue.

Similar reasoning applies to the other three international issues. On the matter of international conflict resolution, the questions is: should we rely on international organizations like the UN, regional treaty organizations like NATO, or a set of temporary, but broad alliances in order to settle international disputes to which we are a party; or should we go it alone with whatever ad hoc small alliances we can cobble together in any particular dispute? Again, your opinion on this issue will likely depend most heavily on how you see its impact on the safety of your family and the nation—regardless of your age when you contemplate the issue. The inconclusive label is appropriate again. Actually, I believe that the general population sees the issue (i.e., international conflict resolution) as more abstract and less worthy of their attention than the previous one (i.e., military spending). Indeed, for this entire group of four, the same comparative comment applies as we progress through the list: unilateralism vs. multilateralism and the fate of sovereignty commands less attention than the second issue, and international trade even less, if possible. Moreover, for the older folks and others who think about it, their opinions on the sovereignty issue will continue to be governed by their perception of the effects on their safety rather than by age. On the last issue here, international trade, we can apply similar reasoning, but this time the inconclusive nature of the opinion pool is determined not by safety, but by economics.

Will free trade better serve my business interests, help to preserve my job, improve my overall economic status? Or will the imposition of domestic tariffs serve my financial interests better? It's a selfish attitude, but it reflects reality. Thus, like the preceding three issues, this one goes in the inconclusive category.

- **Wage Regulations.** *Negative*: This issue and the next are the only non-double-slotted issues that fall in the Opportunist-Egalitarian compartment. Therefore, it should come as no surprise, in light of the discussion of that compartment in Chapter 6, that both issues correlate negatively with our fundamental assertion that aging goes in parallel with political movement from Left to Right. The gist of the issue is whether the government should attempt to equalize salaries by means of minimum wage laws, or even more stringent restrictions like "comparable worth" regulations or caps on executive compensation. The point is that the self-interest of youth, which might conceivably be served by say minimum wage laws, is easily outweighed by their enthusiasm and optimism about their own future. They see themselves in the future as successful, even wealthy, and are not anxious to have impediments placed in their path. Incidentally, some of them are even clever enough to know that minimum wage laws may yield unemployment before they generate a raise. On the other hand, their parents, belying their lack of understanding of economics, may support minimum wage laws because they hope it will increase their children's income without being a threat to their own. So we have a negative correlation.

- **Leitmotif.** *Negative*: This final issue also tracks negatively for our correlation. The explanation is simple. If you are young and have even the faintest shred of self-confidence, you are not an egalitarian. You are more likely a "rugged individualist." You are ready to compete for your piece of the American pie—whether it is in the employment, education, athletic or artistic arena. You do not want to be held down by artificial levelers when you see the sky as the limit. But older people, perhaps a little tired of the struggles of life and more realistic about the chances to catch the brass ring, are willing to countenance a little leveling if it will benefit them and theirs. Thus on this very interesting and fundamental issue, we see that opinions go against the correlation we have asserted.

So let us conclude this chapter as we did in Chapter 6 by summarizing the discussion. We have seen that, among the twenty four issues, when we search for a positive correlation between age and political philosophy—meaning specifically that older folks' opinions on the touchstone issues of the day align with a conservative outlook and younger folks' attitudes are more in line with a liberal point of view—we find a positive correlation in nine issues, a negative correlation in five issues, an uncertain or mixed situation in six issues, and finally four issues on which opinions bear no relation to age. I think it's sensible to combine the last two categories and then if we tabulate the pros, cons and 'abstentions', we get:

Pro	9
Con	5
Abstention	10.

Once again, as in Chapter 6, we do not have an overwhelming endorsement, although there is a clear general trend. I cannot resist reasoning like a mathematician again: the algebraic sum is $9 - 5 + 10 \times 0 = +4$. This shows that the strength of the trend is comparable to what we saw in the compartment study (in Chapter 6). There we had a net +1 among 5 compartments. One in five is 20%. Here we have a net +4 among 24 issues. The ratio this time is 1/6, or 16.7%. Therefore, I shall basically repeat the words that concluded the previous discussion. Overall, the percentage of young people who veer from liberal to conservative as they age should be greater than the percentage who move in the other direction. Of course, many are going to stay right where they started. But when there is movement, the conclusion from our consideration of the touchstone issues suggests that: as you march along with Father Time, more people should be marching from Left to Right than from Right to Left.

At this point, I will pronounce that we have accomplished one of the main objectives of the book—namely, the first objective specified in the Introduction. That is, reasoning non-quantitatively, we have established that there is a moderate tendency for people to become more poltically conservative as they get older. Since I have eschewed polling data to substantiate that assertion, I will argue instead that legitimate quantitative evidence in support of the assertion is provided by the noticeable shift in voting patterns over the last 25 years as the country has aged[1]. Whereas the executive and legislative branches of government were firmly in liberal hands between the first electoral victories of Franklin Roosevelt and Ronald Reagan, that has been increasingly less so since 1980.

Now some might say that I was belaboring the obvious. The continued popularity of the famous quote that has motivated this book must lend it some cre-

---

1.   For example, according to the US Census Bureau the median age of the US population increased from 32.9 to 35.3 during the last decade of the twentieth century.

dence. It should come as no shock that anyone would assert, as I just have, that in very general terms, people tend to get more conservative as they age. I have tried to put some teeth into that vague assertion by examining it in the context of the five compartments, and to a lesser extent the two dozen touchstone issues. My study suggests to me, and hopefully to you, that the purported tendency, while it does not represent a torrent of movement, does suggest a steady stream from Left to Right. Thus as I said, I will consider my first objective to be achieved—the demonstration of at least a moderate trend in the direction I claimed. But what about the second objective? That is, what are we to make of those who resist the trend: young conservatives, and even more interestingly old liberals? Why do these creatures exist? My answers will be the subject of Part III.

But before we get to that, we'll finish up here in Part II as we did in Part I—namely, with an examination of the liberal/conservative divide. In the next chapter, we pick up the thread from Chapter 5. There, we concluded the history of the liberal/conservative divide in the 1990s. In Chapter 8 we will review the history of the last 15 years and then focus in on the status of the divide today. We will render an assessment of the relative strengths of the liberal and conservative camps and try to answer the questions posed earlier: have the conservatives caught up with the liberals who thoroughly dominated the American political agenda from 1932 (or perhaps earlier) to 1980; have the conservatives surpassed them in strength; or are the liberals still the stronger camp? In making that assessment, it will be evident that the bad blood and vituperation between the camps is severe. Is it worse than in past eras? In Chapter 9, we'll answer that question in the affirmative (at least partly) and then attempt to say why.

My grandmother came from Florida to visit my family for a few days in the late 1970s. While driving around Washington, we happened to pass by the Watergate apartment complex. Upon seeing the (then) instantly recognizable buildings, my grandmother fell into spasms of awe, joy, reverence and disbelief. From her reaction you would have thought she was looking at the Grand Canyon, the Taj Mahal and the Western Wall, all rolled into one. I think she felt deeply privileged to be at the hallowed site of the most famous building in America. I found it quite amusing. But it probably reflected the iron grip that l'affaire Watergate held, and still holds for some, on the imagination of the American people.

The term Watergate has come to mean the entire sordid affair that began with a stupidly conceived and poorly executed burglary of the Democratic National Committee office in the Watergate Hotel on June 17, 1972, and ended *in the resignation of the 37th President of the United States on August 8, 1974. It is a story of the toppling of a President, unmatched in US history[2]. It may be inappropriate to use the word 'coup,' but there is no question that a combination of feverish media hounding, hostile congressional investigation, unfavorable judicial rulings, intense criticism by the opposition party, lack of support from his own party, sheer stupidity and bad luck caused Richard Nixon to conclude that the best course of action for himself and the nation was to resign. It was a two-year drama that was captivating, repulsive and—like a train wreck—impossible not to focus on.*

Just like the bussing story, I watched it grow from a small, barely newsworthy item to the major news story in the world. I could not wait to dive into my Washington Post every morning for the squalid, shocking details. Like a soap opera, the story had plot twists, heroes and villains, moral undertones and a remarkable cast of characters: Richard Nixon, John Dean, Judge John Sirica, Archibald Cox, Haldeman and Ehrlichman, Woodward and Bernstein, G. Gordon Liddy and dozens of others, not the least of whom was Deep Throat.

Now keep in mind that Watergate is happening during and immediately after my bussing trauma, but also that the central character is the politician I detest the most. It was a period in which my suspicion of government and the courts had already been honed in the bussing crucible; my faith in the media had been badly shaken by their grossly distorted presentation of the Vietnam War; and my confidence in the liberals of the Democratic Party had been diminished by their deplorable behavior in protest of the Vietnam War, their adolescent violence during the 1968 Democratic convention, and by the already evident failure of the ill-advised welfare and poverty programs they enacted in the mid and late 1960s. So although blood was in the water and liberal sharks were circling the carcass for the kill, and although the protagonist was Nixon, toward whom I was less than favorably inclined, I was prepared to cut him some slack. But Nixon had clearly committed serious blunders, including at a minimum sanctioning attempts to cover up crimes. Just about what I would have expected of him. Why should I defend him? And yet, the pursuit of, dare I say hunt for, Nixon's political scalp was so fervent, so dogged, so relentless, and so single-mindedly obsessive that there was something unholy about it. In the end, I had no sympathy for him, but the method by which he was driven from office was wrought with hysteria,

---

2.   No other US President has failed to complete his term for any reason other than death.

and an almost religious-like fervor. It occurred to me that the liberals were not just running the country, they were running roughshod over it.

I hasten to mention that in my two special milieus, there was no such ambivalence. The Jewish community, convinced that Nixon was an anti-Semite, a conviction that was not refuted by any of his comments on the Watergate tapes, was delighted to see him go down. In the academy, Nixon had even less support. Despite a landslide reelection in 1972, informal polls that I conducted on campus showed McGovern's support as high as 80% or higher. Incidentally, it was at this time that I really began to notice how out of step I seemed to be politically in the university community. (It took my academic friends a bit longer to notice the same thing.) It is human nature to feel comfortable in a milieu where common beliefs, ideas and values are held. It is not rocket science to acknowledge that "birds of a feather flock together." The academic community is so overwhelmingly liberal and has been for a very long time—stretching back further than the mid 1970s certainly—that its residents are very comfortable working and socializing in an environment of like minds. Now when one deals with race or gender, one cannot fail to note differences. But when it comes to political opinions, human beings are not distinguished by their physical appearance. Thus, given that the overwhelming majority of your colleagues are liberal, you tend to forget the small minority that is not, and blithely assume that the individual with whom you are in conversation, or the group with whom you are meeting, naturally must share your political proclivities. Since my "conversion," I cannot count the number of times I have felt myself assaulted on campus by a colleague's presumption that I am a liberal. Sometimes I hold my tongue; sometimes they feel the sting of my conservative wrath. Of course I've been here so long that just about everyone now knows. That off my chest, I return to Watergate and note that: despite my distaste for Nixon, despite his obvious misdeeds for which he merited some form of punishment, I could not escape the feeling that something like an unsavory putsch was taking place. No such discomfort was present among my university or Jewish compatriots.

So here are the lessons I took from the Watergate affair in fall 1974. As you can see, this third trauma (following the Vietnam War and court-ordered school bussing) is continuing to push me to the Right.

- *Although Nixon was impeached in the House of Representatives (well not exactly; the House Judiciary Committee voted three articles of impeach-*

ment, but Nixon resigned before the full House voted), he was tried and convicted in the mainstream media.

- *The liberals celebrated the take down of a conservative, but through the fog of my visceral dislike for Nixon, I recognized that he did not govern as a conservative. He:*

  - *expanded the regulatory powers of the federal government dramatically;*

  - *supported quota-oriented affirmative action policies;*

  - *pursued the Cold War in order to get the "best deal" from the Soviet Union, not to defeat it;*

  - *opened the door to recognition of Red China (that's what mainland China was routinely called in the US at that time);*

  - *and worst of all, instituted wage and price controls—for heaven's sake, there is little in the liberal arsenal that is more collectivist than wage and price controls.*

- *Liberal America was powerful; dangerously powerful.*

It is instructive to compare the Nixon and Clinton impeachment processes, but that would be getting ahead of myself. That will come later. At the end of the next chapter I will reveal the fourth and final nail in my "right-wing coffin."

8

The Liberal/Conservative Divide in the USA; The Present

The goal here is to pick up the historical thread from Chapter 5 and present an assessment of the liberal/conservative divide today. I am writing in summer 2007, nearly thirteen years after the watershed event of 1994. As I explained in Chapter 5, the capture and retention of the Congress by the Republicans—the Gingrich revolution if you will—marked a significant turning point in the history of the liberal/conservative divide. Where are we now somewhat more than a dozen years later?

To answer that question, I first suggest you look back at the description of the 1990s decade in Chapter 5. If you do, you will see that three major themes emerged from my comments there:

- The eruption of World War IV—Islamofascism against Western Civilization.

- Third Way politics—a liberal counter counter-revolution, domestic and foreign.

- Moral decay.

I will couch my review of (some of) the events of the last 13 years in terms of those themes and then I will argue that, during those years, the execution of the conservative agenda has been woefully inadequate in comparison to its articulation—which may be found, for example, in Newt's Contract with America, but also in any of numerous conservative manifestos that were published over the decades following Bill Buckley's seminal founding of the National Review, and of course in the blindingly clear prose of Ronald Reagan's speeches. I'll conclude the chapter with my assessment of which movement is stronger at the moment, liberalism or conservatism.

Before plunging into the review, let us recall quickly the main thrust of Chapter 5. I showed there that America was a fundamentally conservative country for at least two hundred years. This began to change at the start of the Progressive era (circa 1900), after which the changes accelerated as the liberals achieved a broad and deep dominance over the country's political and cultural agenda by the 1930s. That situation continued until roughly the election of Ronald Reagan in 1980—although the incipient counter-revolution started earlier, perhaps with Barry Goldwater's nomination. It's been a battle royal ever since. The conservatives took control of the executive and legislative branches of the federal government, but they have not been able to seize the judiciary. In the other high-profile areas of politics and culture, conservatives have been contesting the battlefield; nevertheless, the academy, the media, foundations, law schools, and even portions of the religious and business communities remain rather solidly under liberal control. The question to be answered is: Who's got or is gaining the upper hand? We'll give an answer at the end of this chapter. Before doing so, we turn to our three-pronged approach to a review of events since the mid 1990s and an assessment of how well the conservatives have done with the power they have wielded in that time.

Third Way Politics. The election of 1994 occurred exactly five years after the fall of the Berlin Wall (November 9, 1989) and slightly less than three years after the dissolution of the Soviet Union (December, 1991). These monumental events signaled the abject failure of socialism and the collectivistic method of organizing society. The inferiority of a Marxist society in comparison to a rule of law/free market society was of course completely evident to all who cared to see it long before the breakup of the Soviet Union. But when the Vatican of Marxism surrendered unconditionally, it became impossible for anyone not to recognize it. Now the key point is that classic liberalism, as practiced in the United States and Western Europe during the better part of the century in which it has reigned, is nothing more than socialism lite. Liberal philosophy teaches that: if we leave the economy to the tender mercies of an unregulated market, then the inequities that will inevitably result are an affront to humanity, and so to forestall that eventuality the enlightened intervention of a benevolent government is required. Well that has a nice ring, certainly more reassuring than "dictatorship of the proletariat," but the fundamental thrust is largely the same. Namely, the people are not completely free to manage their affairs, but must defer to the authority of bureau-crats (under liberalism) or commissars (under Marxism). If you accept the claim that liberalism is nothing more than socialism lite, then in 1994 it is clear that the liberals are on the wrong side of history.

So what did they do? They came up with the cockamamie idea of a "third way." Sayeth the newly reinvented liberal: I shan't renounce my belief that an unregulated market leads to injustices, but I accept that government control of the economy is inefficient and restrictive of economic growth.[1] So we shall deploy a *third way*. Now for the life of me, I cannot figure out exactly what that means. The nearest I can tell is that it translates into: We'll use the government to regulate the economy—but we'll do it more selectively and much more effi-ciently. Right![2]

Surprisingly, the repackaging had some success. Third way politicians won elections in Europe and Latin America by portraying themselves as centrists, not prone to the excesses of the extreme Right, or the extreme Left. (At least they admit there is an extreme Left.) But it's hokum. They were liberals and they gov-erned as such. Schroeder in Germany is a good example. He lowered taxes, but he gagged as he did it, and of course he made no effort to dismantle the gargantuan German welfare state created by his predecessors. I don't know if Chirac ever identified himself as third way; supposedly he was center-right. Sure! I have the impression that if you discount the lunatic fringe represented by Le Pen, then the Right in France is located somewhere infinitesimally to the right of Ralph Nader. Perhaps the only politician who could really lay claim to a legitimate centrist label is Tony Blair. Who knows what Blair's basic philosophy is, but his governing technique was unmistakable. Namely, he acknowledged that Margaret Thatcher saved Britain from economic collapse by dismantling the socialist state that had been built before her and then he proceeded to do exactly nothing to alter the sit-uation she had established—all the while portraying himself as her antithesis. This reminds me of Eisenhower. Ike made no attempt to undo the New Deal; Blair made little attempt to reverse the economic policies of Thatcher. Wise choice, Tony. Unlike the anemic and unemployment-challenged economies of

---

1.   They still do not accept the claim put forth by F. Hayek in *The Road to Serfdom* that collectivism must inevitably lead to tyranny.

2.   If you google "third way," you turn up several representative sites that make for inter-esting reading. But for me, it's the same old same old, except the word 'liberal' is replaced everywhere by 'progressive.' Oh swell, we're back to 1900.

France and Germany[3], which are drowning under the burden of the welfare state, Britain's economy is enjoying robust growth.

What about home sweet home? Was Clinton a third wayer? He certainly claimed the label on occasion. But I'm not so sure. Clinton raised taxes, but not government spending—at least not like his democratic predecessors. And his economic advisors (led by Robert Rubin) were cautious and conservative (with a lower case 'c'). However, in social policy, and especially in foreign policy, Clinton was very liberal. Regarding the former, some of Clinton's actions that justify the assertion include: his attempt to create a gay-friendly military, his attempt to completely nationalize health care, his profuse apologies to numerous countries and groups for perceived past misdeeds by the United States, raising taxes of course, his appointment to the Supreme Court of one very liberal justice (Breyer) and one ultra-liberal justice (Bader-Ginsburg), and his appointment and support of known leftists such as Warren Christopher, Donna Shalala, Andrew Cuomo and the notorious Joycelyn Elders. As for the latter claim, I would cite: his drastic cuts in defense spending and his evisceration of the intelligence services (including the PCification of the CIA), his selection of enemies to engage in conflict—remotely only of course—that consisted of tin pot villains who posed no threat to the United States and countries in which we had no national interest, his determination to treat attacks by Islamic terrorists as crimes rather than acts of war, his coddling of the arch-terrorist Arafat, and his appointments of one pacifist and one incompetent as Secretary of State.

But if the tide of history was flowing against liberalism and the American people knew it, how did Clinton get reelected so easily in 1996? There were several reasons. First, he was perceived (correctly or not) to be much less liberal than his Democratic predecessors Carter and Johnson. Next, maybe it really was "the economy, stupid"; the country enjoyed a very good economic climate in the mid 1990s. Third, the opposition ran a very poor candidate, a so-called "moderate Republican," which everyone knows is code for liberal lite. Why have an imposter when you can have the real thing? And Reagan's regiments, still weary of Bush I, had no enthusiasm for Dole either. Finally, the media constantly repeated the following refrain: the public, after long years of experience with a Democratic Congress and Republican presidents, believes that divided govern-

---

3.   We shall see if the elections of Merkel and Sarkozy, who are more accurately labeled center-right, will make any difference.

ment is effective and now that we have a Republican Congress, it is best to have a Democratic president. Supposedly the public feared control of both branches by the same party. Perhaps they were right; more on that below.

And so the millennium arrives, Clinton is done and George W. Bush, our *compassionate conservative* president, arrives on the scene. I confess that the first time I heard Bush utter that phrase, my thought was, "Oh, oh, that's got to be a euphemism for moderate Republican, or worse, liberal lite." Events have revealed that I wasn't far off base. But let's start at the beginning. Everyone knows the story of W's agonizingly close victory over Al Gore in 2000. You remember Al—he of the loony environmentalism and campaign funding shakedown artistry. What a disaster it would have been if Al had been elected! Had it been so, the Taliban would still be terrorizing Afghanistan, Saddam would still be terrorizing Iraq, and Osama would be terrorizing us far worse than he already is. But let's get back to W. He certainly cut a large swath across the first half of the first decade of the 21st century. However, it seems very likely that had 9/11 not occurred, the Bush presidency would have been very much like his father's—undistinguished, faux conservative, and abbreviated if he failed to retain the enthusiastic support of his conservative base. But September 11 did happen on his watch and whether you agree with the policies he developed in response or not, it is indisputable that his reaction has been bold, energetic, risky, violent, and with the potential to effect enormous changes in world politics.

There is nothing third way about George W. Bush's foreign policy since 9/11. It asserts unequivocally that we are the good guys, that Islamofascists have declared war on us and our way of life, that our intention is to defeat them by seeking them out on their grounds and destroying them there instead of waiting for them to come to us, that we shall do this preferably with widespread international support, but without it if necessary, and that we intend to drain the swamps that bred these evil monsters by converting the political systems of the host countries that nurtured them into ones that more closely resemble our own. By any measure laid down in this book, that is a staunchly conservative policy.

We'll say more about W's foreign policy when we explore the next theme, but for now what about his domestic policies? How have they affected the liberal/ conservative divide? George W. Bush advertises himself as a conservative—albeit one with a compassionate side. This suggests of course that your garden variety conservative has no compassion. I beg your pardon! Moreover, I believe that the results of his presidency show that, with several important exceptions, W is cut from the same cloth as his father and all the other big government Republicans that have tortured and teased bedrock conservatives for more than 50 years. I think that deep down, big government conservatives (an oxymoron if there ever was one) like W have an essentially conservative philosophy—again according to the definitions, compartments and issues described in this book—but they govern otherwise. I'm not sure why their actions don't follow their words, but here are some possibilities:

- the liberal hegemony has been so mesmerizing for so long that they are literally programmed to look for big government solutions to societal problems;

- if you're elected to government, what is there to do but … govern, which means starting programs, spending money, nosing around in the people's business;

- the electoral system guarantees it because to get elected and reelected you must ingratiate yourself to special interests, which requires that you spend other people's money;

- they want to be liked;

- they are not well-schooled, neither in basic economics, nor in political philosophy.

Anyway, W is one of them. Under his administration: government spending has exploded; new government programs have proliferated (Medicare drug prescription, No Child Left Behind, the plethora of programs and agencies under the new Homeland Security Department, and of course we're going to the moon again); business is regulated more closely (under Sarbanes-Oxley); free speech is curtailed (by the notorious McCain-Feingold campaign finance reform law, not to mention the Patriot Act); yes, taxes have been cut—but only temporarily; immigration policies, for both legal and illegal immigrants, are a disgrace that pose grave dangers to our country; and King George has not vetoed a single domestic spending bill.[4] If it were not for the exceptions I'll mention momentarily, you might think that Al Gore actually won the 2000 election. So maybe W really is, like his good friend Tony Blair, a third way kind of guy. Or does he represent a fourth way? (Tongue in cheek there, folks.)

---

4.   Actually he has cast only three vetoes in six and one half years; none at all in his first term.

Now for the exceptions. There are three main ways that W separates himself from your standard big government or moderate Republican. The first is in foreign policy. I commented on this already above and will say more in the next theme below. The second is that in certain well-defined places, Bush has proposed economic plans that qualify as mainline conservative. I have in mind his proposals to: make permanent the tax cuts passed early in his administration; reform Social Security by allowing diversion of contributions to personal accounts; and at least talking about the possibility of drastically simplifying if not abolishing the current income tax code. However, his leadership in those matters has been abysmal and none of these initiatives looks to have a ghost of a chance of coming to fruition. The third exception stems from the fact that Bush is clearly a very religious man. Not that this guarantees a conservative philosophy—consider for example the deeply religious, but extremely liberal Jimmy Carter. However, in W's case, it would appear that his religious beliefs have led him to take strongly conservative positions on fundamental cultural issues like abortion, family values, separation of church and state, etc. But as Ronald Reagan knew, one's position on cultural issues is very different from one's policies on the bread and butter economic and social issues that are the proper domain of government. The battle for the culture should be played out in the homes, churches, schools and local communities of the country, not in the chambers of the federal government. That statement itself represents a conservative opinion, which is not at all subscribed to by liberals who want all three branches of the federal government involved in the morals of the people. The only weapon the president should wield in that struggle is that of the bully pulpit, and even that should be unsheathed sparingly and with caution.

Ronald Reagan once said that "Government is not the solution, government is the problem." This is not an opinion with which George W. Bush would agree. Moreover, there are many of his ilk, big government Republicans, in both the executive and legislative branches of the federal government. I don't know whether these politicians are third way, fourth way, no way, or they've lost their way. But their presence and works have made the task of evaluating where we are and which way we are going across the liberal/conservative divide into a more difficult one.

World War IV. *September 11, 2001*. The date screams at you and commands your attention. Not unlike the effect *December 7, 1941* had sixty years earlier. On

9/11 the Islamofascists achieved something that none of Nazi Germany, Imperial Japan or the Soviet Union could bring off—a planned and unprovoked attack on the continental United States in which three thousand innocent American civilians were slaughtered. It had been 187 years since a foreign power had successfully invaded the mainland. That day, September 11, 2001, and that attack marked the official start of World War IV. The opening skirmishes occurred earlier, but the first battle of the war took place on September 11. No one except the certifiably insane questioned that December 7, 1941 was an invitation to war that we were compelled to accept. There are now many in the United States who wish to decline the invitation dished out by Osama Bin Laden on that fateful, sunny day six years ago. George W. Bush is not one of them.

Bush's stand on World War IV is summarized succinctly in the paragraph in the last section that begins, "There is nothing third way about George W. Bush's foreign policy since 9/11." He accepted Osama's invitation quickly and eagerly. He did not vacillate or procrastinate or lob cruise missiles at pharmaceutical plants as did Clinton when Osama supplied less assertive and more veiled invitations in earlier years. (Although the bomb in the basement of the World Trade Center in 1993 was a pretty clear signal.) He did not plan indictments or send FBI agents to question suspects in Saudi Arabia. No, he sent a more formidable force, the United States military. The take down of the Taliban in Afghanistan, the nest in which the viper had made his home, was nearly unanimously applauded and supported in the nation. It was clearly the appropriate first response to the challenge posed by the malevolent Bin Laden and his Islamofascist thugs. But then the situation, as situations are wont to do in the pursuit of war, became much less clear. Why? Well, precisely because of the nature of the enemy we faced.

In World Wars II and III, the battle was all over the globe. But the heart and brain of the enemy were located in Berlin, in Tokyo, in Moscow and in Peking. Cut out the heart and/or immobilize the brain, and victory was assured. At least we knew where to go to do that. Not so in WWIV. We have only a vague sense of who is making war on us; of whom their leaders are; where to find them; and exactly what it means to defeat them. They are everywhere and they are nowhere. They are many and they are few. They are powerful and they are weak. Confused by these contradictions, Bush made his first mistake, a big one actually. He named the conflict the War against Terror and he identified the enemy as terrorists who follow madmen that have hijacked the Islamic religion. This was palpable nonsense. One can no more make war against terror than one can make war against espionage or skullduggery. We are at war with the people whose ideology spawned the terrorists that murdered Americans on September 11. Now understandably, Bush did not want to proclaim a war between America or Western Civilization on the one side and the Muslim world on the other. There was no need for that; moreover, it would have been unjustified. But by not naming the enemy as Radical Islam, or Islamism, or Islamofascism—meaning of course that branch of Islam which: sees itself at war with Western Civilization in general and the US and Israel in particular; wants to establish a Muslim caliphate throughout the Middle East; seeks to expand the caliphate to all the corners of the Earth; proposes to achieve these goals through Jihad or holy war; and considers the liberal democracies to be an infidel empire worthy of destruction—by not clearly identifying that enemy, Bush sacrificed the moral clarity that is so indispensable when galvanizing the American people's will to pursue a mortal struggle.

I will resist the urge to go into the following thought in great depth, but one consequence of the lack of moral clarity is reflected in Bush's attitude toward Israel. While he shunned Arafat, a welcome change from the obsequious groveling that Clinton did at Arafat's door, Bush treats Arafat's successor, who is nothing more than Arafat in a suit, with respect. Abbas, a Holocaust denier, leads a pseudo-nation of people who overwhelmingly identify with and support our enemy in WWIV.[5] Indeed they are part and parcel of the enemy army. What could be more heinous than strapping on an explosive belt, dressing up in Jewish religious garments and then walking into a religious celebration, detonating the belt and killing dozens of innocent Jews? This monstrous evil known as the suicide bomber was invented by the Palestinians. The Bush administration's attempt to be even-handed in its approach to the Israeli-Palestinian conflict betrays its lack of moral clarity in the prosecution of WWIV.

Now back to the main train of thought. With the Taliban disposed of—or at least chased into the desolate mountains of Pakistan, Osama confined to his cave, Afghanistan on the road to democracy—sort of, Bush ponders his next move. I believe he was motivated by two powerful concerns and one strategic decision. Concern number one was the possibility that the Muslim terrorists could acquire and deploy weapons of mass destruction against us. He had little doubt that if they obtained them, they wouldn't hesitate to use them. This dire possibility,

---

5.   as the election of a Hamas Parliament proved.

which was in some sense a short term concern, had to be prevented at all costs. A second more long term concern was how to do something about the fundamental conditions that caused these vermin to crawl out of the slime that incubated them. Bush's answer was Wilsonian. We'll export democracy and capitalism to the Middle East; then the Arabs/Muslims will eagerly vote, shop at the Mall and drive SUVs instead of (mis)reading their Koran and learning to hate us. Finally, the strategic decision: he vowed not to wait for them to come to us, but instead to go get them first. So with these parameters, where was the next stop after Kabul?

What were the choices? They were, roughly from east to west: Pyongyang, Tehran, Baghdad, Damascus, Riyadh, Tripoli. All of the regimes headquartered in those cities had fomented terror against the West, and the destruction of any one of them would serve the interests of our side in this war—provided, of course, that it was not replaced by something worse. So let us speculate on how the thinking might have proceeded. First the Saudi regime. What an odious place! It gave birth to most of the perpetrators of September 11, not to mention Osama Bin Laden himself. It favors and perpetrates the most noxious form of Islamism, Wahhabism, whose poison has infected millions across the globe. Its blatant discrimination against Christians and Jews, and its maltreatment of women are on display for all to see. But, we have collaborated with them since the time of Roosevelt and Saud. They (pretend to) play nicely with us, sort of like Egypt and Jordan do. And finally, how would it look if we went after our "friends" before dealing with our enemies? So Riyadh was out. Tripoli was out too. Qadaffi was not nearly the bad boy he had been 20 years earlier. Indeed, events would prove later that not specifically targeting Libya was the right strategy in that case.

That left North Korea, Iraq, Iran, and Syria, the (augmented) "axis of evil." But Iran and Syria certainly had no nuclear weapons. One or both of them might have chemical or biological weapons, but they were not advertising it, nor were they under the domain of a demented leader. Perhaps an evil leader, but not a demented one.[6] As were both North Korea and Iraq, each of which professed to have WMD—nuclear or otherwise. Both countries were led by certifiable lunatics who posed a real danger in regard to the first concern—making WMD avail-

---

6.   although the current President of Iran might fit both labels. And of course, it is now common knowledge that Iran is assiduously pursuing the acquisition of nuclear weapons.

able to terrorists. In fact Saddam had already used WMD against the Iranians and also, unbelievably, against his own people. So it was not a hard decision. Simply put: Iraq offered the possibility of addressing concern #2 that North Korea did not. Thus Baghdad it was. Well, I don't mean to imply that the decision to go after Saddam was made as cavalierly as this scenario suggests, but I'm sure the line of thinking I outlined played some part in the analysis.

Bush tried to assemble a broad international coalition for the venture, but he was only partly successful. He tried to get the UN to take a prominent role, with even less success. Following the precepts of his own policy, he decided to go after Saddam with what he had. The war itself proved remarkably easy—at least in comparison to what was predicted. What came next has been anything but.

Clearly one could write a whole book on the war in Iraq, and many have. My purpose here is merely to point out the major thrust of Bush's foreign policy and the actions that flowed from it. Seen from the vantage point of the two concerns and the one strategic priority, Bush's invasion of Iraq is logical and not surprising. But it constitutes a huge gamble. Converting Iraq into a pluralistic democracy, even with an Islamic slant, would be a phenomenal achievement, with the potential to fundamentally alter the Middle East, secure victory for us in WWIV and change the world for the better. But if the gambit fails, the downside potential is correspondingly awful: the strengthening of our enemies and the spread of tyranny, an increased danger to the homeland, and a tremendous setback for Western Civilization. Which way will it go? As I write, the jury is still out, but the trends are not favorable.

Next I want to go back in time. After all, this review purports to treat the years since the mid 1990s. I started the discussion of this theme with 9/11—how could I not? But what about foreign policy in the Clinton years? Was there a foreign policy in the Clinton years? In fact, there was, as we shall see, but it took a back seat to domestic policy. Savoring the hard won victory in WWIII, Clinton was determined—as was most of the country—to enjoy the peace, and use the bounty in the federal budget created by the disappearance of the Soviet Union (the so-called peace dividend) to address domestic concerns. Actually, Clinton spent less of it than one would have expected (in part due to the resistance of a Republican Congress). Nevertheless, despite his intention to "focus like a laser on the economy," the world did not disappear. The United States, as the leader of the free world and the Earth's sole superpower, could not ignore the international crises and foreign despots that beckoned for its attention. So what were the main tenets of Clinton's foreign policy and the consequent actions he took? The tenets are easy to describe: multilateralism, ecumenicism, and a liberal dose of free trade (pun intended). The first two are solidly liberal, whereas the third was, well, third way. To his credit, Clinton pursued free trade agreements much more aggressively than any Democratic predecessor, and the country and our trading partners benefited from it. In that regard, Clinton often had more Republican than Democratic support. As for the first two liberal principles, you certainly know what I mean by multilateralism. Specifically, the US shall not act unilaterally in foreign affairs. It will consult with and act in concert with its allies. It will support international bodies and treaties like the International Court of Justice and the Kyoto Protocol. That much is clear. Now, what do I mean by ecumenicism? It means we shall not focus exclusively on our major allies (NATO, Japan, Australia, etc.), nor excessively on our major adversaries (China, Russia—perhaps, or even Iran or Iraq), but we shall also pay close attention to third world countries that are in such desperate need of our help and guidance—places such as Haiti, Bosnia and Somalia. It would appear that Clinton and his two distinguished Secretaries of State considered America's *most important* international task to be helping formerly oppressed victims of colonialization to overcome their past disadvantages—fairly standard liberal foreign policy. What did these principles lead to in the way of action?

- The identification as principle adversaries of pipsqueak despots such as the warlord General Aidid who posed no threat to us, or countries such as Serbia which were completely outside our national interests.

- An obsession with the Israeli-Arab/Palestinian conflict that resulted in: constant pressure on Israel to treat those of its citizens who bemoaned the maimed and broken bodies caused by Palestinian suicide bombers as "obstacles to peace"; Warren Christopher crawling to Damascus two dozen times; and the humiliation of the President by Yassir Arafat at Camp David.

- The drawing down of US military capabilities to dangerously low states of readiness.

- A lack of seriousness in its attitude toward the military, thinking of it as no more than a social laboratory in which to tinker with policies that could render it more hospitable to homosexuals and females.

- The marginalization, demoralization and radicalization of the CIA.

- The treatment of China like a special interest group with whom we had to curry favor in order to assist reelection efforts.

- Worst of all, the refusal to recognize the looming threat from Islamic radicals.

It's not a pretty picture.

Moral decay. Let me tread cautiously here. I'll begin by quoting George Washington's Farewell Address.

> *Of all the dispositions and habits which lead to political prosperity, religion and morality are indispensable supports. In vain would that man claim the tribute of patriotism who should labor to subvert these great pillars of human happiness—these firmest props of the duties of men and citizens. The mere politician, equally with the pious man, ought to respect and to cherish them. A volume could not trace all their connections with private and public felicity. Let it simply be asked, Where is the security for property, for reputation, for life, if the sense of religious obligation desert the oaths which are the instruments of investigation in courts of justice? And let us with caution indulge the supposition that morality can be maintained without religion. Whatever may be conceded to the influence of refined education on minds of peculiar structure, reason and experience both forbid us to expect that national morality can prevail in exclusion of religious principle.*

Washington was expressing the opinion, held by virtually all of the founders, that the new self-governing democracy they had established in the United States could not succeed unless the people were virtuous and moral. Moreover, the measure of their virtue and morality was to be found in religion. Said otherwise, for the society to work, the people must behave virtuously, for example, be respectful of one another, practice modesty and humility, conduct their business fairly, be charitable toward the less fortunate, and show tolerance toward those with whom they disagree. The guide for their moral behavior was to be religious principles. Naturally, they were thinking of Christian religious principles, but the emphasis was more on *religion* than on *Christian*. To many today, these notions seem quaint, old-fashioned, out-of-date. But they were commonly accepted by the great majority of Americans well into the 20th century and are still highly regarded by many Americans today—although whether those constitute a majority is open to question. For the fact that they are also out of favor with many, I cite as evidence the paragraph I wrote in Chapter 5 and which I repeat now:

> *Despite, and maybe independent of, the apparent move to the Right, the US is afflicted by moral rot: rampant pornography on the Internet, violence and promiscuity celebrated in the media, a vicious assault on traditional marriage, schools that teach multicultural drivel instead of pride in America, more than a million abortions per year—including the particularly heinous practice of "partial birth" abortion, pervasive gambling, an unwillingness to protect our borders, the banishment of religion from our schools and the public square, and the lack of concern at the behavior of an amoral president who compromises the morals of a naïve young lady.*

The trends I describe in the last paragraph are indisputable. But I will strengthen the partial disclaimer in the first sentence as follows. I do not see the increasing moral rot as a consequence of either liberal or conservative philosophy. To assert otherwise would be a dangerous and an incendiary accusation that would violate the very precept set down by President Washington. But if Washington is right, and I think he is, then this development—that is, the apparent weakening of the moral fabric of the nation—has potentially momentous political implications. Now, my point in placing this theme here is to observe that the decay has proceeded apace during the last decade or so, and does not appear to be abating. It started during the liberal reign and continues undiminished during the conservative comeback. Thus it is a bipartisan concern and a major political issue that is just lying there, waiting to be picked up in earnest by either the Left or Right. Well, both sides have to some extent. But neither has run with the ball particularly well. If the rot continues, then whichever side addresses it more effectively may gain a leg up in the future liberal/conservative battle.

Now before trying to assess which side is currently ahead, I wish to provide two reminders. First, I want to remind the reader of the points of political commonality that I laid out in Chapter 2. Yes, the liberal/conservative divide is very deep, but the points of commonality provide a sturdy bridge that often enables us to navigate the chasm. Second, I want to remind myself, as well as the reader, that the blot of moral decay is also countered by a streak of decency, generosity, piety and heroism that is always on display in American society. When I contemplate what the future holds in store for my grandchildren and I am dismayed at the moral decay in society, I slap myself upside the head and remind myself that this is still a pretty amazing country. In fact:

- The rates at which Americans make charitable gifts, set up charitable organizations and assist one another in times of personal crisis far exceeds the rates in other countries.

- When major crises hit, like September 11 or Hurricane Katrina, Americans always respond instantly and generously.

- Similarly, when tragedy strikes anywhere on the globe, America is always first on the scene to provide assistance.

- America is still a far more religious country than any of our allies—meaning of course not that there is an official religion, but that the percentage of citizens for whom religion plays a major role in their lives is much higher than in other Western nations.

- The wealthy in America are renowned for their public works in the arts, education, religion, civic affairs, etc. It is just expected in the US that if you make a fortune, you give back (see e.g., Bill Gates and now Sergey Brin and Larry Paige).

- America has sacrificed the blood of its sons twice to save the world (WWII and WWIII). Unfortunately, we have to do it again—and we are doing so.

- America sets a shining example for the world in how it cares for its disabled, welcomes foreigners, attends to its minorities, corrects its mistakes (e.g., abolishing slavery and segregation, compensating the families of unjustly interred Japanese-American citizens, and atoning for its less than heroic performance during the Holocaust by honoring its victims), and successfully runs what is surely the most ethnically diverse, large society that has ever graced the face of the Earth.

I could go on, but let me just say that in summary, we haven't reached the level of Sodom and Gomorrah quite yet. But we do seem to be heading down a slippery slope. Some people, perhaps impressed by a list such as the above, have asserted that, au contraire, there is a rejuvenating moral awakening going on across America. I am not convinced. I think we are at a crossroads. And to reemphasize a point made earlier, we will be led up the righteous path to redemption primarily by religious and civic leaders, not by politicians. However, since the consequences at the end of the slippery slope are political, there is a role for politics in this struggle. Which political persuasion will contribute more positively? The future will tell.

Now that the historical review of the very recent past is complete, two main tasks remain in this chapter. I shall supply a justification for my belief that conservatives have failed to govern conservatively, and an assessment of the relative strengths of the liberal and conservative movements today.

The Conservative disappointment

I am not going to beat around the Bushes here; I am going right at `em, pere et fils. Fifteen years ago George H. W. Bush was a great disappointment to hardcore conservatives; in recent years, George W. Bush has also been a disappointment to the current crop of bedrock conservatives. I'll not dwell on the father except to highlight three points: he reneged on his no new taxes pledge; he spiked the ball before he reached the end zone in Iraq; and generally he deferred to the liberal agenda and thereby betrayed his supposed mentor, Ronald Reagan. What Bush characterized as "voodoo economics" has helped to create and sustain 25 years of nearly continuous economic growth. In short, there is no question but that George H. W. Bush was a big government, faux conservative Republican in the mold of Nixon, Ford, Dole, etc. The media portrayed him as a conservative, but it was not true. What about his son?

The verdict there is not as cut and dried. In many ways, W has been true to basic conservative principles. In that vein I would cite:

- his support for a strict interpretation of the Constitution and the conservative jurists he has appointed to the federal bench;

- much of his foreign policy, for example, his aggressive reaction to the September 11 attack on the homeland, his (admittedly qualified) support of new free trade agreements, his willingness to take unilateral action when he deems it in the national interest, and his unwillingness to endorse feel-good international treaties and bodies that are manifestly damaging to the national interest;

- his conservative positions on cultural issues;

- his advocacy of a return of religion to the public square; and

- his willingness to promote (albeit with little in the way of successful implementation) conservative policies on Social Security and tax reform.

But these are counterbalanced by a host of activities that peg W as yet another big government, moderate Republican. These include but are not limited to:

- Runaway government spending. The federal budget and the national debt have exploded on W's watch—far more than under Clinton. (In the first three years of Bush's presidency expenditures rose nearly as much as in all eight of Clinton's. Also the federal deficit under W reached a level nearly double the worst annual amount that Clinton ever generated.) Moreover, this cannot be blamed on the outbreak of WWIV and the requisite increase in defense spending. The growth in other spending, entitlement and discretionary, has been just as feverish. This criticism is absolutely fundamental. If a politician does not believe in or pursue limited government, then it is totally unjustified for that politician to classify himself as conservative.

- Myriad new government programs. The plethora of major new federal programs, agencies and legislation initiated by the Bush administration also belies any claim to the conservative label. To name just a few, there is: No Child Left Behind, the Homeland Security Department, the Patriot Act, Sarbanes-Oxley, the Medicare Drug Prescription Program, and the McCain-Feingold Campaign Finance Reform act. These are significant, if not draconian new initiatives that have dramatically increased the power of the federal government at the expense of the people. To characterize an administration that is responsible for this avalanche of enhanced government power as conservative is ludicrous.

- Diversity. Bush has made no effort to dismantle the diversity machine that mocks the 14th Amendment to the Constitution. His Justice Department argued tepidly before the Supreme Court against reverse discrimination in the Grutter vs. Bollinger case, a critical case that had the potential to drive a stake through the heart of the diversity machine.

- Repeal of the New Deal, and the Great Society as well. He has utterly failed to bring to fruition Social Security and income tax reforms that a truly conservative administration would go to the mat to achieve. He talked a good game, but failed to deliver. This calls into question his true commitment to the conservative ideas that underlie such reforms. Indeed he has worsened the situation with his profligate Medicare Drug Prescription program. It should be an embarrassment to Bush when I point out that his liberal predecessor, Clinton, by signing Welfare Reform, had a greater impact on repeal than Bush has had.

- Immigration. Bush's position on illegal immigration is an abomination that qualifies him for membership in the Democratic Party. Illegal aliens are exactly that—illegal. His proposal for dealing with them is nothing less than amnesty. Shall we also ignore tax cheats for years and then grant them amnesty? Supposedly the US is a society under the rule of law. Now the current regime that fosters instead of inhibiting illegal immigration did not originate with Bush. This has caused a problem that has been festering for decades, and has resulted in the accumulation of millions of illegal aliens in this country. No one knows how many. Estimates vary between 12-15 million. It could be more. Many have spawned children who, according to our exceedingly lenient rules, are citizens, yet in principle vulnerable to losing their parents to a deportation order. How shall we humanely deal with this problem? Reasonable suggestions have been put forward. All of them include the requirement that illegals depart our shores and then reapply for legal entry, whereupon favorable consideration could be given to those who were productive and law-abiding while in residence. W's plan falls woefully short. Moreover, in parallel fashion, he has made no attempt to formulate a decent policy on legal immigration either. Instead of emphasizing lotteries and family reunions, which terms have been very loosely interpreted, a good plan would focus on people with the skills we need for economic development in the 21st century. It should also emphasize countries of origin like ours—rule of law democracies with free market economies. Of course we can continue to accept political refugees and victims of political and religious persecution as we have in the past. Finally, the Bush administration has made no attempt to put out of business the bilingual education industry, which has done so much to retard the assimilation and acculturation of legal immigrants. This is another egregious violation of conservative principles.

• Moral clarity in the war. I discussed this earlier. Let me just say here that by not naming the enemy and by cavorting with suspect, fifth column elements like CAIR, Bush has appeared more PC than conservative.

Of course the conservative disappointment goes deeper than just disillusion with George W. Bush. It extends to the legislative and judicial branches of government as well. After a wonderful start in the House under Gingrich the Republican Congress behaved more and more like its Democratic predecessors, for which it was rebuked by being thrown out. The substantial cadre of faux conservatives and big government Republicans in Congress, especially in the Senate, are guilty of blatant contempt for conservative principles. And finally, turncoat jurists, such as John Paul Stevens, David Souter, and (at the end) Sandra Day O'Connor, who succumb to the lure of liberal popularity, enable the Court to legislate from the bench instead of delivering original intent interpretations of the Constitution and the nation's laws. So in summary, although it might be argued that Republicans are the majority party, the conservative movement has not captured the Republican Party—certainly nowhere near to the extent to which the liberal movement has captured the Democratic Party. Thus although conservatism may be on the rise in the nation, it is not at all clear that it has eclipsed liberalism as the reigning political philosophy—which is a perfect segue into the final section of this chapter.

An Assessment

The liberals began their ascent a little more than a hundred years ago, achieved dominance within 35 years and had their way for nearly 50 more years. The conservative counter-revolution was sparked by the (re)emergence of an intellectual movement in mid-twentieth century, highlighted by the works of Friedrich Hayek, Russell Kirk, Milton Friedman and William F. Buckley. Conservatives arrived politically with the election of Ronald Reagan, followed by the Gingrich-inspired capture of Congress in the mid 1990s. However, the liberal reaction to its loss of hegemony has been furious and the battle between competing ideologies has been spirited and yes, nasty. Who is wining? Has the conservative philosophy been adopted by enough people to qualify it as the leading philosophy? Is it dominant? Or, despite the obvious inroads, is it still a minority philosophy? In addition to the position vector, we can also inquire after the velocity vector. That is, who *will* be ahead in the future? The answer to the latter question must wait until Part III. Here our task is to assess where we are today?

It is a difficult task. There are conflicting signals and people of good judgment can and have come to contrary conclusions. Before we draw up the ledger sheet, let's mention two reasons as to why the picture is so cloudy—reasons which did not apply 75 years ago when the balance of power was shifting from conservative to liberal. The first is the concept of the faux conservative. In FDR's first presidential campaign, he often spoke in conservative tones, but once he gained power there was nothing faux liberal about his mode of governing. He pursued liberal policies with vigor and conviction. On the other hand, many of today's conservative politicians do not seem to have the same courage of their convictions. Ironically, like FDR, they speak in conservative hues, but the canvass they paint by their governing actions is colored liberal. The confusion caused by putatively conservative politicians advocating and implementing liberal lite policies makes it difficult to determine if conservative ideas are truly ascendant. The second difficulty is the mainstream media. It is ubiquitous and much harder to ignore than it was 75 years ago. And it has become and remained staunchly liberal. Thus it skews the playing field to a substantial degree, making it hard to get a good reading on the prevailing political winds. For example, one could argue that the NY Times was conservative in 1930, but its ability to hold the line for conservatives was very limited. Today, the Times is ultra-liberal, and it is doing a very good job of holding the liberal line.

OK, let's add up the wins and losses.

Places where conservative philosophy has been triumphant since 1980 and remains ascendant (in no particular order):

- America has not adopted gun control.

- The people's respect for and admiration of the military has been restored.

- Nationalized health care has been defeated.

- The growth of the investor class has been spectacular.

- Instigated by tax cuts and the Fed's close attention to inflation, we have had 25 years of sustained economic growth, punctuated by only three recessions, two of which were very minor.

- True welfare reform has been enacted.

- The cause of free trade has advanced and protectionism has declined somewhat.

- Teen sex and drug use has diminished.

- Capital punishment is still the law of the land.

Places where liberal philosophy has been triumphant since 1980 and remains ascendant (in no particular order):

- The elite opinion-making institutions, such as the media, Hollywood, higher education, foundations and law schools, have remained solidly in the liberal column.

- Abortion remains legal and widely practiced.

- Homosexuality is increasingly accepted as a lifestyle rather than as an aberration.

- The multicultural agenda has flourished and programs to *diversify* all manner of American institutions are proliferating.

- Legal immigration is at very high levels, especially from brown countries.

- The government continues to grow rapidly as new programs, new revenues and expenditures, and new regulations give testimony to the central role Uncle Sam plays in American life.

- The New Deal/Great Society entitlement programs are alive (even if not completely well).

- Judicial activism has enabled the enshrinement of liberal ideas into law.

And now here are a few places where the competitors have fought to a draw:

- The circle of ideas surrounding the separation of church and state and the role of religion in the public square;

- The environment; does it take precedence over economic growth and human pleasure?

- What to do about illegal immigrants;

- How are we doing in WWIV, is there even a WWIV, and if so or even if we are only combating sporadic terrorism, how should that fight be conducted?

- Leitmotif—are we a nation committed to social justice or rugged individualism? Incidentally, if we ever really settle this one, everything else will fall into place.

So who is winning? Like I said, a very difficult question to answer. The balance sheet above suggests a draw. In fact, it is undeniable that the liberal hegemony of the mid-twentieth century has been demolished. (It pays to keep in mind that the hegemony was never total; we did not go down the socialist road nearly as far as they did in Western Europe.) Conservative ideas and conservative politicians have been gaining strength in the last quarter century. But have the people rendered a verdict on which set of principles—liberal or conservative—should dominate in the governance of the country? I think not. You might say that the people want to have their cake and eat it too. They want to keep their guns, but they also want easy access to abortion. They want low taxes and robust economic growth, but they also want the social services provided by government programs. They want their individual freedom and the right to be left alone by the government, but when the wolf is at the door (whether in the form of an Al Qaeda terrorist, Hurricane Katrina, or high prescription drug prices), they look to the federal government to play a major role in keeping the wolf at bay.

The matter is clearly unsettled. Let the games continue.

Before concluding this chapter with a personal reminiscence, I want to make two more points. First of all, we are in the midst of a major internal debate, one heralded by passion and conviction that could and occasionally does spill over into invective. At this juncture, we need to keep in mind the points of commonality spelled out in Chapter 2. And all of us have to remember that this is a family dispute. Its outcome is of vital importance to all of us, but we must not forget that we are all Americans, and the ultimate goal for everyone is continued prosperity and the success of our free and one-of-a-kind nation. The second point is the following. I have been pretty hard on Mssrs. Bush in this chapter. But not nearly as hard as the vicious, vociferous critics of W on the Left. In fact, George senior is clearly a very decent man, devoted to his family, a dedicated public servant who has indeed served his country ably in many roles. Anyone who jumps out of a plane at age eighty is alright in my book. And George junior is also a decent guy, a good family man, a man who rescued his life from dissolution, who has been dealt a very difficult hand and has confronted it with determination and courage. Both father and son also clearly have the courage of their convictions. It's just that I don't particularly agree with many of those convictions.

One of the advantages of the academic life is its easy compatibility with travel. Like most of my colleagues, I have had the good fortune to travel to many corners of the globe in order to attend mathematical conferences and to pursue joint research with professional collaborators. In the academic year 1975-1976, I combined a NATO Fellowship with a sabbatical leave from the University of Maryland in order to teach and do research in mathematics at the Hebrew University of Jerusalem. I spent the year on the faculty there, my children spent the year in Israeli schools, and my wife spent the year converting kilos into pounds, centimeters into inches and Celsius into Fahrenheit as she coped with the non-trivial difficulties of running an Israeli home for three spoiled American males. While 30 years ago Israel was certainly not a third world country, it was also plainly far behind the United States in providing the creature comforts that we were accustomed to. But that is not the main point of the story.

I went to Jerusalem for both professional and personal reasons. Professionally, there were several distinguished Israeli mathematicians with whom I was anxious to interact. Personally, I was eager to delve more deeply into the Jewish society to which I had been introduced 10 years earlier, and also to spend more time soaking up some of the wisdom I knew that Arieh Rigevsky could impart. As it turned out though, I was not fully prepared for the intense experience the year proved to be. By its end, it supplied the fourth traumatic event, which together with the three I've already described (Vietnam, court-ordered bussing, and Watergate) caused a turnaround in my political thinking. This one, like court-ordered bussing, was deeply personal—not abstract and theoretical like Watergate and Vietnam were for me.

The nature of the trauma is easy to describe. When I arrived in Israel to live for an extended period, I was determined to keep an open mind. Was this a good society? Was it democratic? free? tolerant? Did its people behave honorably and generously? Were they militaristic without just cause? Was the place run according to the rule of law? How did they treat the Arab minority? I knew that as a Jew I would be accorded certain privileges, but I also knew that as an American I would be viewed as naïve and soft. Would they be interested in my point of view? And perhaps most important of all, was there any justification whatsoever for the unbridled hatred to which it was subjected by the Arab world, or for the more veiled opprobrium heaped upon it by almost every other country besides the United States?

I won't go into an elaborate description of my methods for answering these questions, but I will report that Israel passed with flying colors. Don't get me wrong, Israel is very far from perfect. The flaws I identified then are still present. For example, its economy is way too socialistic, its political system far too chaotic, the intensity of everyday life is occasionally hard to bear, the religious-secular divide is often bitter and of course it struggles with the seemingly never-ending threat of annihilation by neighbors bent on its destruction.

But Israel is also:

- *an open society where people of every political stripe express their ideas freely, forcefully and without fear of retribution;*

- *a socially mobile country where people of humble origins rise to unexpected heights;*

- *full of scientists and musicians, poets and journalists, farmers and industrialists, lawyers and doctors, and yes soldiers, who exemplify the diverse and dynamic society that nurtures them;*

- *a nation that has lifted itself from third to second to first world status in a remarkably short time;*

- *a democratic nation governed, under the most trying circumstances, according to the rule of law;*

- *unique in that its creation provided redemptive hope for a people dispossessed from its land for two millennia;*

- *a nation, which while subjected to the most perverse slaughter and horrific slander by its Arab neighbors, still manages to treat its potentially fifth column Arab citizens (mostly) with respect;*

- *a nation of immigrants that has successfully absorbed people from more than a hundred countries;*

- *a country full of creative people who generate intellectual property at a per capita rate that is unmatched in the world;*

- *an interesting, exciting place to live, full of friendly and helpful people.*

I learned these things at the same time as I watched the world increasingly designate this wonderful country as the most racist, xenophobic, ruthless, intolerant and illegitimate nation on the face of the Earth. Moreover, almost without exception, that vitriol came from the Left. The infamous "Zionism is Racism" resolution passed at the UN (while I was living in Israel) was largely the work of the socialist governments of the world. As a Jew growing up in New York I had been taught that the danger to my people always came from the Right. This was now manifestly no longer the case in the US or Western Europe. Beginning with the 6-Day War (1967), and culminating during my year in Israel, it became crystal clear to me that the further left any person or organization stood in the political spectrum, the greater the likelihood of anti-Zionist sentiment and hatred of Israel. Increasingly, political and religious conservatives defended Israel in the forums of the US and the world, while liberals of all stripes saw Israelis as at best obstacles to peace, and too often as Nazi-like oppressors of the poor Palestinians. The Right applauded while the Left booed when Israel braved distance, logistical complexity and fanatical terrorists to rescue the Jewish hostages at Entebbe. (The same difference in reaction was evident when Israel destroyed the Iraqi nuclear reactor six years later.) Incidentally, the drama at Entebbe occurred just as my family left Israel to return to the United States. The event had additional meaning for us because we took the exact same flight from Tel Aviv to Athens three months prior to the hijacking.

I returned from Israel in the summer of 1976 with all the liberal programming of my youth expunged from my mind, feeling quite comfortably conservative, and I have never looked back.

9

Acrimony between the Camps

I cannot tell you how many times I have heard colleagues state matter-of-factly that George W. Bush is a "moron" or an "idiot." Bush-bashing is ubiquitous on campus and faculty dialogue is *liberally* sprinkled with derogatory comments about the President. Moreover, this treatment is mild compared to the routine excoriation of the President that emanates from the mainstream media, senior leaders in the Democratic Party and of course the entertainment industry. The residents of those quarters regularly, impolitely and disrespectfully accuse Bush of: promoting tax cuts for the rich at the expense of the middle class and the poor; lying about WMD in order to coax the country into war in Iraq, presumably to benefit his oil buddies; allowing his religious beliefs to interfere with his Constitutionally mandated duties; trying to destroy the Social Security system and impoverish the elderly; consigning the afflicted to permanent illness or death by stymieing stem cell research; and the list goes on and on. In addition, he is accused of doing these terrible things in the most fiery and intemperate language. Unfortunately, the verbal and written assaults on the President's policies and character are merely representative of the acrimonious relationship that currently exists between liberals and conservatives. The bitterness and hostility between the camps are expressed daily as Democrats and Republicans say the most outrageous things about one another.

What is going on here? Is this normal discourse for our two-party system? Does the current level of vituperation mirror what has happened in the past, or is the invective being hurled more ferociously than usual? The answer: from a short-term perspective, the current debate is nastier than it was; but from a long-term perspective, it's about par for the course. For example, Thomas Paine's comments about George Washington's farewell presidential address were, "The world will be puzzled to decide whether you are an apostate or an imposter, whether you have abandoned good principles or whether you ever had any." Despite the fact that they had a 50-year relationship, Adams and Jefferson fought like cats and dogs; once Jefferson referred to his political rival as "a hoary incendiary who wanted to be president for life." Speaking of cats and dogs, few rivalries could match that of Andrew Jackson and his Whig enemies John Quincy Adams, Henry Clay and Daniel Webster, the first of whom made an unsubstantiated charge of adultery against Jackson. Like our greatest president (Washington), Lincoln was not spared the calumny of his opponents. But even members of his own party could be cruel as exemplified by his Secretary of War, Edwin Stanton, who called Abe "a long-armed ape." A president, now viewed quite favorably, but who suffered the slings of outrageous fury during his presidency was Harry Truman. My favorite sling though was aimed at his Secretary of State, Dean Acheson, who was called "a pompous diplomat in striped pants, with a phony British accent" by Senator Joe McCarthy. Finally, we should not forget the devastatingly mean barbs directed at both Lyndon Johnson and Richard Nixon for their prosecution of the Vietnam War.

My point here is not to accumulate a long list of scurrilous quotes about our past presidents, great and small. Rather it is to illustrate that the verbal and written assaults on George W. Bush are no worse than those aimed at even his most illustrious predecessors. Yet, over the last few years the opinion is continuously expressed that the civic discourse has deteriorated. What accounts for this perception? I think we can unravel the mystery if we review the treatment accorded our presidents during the last 60 years.

Truman was a firebrand, an unexpected president and of course a surprise winner in 1948. All this opened the door to vicious criticism by his opponents. But then things quieted down for Ike—a legendary war hero, greatly admired and beloved by most Americans. Eisenhower's (seemingly) casual approach to the presidency elicited playful ridicule from his detractors, but little in the way of sharp personal criticism. The atmosphere stayed more-or-less the same for Kennedy, who was also widely admired—although his set of admirers had a rather different profile from Ike's. Also, people thought twice about engaging JFK in a p-ssing contest for they might feel the sting of his rapier wit. Then, as remarked already, the fire heated up for Johnson and Nixon, whose terms spanned one of the most politically tumultuous periods in our nation's history. But later, with Nixon gone and the very bland Gerald Ford in the White House, things quieted down again. In truth, it was hard to get worked up about Ford—although two women did get sufficiently worked up to try to kill him. Next comes Jimmy Carter, a bit of an anomaly in the following sense. The Ford presidency afforded the country a period to recuperate from Watergate and Vietnam, after which it was ripe to get worked up again at the President.

But Carter is so obviously one of the most incompetent presidents in US history, to the point of pathetic. How can you get angry at a child trying to do a man's job? So he got off relatively lightly. Reagan dismissed him like a zephyr. Ah, Ronald Reagan, he certainly should have generated some serious heat. The liberals were incredulous that this "amiable dunce" could be elected president. They treated him derogatorily, but it was impossible to hate him—he was just so charming and likable. Moreover, it was clear that the people adored him, making it difficult to fiercely attack him (the Teflon President they called him). And there is another salient point. The liberals did not yet appreciate that their grasp on nearly complete political power was really ending. So they were not as desperate and angry as they would be 20 years later. Next, Bush senior was another Gerald Ford—a really nice guy, about whom it was hard to get worked up.

The atmosphere headed south with the arrival of Bill Clinton—especially after the 1994 Gingrich revolution. Unlike in1980, the liberals' confidence is shaken badly and they can't ignore any longer that their day of dominance is over. Correspondingly, the conservatives sense that their turn in the sun has arrived and they are much more inclined to swing back than they were under Taft or Eisenhower or Ford. Conservatives attacked Clinton aggressively. They questioned his morality (Whitewater, Vince Foster, sexual misconduct, inappropriate fundraising practices). They let him know that he was holding back the conservative revolution; that he behaved like an overgrown adolescent porn/rock star left over from the 60s; that he hadn't had a real job for a single day in his life, thus he was unqualified to lead the nation; that he was eviscerating the military and intelligence services; and that the attempt to nationalize health insurance by the Dragon Lady to whom he was attached would not succeed. They even impeached him. But Clinton could give as well as he got. He whipped Newt solidly in the government shutdown crisis; he was the true Teflon president as none of the sexual or criminal accusations stuck; he galvanized his party to easily defeat the impeachment conviction; and he tricked the conservatives into confirming two very liberal justices for the Supreme Court. Regarding these last two items, it is interesting to make a comparison. In the matter of confirming justices to the federal bench, Republicans have a much more difficult time getting conservatives past liberal Congressmen than vice versa. And regarding impeachment, Nixon was driven from office by a Democratic Congress for infractions no more and perhaps less serious than Clinton's, which occurred at the time of a Republican Congress. Obviously, Democrats have greater taste for and facility at fighting hard on existential matters. All the same, the acrimony during Clinton's presidency was barely a warm up for George W. Bush. The political atmosphere now is more poisonous than it has been for 30 years—although let's keep in mind, not out of line with comparably nasty times during the overall history of national politics.

Now that we've placed the recent acrimony in some historical perspective, let's examine the Bush hatred a little more closely. And hatred it would seem to be. Any objective reading of the liberal pulse, for example among my liberal colleagues, points to the fact that George W. Bush is soundly despised in those quarters. Aside from the political reasons, which I'll get to momentarily, there are personality defects that engender much contempt. To explain, let us compare Bush with Reagan—who was far more conservative than Bush and thus presumably at least as worthy of liberal disdain. But where Reagan was charming, Bush is awkward; where Reagan was naturally eloquent and a great communicator, Bush is stiff and stumbles over his words; where Reagan appeared genuine and sincere, Bush comes across as arrogant and smug. Moreover, he has that terrible smirk that makes you want to wipe it off his face. In short, unlike Reagan or Kennedy or Ike, whom people looked at and listened to and instinctively liked, Bush lacks any natural charisma or the kind of charm or grace that attracts instinctive affection. Au contraire, his manner and style seem to alienate many people. But that's not really why liberals hate him. They hate him because:

- They view his elevation to the presidency in 2000 as tainted, that he was installed in office by a biased Supreme Court rather than elected to it by a majority of the people.

- In a galling reprise, he managed to win reelection in 2004 with an equally narrow electoral majority.

- That of all the people to be standing on the watchtower when Osama struck, it should happen to be this dreadful man who then automatically received the allegiance of the American people, since they would have rallied around whomever was President at that critical juncture, whereas Bush was totally undeserving of that unfair advantage.

- He wears his religion on his sleeve and cites Jesus as his favorite philosopher.

- He cares more about tax cuts, private Social Security accounts and aborted fetuses that he does about helping the poor, fighting discrimination against homosexuals or protecting American workers whose jobs are endangered by globalization.

- He has, through deceit and deception, led us into an unwinable war of questionable legitimacy and spilled the blood of American youth in a worthless cause.

- He has alienated our European allies and promoted policies that engender fear and hatred of America throughout the world.

Bush backers survey the scene created by the Bush whackers and, whether they are hardcore conservative, moderate Republican or elsewhere at or to the right of Center, they are appalled by the venom directed at the President. Some turn the other cheek. But many do not. They unleash a torrent of accusations at the President's liberal opponents, which run something like this. We hold the liberals in contempt because:

- They appear to hate America, the land of freedom that affords them the liberty to viciously and publicly criticize the President; how else to explain the fact that they seem to be rooting for the enemy in WWIV.

- The constantly emphasize America's shortcomings, whether real or perceived, such as the fact that there are still poor people in this incredibly rich country; or that the government never does enough to aid citizens caught in a natural disaster; or that we waste natural resources because we prefer SUVs and build well-equipped, large homes; or the fact that the post invasion planning for Iraq was bungled.

- But they never take pride in or boast about America's world-leading economy, the fact that it is the most successfully integrated and tolerant multicultural country on Earth, its unbelievably charitable reactions by individuals and organizations to crises, domestic and foreign, and the economic mobility of its people—we constantly create new millionaires. Liberals focus on the perverse actions of a few renegade soldiers at Abu Ghraib, but begrudge the achievements of superstars like Bill Gates and Sergey Brin (the co-founder of Google, who immigrated to America with his family when he was a small child).

- They insist that all the problems of America are to be solved by the federal government and they downplay the role of churches, schools, civic and charitable organizations, and of course business.

- They preach tolerance, but they are blatantly intolerant; they have fought tooth and nail to limit any conservative presence on campus or in the media.

- They will not face the reality that the American people have repudiated socialist philosophy, lite or heavy.

- They fight dirty—they filibuster judges, editorialize on the front page and limit free speech with bogus hate speech laws and regulations.

- They are pacifists who will not defend America.

- They claim that the New York Times and CBS News are fair and balanced, but that Fox News and Rush Limbaugh are biased. Puleez.

- They blame Katrina, global warming (if it exists), the trade deficit and probably ring around the tub on President Bush.

- They criticize Bush initiatives like Social Security reform, income tax reform and the aggressive promotion of democracy in the Middle East, but instead of offering alternative plans to solve real problems, they stoop to meanness and call Bush a moron.

Well, there's not a lot of middle ground here. We have two very different and competing visions of history, of morality, of justice, of truth, of how the country should be run, now and in the future. This schism occurs not only in a period when there is no public consensus in the field of political philosophy, but at a time when majority opinion is moving from one side to the other, from liberal to conservative. Of course this is not unprecedented. If my version of history presented in Chapter 5 has any merit, then we went through a similar seismic shift in the 1930s, except that the progression went in the other direction. We should therefore have had the same kind of seemingly irreconcilable differences and the same rancorous and fractious disputes that we have today. But we didn't. The bad feelings toward FDR then among the suddenly minority conservative population was nowhere near as intense or widespread as the corresponding feeling among liberals toward Bush today. In fact, the conservatives of that era surrendered to the liberal takeover without firing nary a shot, figuratively speaking—a very mild level of reaction compared to today's liberal counterattacks. It is interesting to explain why this was so, and that is our next chore.

I will offer five reasons for the relatively tame acceptance by conservatives in the 1930s and 1940s of the liberal ascendance and increasing dominance at that time:

1. They didn't appreciate what was happening to them. If you have a 200 year run of the farm, it is easy to take things for granted. While the progressive era of the early part of the century shook things up, and while the upheavals caused by the Stock Market Crash and Great Depression were severe, many conservatives just didn't believe that the American people

were losing their faith in basic free market capitalism, limited government and traditional American culture.

2. Eventually conservatives did come to appreciate that the nation and the world were being subjected to revolutionary and potentially cataclysmic forces. The period witnessed not only the Great Depression, but also the birth and growth of the twin evils of fascism and communism. Conservatives vaguely sensed (perhaps feared would be a better word) that laissez faire economics, isolationism, and circumscribed government would not be up to the task of combating these powerful forces. Thus they came to doubt the worthiness of their conservative principles vis-à-vis liberal policies that their opponents claimed were designed to cope with the Depression and totalitarianism.

3. Like any group in power for a long period, conservatives had grown "old, sloppy, lazy and fat." Perhaps also corrupt. It is in the nature of things. The Roman Empire lasted 500 years, the British Empire 300, the conservative era in America more than 200. Nothing lasts forever. Political movements, however successful, eventually fall prey to the forces of attrition that render them old, sloppy, lazy and fat.

4. They were out of ideas and running low on faith. This is related to the previous reason, but is not exactly the same thing. You can be old and sloppy without being out of ideas. The declining empires mentioned in the last item were in poor shape before they completely ran out of ideas. But once devoid of ideas, loss of faith follows inevitably. And when you no longer have confidence in your own system, you are easily dislodged from your pedestal.

5. Finally, when your faith in your system is shaken, you begin to give credence to the other guy's ideas. Conservatives in the first 30 years of the 20th century began to see liberalism as less of a threat. They worried that classic conservative principles weren't working and perhaps went as far as to think "Well, let's give the other guy a shot and see if his ideas will play any better."

In retrospect, in light of these reasons, it is not altogether surprising that the conservatives surrendered so meekly. Therefore, we may ask why the liberals haven't followed the mold and gone down like pussycats in the current era. The answer is because the analog of only one of the five cited reasons for the conservative collapse applies to today's liberal movement. Namely, they are definitely old, sloppy, lazy and fat. And they are corrupt also. But that is the only condition that obtains. None of the other four applies. Indeed, after a period of denial, liberals have come to appreciate precisely what is at stake in the current battle. For example, I've mentioned that their dominance in the executive and legislative branches of government has been broken. But they are fighting to the death to maintain their hold on the judiciary—the branch that has been the most effective in furthering their agenda. Regarding whether there is a major crisis in the world or nation that their policies are insufficient to address, liberals have not given an inch. They see the major crises of the world (Iraq, disputes with Allies, terror, rogue nations, globalization) and of the nation (abortion rights, homosexual rights, illegal immigration) as being caused by the newly ascendant conservatives. Moreover, they believe that the crises could be ameliorated by a return to liberal policies. Next, I do think they are out of ideas; virtually all of what they espouse is retreads of classic liberal dogma. But amazingly, they are not out of faith. This may be because their political faith and their religious faith are one and the same—secular humanism. Their religion is alive and well and the worshippers are as fervent as ever. Finally, they have no inclination whatsoever to "give conservatism a chance." Since their faith is intact, such an inclination would be tantamount to apostasy. Ain't gonna happen. In any event, taken together these explain why, unlike the meek surrender by conservatives 60-70 years ago, liberals today are in full counterattack mode. What this augurs for our nation will be examined in Chapter 12.

The following analogy is a little far-fetched, but there is some validity to it. One could say that the conservatives surrendered 60 years ago in a similar fashion to the German and Japanese surrenders at the end of WWII. Namely, although it would be incorrect to call it *unconditional*, it would be correct to describe it as I did in the personal reminiscence in Chapter 4, namely, the stance adopted was, "OK, you win, we lose, tell me what comes next." On the other hand, the liberal surrender today imitates the Arab surrenders after all the wars they have lost to the Israelis—namely, there is no surrender. At most they acknowledge defeat in a battle, but then they vow that the war goes on.

So the liberals fight on—ferociously and tenaciously. The retaliation by conservatives is perhaps not as ferocious, but unlike their forbearers 60 years ago, there is no hint of retreat. Conservatives clearly believe that their era has arrived and they are not about to squander the opportunity. More specifically, conservatives are motivated and inspired by their interpretation of history over the last two generations. They believe that the course of WWIII and especially its denouement proves that the liberals are on the wrong side of history. The accretion of power in the hands of the central government, the collectivist method of arranging either an economy or a social structure, the faith in secular humanism, the willingness to trust our country's safety to collective security agreements and international agencies, the eagerness to cast off the wisdom, mores and culture of our founding fathers, all of these notions have been proven to be wrong-headed. Even if motivated by good intentions, they are ultimately misguided and dangerous to the Republic. Conservatives are aghast that more liberals do not acknowledge the evidence and change their way of thinking. Conservatives place much of the blame for that failure on the so-called "mainstream media" (MSM)—the major network news organizations (CBS, ABC, NBC, CNN), the leading American urban newspapers (NY Times, Washington Post, LA Times), and some would include the entertainment industry, and perhaps also the major publishing houses. I don't think any sensible conservative would question the concept of freedom of the press, or not acknowledge the salutary role in our history played by a robust and free press. Indeed freedom of the press occupies an exalted spot (in the First Amendment) in the Constitutional law that conservatives revere. But for various reasons, one of which is certainly the liberal capture of the journalism schools and humanities departments in the nation's universities, the MSM lurched sharply to the left during the last 60 years, where it remains firmly entrenched. The apogee of its power occurred during Watergate and Vietnam—during which time it is only a mild exaggeration to assert that the MSM terminated a war on unfavorable terms and engineered a coup.

Necessity being the mother of invention, conservatives found clever and original ways to circumvent the influence of the MSM. The main vehicles were: Fox News, Talk Radio, the Internet, direct mailing and think tanks. The conservative message was widely disseminated by, among others: Rush Limbaugh, Larry Elder, Michael Savage, Thomas Sowell, Ann Coulter, right wing bloggers, Paul Weyrich, the Heritage Foundation and the Cato Institute. These people and organizations broke the liberal lobby on the news. However, the MSM is still very powerful. So the battle between liberals and conservatives clearly will stay red hot for at least the near future.

I will conclude this discussion with two contradictory observations, one hopeful, one not. The latter is a reinforcement of the point I made earlier, namely, there is not a lot of middle ground here. Indeed, the nasty fact that is glossed over by third way and other "why can't we just get along types," and with which many people will be uncomfortable, is that in actuality *there is no viable middle here*. Take a look back at the table of touchstone issues. It is quite remarkable how clearly demarcated are the lines separating the two sides of an issue—for many if not most of the issues. For example, you are either in favor of expanding the scope of government or you favor reining it in. It is a cop out, and shows that you haven't really thought about the issue seriously, to say that the present size of government is about right. Or pray tell what is the intermediate position between revoking and affirming the citizen's right to bear arms? Perhaps a nine millimeter is OK, but an AK47 is not. Another cop out. How about the Constitution? Is it a living document or not? You can't declare Articles I, III, V, VII and Amendments I-X as sacrosanct, and then assert that all the rest is fair game for reinterpretation in light of modern times. That would be ridiculous. Consider one more example: capital punishment. You are in favor of it or not. A position like, "I oppose capital punishment except for the murder of a policeman or correctional officer," is yet another cop out. (Bad pun.) Why not firemen? Or teachers? Or the President of the United States? There are many more issues that qualify—think about abortion or animal rights—for which it is hard to see meaningful middle ground between the current liberal and conservative positions.

So what am I saying? Simple. There is no third way. Modern liberalism and modern conservatism are diametrically opposed philosophies—at least at this moment. There is not a lot of common ground. And really no solid ground between them. So it is not at all surprising that the debate between these competing philosophies is harsh, hyperbolic and uncompromising.

And yet … the more hopeful observation is that while the debate is nasty and unforgiving, it has remained a *debate*. No one is lobbing Molotov cocktails, no guerilla war has erupted, no one is under house arrest, and neither side is challenging the assertion of the other that its primary objective in furthering its goals is to build a better and stronger United States of America. The points of commonality described in Chapter 2 are holding firm. While I may believe that the policies espoused by my liberal colleagues and fellow tribe members are misguided, I absolutely do not question that their motivation is to build a better America. I simply question whether their tactics will achieve their objective. I am confident that the feeling is mutual. Clearly they think my ideas are wrong and counterproductive, perhaps even stupid and dangerous. But they still inquire after the health of my family and laugh at my jokes. We are all Americans, privileged to ride the greatest ship of state ever launched and we'll continue the battle by trying to convince the other not by convicting the other.

> *Picking up the thread from the previous reminiscence, I reiterate that I returned from Israel in the summer of 1976 a hardcore conservative, and I have never looked back. But I did blink once. I abstained in the presidential contest that fall between Jimmy Carter and Gerald Ford. I did so for several reasons. First of all, I felt somewhat out of it. For a whole year I had been immersed in Israeli life and paid scant attention to American politics. To be honest I felt unfamiliar with the candidates and (to some extent) with the issues. In fact, I had never heard of Jimmy Carter until late spring `76. Moreover, because of family commitments that fall, I had little time to get up to speed politically. What little I could glean made clear to me that neither candidate came close to embracing the conservative ideas and themes that were new and true to me. Carter was a classic tax and spend liberal and Ford was a big government Republican. Incidentally, I was almost completely unaware that Ronald Reagan had run a vigorous primary campaign against Ford during my absence and that he had embraced conservative ideas and themes avidly. I certainly sensed that Ford was "the lesser of two evils," but he was clearly not the kind of conservative candidate that I was looking for. So I abstained. There may have been many who reasoned as I did and if so, then we put Jimmy Carter in the White House—an outcome that I, and the country, would come to regret.*

> *Fast forward four years. There I am casting the most enthusiastic presidential vote I had ever cast, or would again—although the successor vote another four years later was cast was with nearly equal gusto. Yes, I voted for Reagan twice, and with deep conviction each time. In fact the events of the four years of the Carter administration were ironclad proof that my newfound conservative political philosophy was right on the money. For, by any objective standard, Carter had to be one of the most inept Presidents of the 20th century. Actually, I think he takes the booby prize. Others might argue for Harding or Hoover, but for my money, Carter was the worst. Let us run down the "accomplishments" of the Carter Presidency.*

> - *His tax and spend profligacy pushed interest rates and inflation to record levels while it strangled the economy and heightened unemployment. The term "stagflation" was coined to describe the dire economic mess; but Jimmy Carter's economy was best described by Ronald Reagan in his convention speech in 1980 as "a new and altogether indigestible economic stew—one part inflation, one part high unemployment, one part recession, one part runaway taxes, one part deficit spending, seasoned with an energy crisis; it's an economic stew that has turned the national stomach."*

- *Jimmy decided the people of America were suffering from "malaise," and after secluding himself at Camp David to dream up a cure, he delivered what is universally acknowledged to be one of the most pathetic addresses ever delivered by an American President.*

- *He cut defense spending, military pay and weapons systems mercilessly. Under his tutelage the state of our armed forces deteriorated into the sorriest condition since before the Second World War.*

- *He encouraged the downfall of the Shah and helped to bring into being the Islamofascist regime that has ruled Iran ever since, and which is one of the main fonts of the evil that besets us today in WWIV.*

- *He acquiesced in the brutal capture of our embassy in Tehran and the savage imprisonment of our diplomats for more than a year; thus he ignored a blatant act of war perpetrated against us.*

- *When he relented and permitted the military to attempt a rescue, it was foiled in large part by the sorry state of the military to which he had condemned it.*

- *He appointed a pacifist as Secretary of State, Cyrus Vance. Vance resigned in protest of Carter's feeble attempt to use force to rescue American civilian hostages.*

- *Carter preened that America's foreign policy would be guided by a moral code, when all he achieved by his hypocrisy was represented by a CIA that could no longer engage operatives overseas if they had so much as a parking ticket.*

- *Like his illustrious predecessor, Richard Nixon, he attempted to ration gas, once again driving up prices and causing long lines at the pump.*

- *He set us on the road to the disastrous energy policies that still straightjacket the country today: no new nuclear power plants, no new oil refineries, restricted offshore drilling, no drilling where snail darters or caribou might say peek-a-boo, and the pursuit of cockamamie ideas like wind power.*

- *He coped with the resulting energy shortage by donning a cardigan and instructing us to turn down our thermostats.*

- *He was unable to check the advance of the Soviet Empire deep into Africa, Asia and Latin America, and then he professed to be surprised when the Soviets invaded Afghanistan. He was so incensed by the latter aggression that he unleashed a lethal weapon—he kept American athletes at home during the Moscow Olympics.*

Can you say Peter Principle? Carter's presidency was a complete, unmitigated disaster. As if to add an exclamation point on it, he has gone on to an equally distinguished post presidential career. I speak not of his allegiance to various ultra-left wing causes or his frantic efforts to monitor rigged elections in third world countries; but rather of his shameless coddling of bloodthirsty dictators like Castro and Kim Il Sung, his barely disguised animus toward Israel and Jewish people, and perhaps worst of all, his inexcusable public criticism of his country and its president when he is overseas. This behavior is unprecedented among former presidents.

Now during the late 70s and early/mid 80s, I was vociferous in my criticism of Carter and praise for Reagan. Most of my colleagues at the university did not appreciate my point of view. I would make points that I thought they would resonate to, like the following:

- *Under Carter we had high inflation and small raises, whereas under Reagan we have low taxes and big raises;*

- *Under Carter, university support by federal agencies was constricting, but under Reagan as government receipts grew from the booming economy, our federal grant support is greater;*

- *Carter was religious but Reagan rarely went to church; why do you like the first guy better?*

- *Under Carter the academic job market was a disaster, but under Reagan jobs grew plentiful.*

Their reaction: they thought I was nuts. Hardly anyone agreed with me. Political discussions grew testy and unpleasant. I decided that it was not worth the bad feelings. And so I drastically curtailed my participation in political discussions on campus. Then it vaguely dawned on me that I had been muzzled—albeit, the muzzle was largely self-administered. Can you say "chilly climate?" Ah, one of the favorite phrases of the campus diversity fanatics. They do everything in their power to stamp out the chilly climate (which is more in their minds than in reality on campus) as it applies to homosexuals, minorities, women or any other of their favorite groups. But the chilliest climate on campus is the one encountered by political conservatives.[1] How ironic! In the university, where free expression, the exploration of all ideas in the search for truth, openness and tolerance for unusual points of view, where all of these ideals are supposed to be the hallmark—well, I will not be the first to tell you that "it aint necessarily so."

---

1.   It's pretty chilly for religious Christians too, but that is another story.

But I don't want to end this reminiscence on a negative note. During the 1980s I was thrilled when Reagan was elected and reelected, and I was delighted by his triumphs: the rescue of the economy and the initiation of 25 years of nearly continuous economic growth; the resistance to the Soviet Union, the roll back of some of its successes and the implementation of policies that would drive it out of business forever shortly after Reagan left office; the restoration of pride in America and the putting to rest the idea that we had passed our zenith—all of these accomplishments despite a liberal Congress and an increasingly liberal MSM.[2]

---

2.   To preserve the happy ending of this reminiscence, I have consigned to a footnote the mention of some of Reagan's disappointments. In fact he suffered three major failures and made one major mistake. The first failure was his inability to permanently limit the growth of government; he engineered a slowdown, but it proved temporary and the government behemoth continues to expand. The second failure was that he made little progress in the Culture Wars. To be fair, I think he thought that this was more a job for private, religious, civic and charitable organizations than for the president; nevertheless, the fact remains that the rot has not diminished. The third failure was his inability to foresee the rise of global, radical Islam. Hezbollah gave him a taste in 1983, but he ducked that fight. He did go after Qadaffi, however. His major mistake: choosing George Bush as his Vice President. No true conservative successor to Reagan was groomed and we are paying dearly for that. He picked Bush for the same reason that Kennedy picked Johnson and Ike picked Nixon; the former felt he needed the latter on the ticket to win. All of these selections backfired. Reagan didn't need Bush to win. We would have been far better off if he had picked a real conservative like Phil Crane, Phil Gramm or Jack Kemp.

PART III

Young Conservatives and Old Liberals

10

Premature Conservatives

If you examine the voting record of a single American voter over the course of a few decades, you will see, with rare exceptions, one of three possible patterns:

   a.   the voter stays constant in his allegiance to party or political philosophy;

   b.   the voter starts out casting her ballots at one end of the political spectrum, but migrates (slowly or rapidly) to the other and then stays there; or

   c.   The voter switches back and forth many times between the two parties or philosophies.

From the point of view of our study, there is no need to examine carefully voters who manifest pattern (c). This is because any voter who repeatedly switches between liberal/Democratic and conservative/Republican candidates is not operating according to a well-thought out political philosophy. It is a rare and confused citizen who repeatedly flip-flops his political axioms. Furthermore, both conservative and liberal philosophies have not changed that much over the decades. Hence, the voter who is changing allegiance constantly is casting ballots based on considerations other than political philosophy. His motivation is likely to be: personality, appearance, debating skills, ability to deliver pork, "trust," believability, likeability, a single issue, or some other criteria that bear little resemblance to a well-defined political philosophy. These voters are irrelevant to our considerations and are of no interest to us here.

That leaves patterns (a) and (b), each of which has two different manifestations. Thus the possibilities are:

   1.   Voters who start out liberal and stay that way forevermore;

   2.   Voters who start out conservative and do not stray from that path;

3.   Voters who start out liberal, but then adopt a conservative preference;

4.   Voters who start out conservative, but migrate to the liberal camp.

Our fundamental conclusion in Part II (Chapters 6 & 7) was that, for voters who do shift allegiance over their lifetime, somewhat more will shift from Left to Right than vice versa. Thus of the four categories, number 3 corresponds to exactly that progression. Now presumably all the argumentation offered in Parts I and II of the book lend legitimacy, credence and rationality to that kind of movement and we shan't concentrate any further on providing any rationale for those migrants. Remember: *If you are young and not liberal, then you have no heart; but if you are old and not conservative, then you have no brain.* Thus we shall refer to the folks in category 3 as those who have completed the "normal political progression."

Now what about the other three categories? It may very well be that constancy is more common than change. That is, the folks who dwell in the first two categories are likely to be more numerous than those who inhabit the latter two. But constancy itself is a form of negation of the normal political progression. On the one hand, if you start out liberal and stay that way, why didn't your head take over from your heart? If, on the other hand, you start out and stay conservative, then did you start out as a heartless wretch? Finally, what about those who truly violate the maxim, that is, they start out conservative and wind up liberal? What kind of "deviancy" accounts for that transformation? In summary, all the people in categories 1, 2 & 4 are bucking the basic trend described in these pages and therefore worthy of examination.

In this chapter we will consider the voters in categories 2 and 4, lifelong conservatives and conservatives who convert to liberalism. We shall postpone the discussion of those in category 1, lifelong liberals—arguably the most interesting characters we explore, until the next chapter. In this chapter we will also pay attention to the residents of my two special environments, Jews and academicians.

We have observed that many, perhaps most people don't change their political stripes over time. In particular, lifelong conservatives can only be so if they start out as conservatives. But we've already agreed that youth and idealism go hand in hand, thereby suggesting—as our fundamental axiom asserts—that youth lends itself to liberalism. So how do young conservatives avoid the natural tug of liberalism on their fertile young minds? Must they be hard-hearted wretches, devoid of compassion for the poor and lacking in utopian desires to fix the world? I think not. Indeed young conservatives have always been with us. The Young Americans for Freedom and the (somewhat less conservative) Ripon Society have long and venerable traditions. They may not be as well populated with young people as the Americans for Democratic Action or the American Civil Liberties Union, but they are not wanting for membership either.

So where do these young conservatives come from, both those who retain their political bent all their lives and those who (contrary to form) succumb to the liberal call later in life? I am even willing to posit that, left to his own devices, especially if those devices are found on an American college campus, the "average young person" is apt to develop a liberal philosophy. What mechanisms intervene to deflect that natural tendency toward liberalism in order to produce a young conservative? I will outline four scenarios that can account for such an occurrence. There are probably more.

Programming. A young person might be conservative because she was programmed to be. This could happen in numerous ways. For example, she grows up in a household where one or both parents are very conservative. Children pick up their parents' tastes, habits and proclivities—against which they don't always rebel. This would be especially so if the breeding was reinforced by an extended family, e.g., aunts and uncles, grandparents and cousins. If all the members of the family are demonstrably conservative, it's going to take a strong-willed and/or rebellious child to resist that kind of programming.

Political programming could also occur in a religious environment. This might be overt or covert, planned or unplanned. In many communities, religious organizations have a powerful influence, especially on those parts of the political scene that involve cultural matters. It is not hard to imagine a young person emerging from a strong religious environment with very conservative tendencies. Incidentally, I'm not talking about brainwashing by a cult here—just the natural, seductive power of persuasion that people you respect, trust and want to emulate often exert upon you.

Growing up an army brat makes you a likely candidate for conservative programming. It is common to see families of multi-generational soldiers—fathers and sons, brothers and cousins, and these days, women too. Such environments are often quite conservative and if one has the inclination to continue the family's military tradition, conservative politics goes right along with it.

Another possible conservative programming environment is provided within a business setting. If the young lady comes of age in a place where almost all of her friends and relatives are in business, even if say they are all farmers, she is probably embedded in a milieu where the natural tendency is toward political conservatism. If the environment is sufficiently saturated with business, its attendant conservatism will be a tug that will be hard to resist.

Finally, one could imagine an all-embracing educational environment—e.g., living with your professorial parent(s) on a campus, or in an apartment complex housing the members of a think tank or some focused NGO. Politics may be an intense part of such an environment. If that environment is suffused with the conservative spirit, it could serve as a strong political training ground for a young person. Incidentally, if it is an environment of higher education, then in order for it to be conservative, it had better look like Hillsdale College or Grove City College and not like Harvard or Yale.

Personality traits. Recall that in Part I we associated certain personality traits with political tendencies. Indeed these played a central role in the construction of the five compartments by which we correlated age with political philosophy in Part II. Well, human personalities take an infinite variety of forms and predicting the personality of a youth based on family history, or any other supposed predictive factor, is exceedingly unreliable. So, paying homage to our compartments, a young person from any home or family may turn out to be pragmatic and not idealistic, or he may be opportunistic and not egalitarian-minded, or he might be an absolutist and not a relativist, or he may manifest any combination of these "contrary" traits. But if so, then these tendencies are likely to steer him toward a conservative path, which will not be the fate of his brethren who manifest the more common traits of youth. For him, following his head before his heart comes naturally. Moreover, no programming is necessary, his natural tendency is to identify with and adopt a conservative agenda.

Personal experience. The lead example here is described by the classic phrase, "a conservative is a liberal who has been mugged by reality." There may be an event, person, place or object in the young gal's experience that is so powerful and influential, that it produces a conservative temperament. The possibilities are endless.

The classic is of course the mugging. Although, it is not axiomatic that a mugging must produce a conservative. The mugging needs to have occurred in a circumstance that discredits liberalism. For example, the mugger is on welfare, or has benefited from a lenient sentence from a previous crime. Another possible experience is court-ordered bussing. I've told you about the consequences of that experience in my reminiscence in Chapter 6. Yet a third possibility is a military experience. I'm not talking about a military family; merely an individual who finds herself in the military. The entire experience, or even a segment of it, could easily create an instant conservative. Here's one more: a calamitous liberal mentor. By that I mean to suggest the following. You are a liberal, but one of your most important mentors—say a teacher, group leader, or your supervisor, who is your liberal guide and whom you admire—does or says something dreadful or hypocritical or heaven forbid, something patently conservative. You realize that her liberalism is a sham and in a moment of cathartic clarity, you associate the whole liberal gestalt with this failed mentor and decide to throw it all out.

Premature conservative. Those guys in the Young Americans for Freedom may not qualify under any of the above scenarios. They may have arrived at their conservative politics in a more premeditated, analytical fashion. That is, they studied history, politics, economics, and maybe even sociology; then they matched what they learned against current events; and finally they methodically evaluated the contrary theses of the two philosophies and came to the conclusion on their own that conservatism is more worthy of their support than liberalism. When that happens, the allegiance to conservative principles is strong because the personal convictions are deep. I knew a few people like that in college, even one or two in high school. I thought they were crazy. In fact, I now realize that they were prematurely wise.

So what about these young or premature conservatives? Are they stone cold, heartless rats? I don't think so. Young conservatives can be just as compassionate, tolerant and caring as young liberals. And I don't mean compassionate in the sense of President Bush's "compassionate conservatism." What a bunch of hooey! That's his code to identify himself as a big government conservative. A true conservative is compassionate in the following sense. He understands that the policies devised and implemented by liberals hurt the poor, hold back the middle class, taint members of underrepresented groups, drag down the economy and subject the country to danger. How in heaven's name can any of that be classified as compassionate? Yes, liberal plans are well intentioned—motivated by idealistic and egalitarian impulses. They are also abject failures. And exactly what about failure makes it compassionate? Au contraire, establishing policies that give the greatest number of people the maximum chance to succeed is true compassion. Level the playing field, open all possible doors to opportunity and then get out of the way to let people compete and thrive. Some will fail, but the percentage that do will be much lower than in a liberal system, which drags down the high achievers to the level of the mediocre. Now recognizing that in a conservative system, some will fail, perhaps even through no fault of their own, the system encourages and empowers various types of NGOs to help catch and aid those who do fail to compete successfully. America has a phenomenal history of this kind of private intervention, both before and since the advent of expensive and counterproductive government generated compassion. Government compassion amounts to redistribution schemes that have the effect of dragging everyone down toward the level of the downtrodden so that shared misery becomes the norm. Private compassion strives to help the less fortunate lift themselves up closer to the level of the more fortunate. Which compassion do you prefer?

Thus far in this chapter we have focused on young conservatives. Discounting those who flip-flop in their political preferences, we identified two paths that a young conservative might take as he ages—remain a lifelong conservative or convert to liberalism. Let's address these two briefly now. In fact, there is nothing surprising about the first path. Our basic conclusion supports the idea of a rightward drift in political preference with increasing age. Therefore, if you start out conservative, the normal expectation is that you would stay that way, perhaps become even more so. So what is remarkable about lifelong conservatives—if there is anything remarkable about the concept at all—is not the lifelong constancy, but rather the starting point. I gave several plausible explanations (earlier in this chapter) for how such a starting point might be arrived at and I will have little more to say about lifelong conservatives.

Now what about those who cast off the conservative mantle, convert to liberalism, and maintain that course? Such a sequence flies in the face of the normal progression that I have outlined. But it happens. Just not very often! I challenge you to draw up a list of well-known figures who have made that trip. Then compare it to an analogous list of those who have traveled in the opposite direction. For every David Brock or Arianna Huffington, there are dozens and dozens like David Horowitz or Ronald Reagan. The number of politicians who abandon the Democratic Party for the Republican Party dwarfs the number who make the opposite choice. To my way of thinking, this is as it should be. But let's, for the sake of completeness, spend a few words on possible motivations of those who make the Right to Left trek. It is only fair to acknowledge some of the causes for this choice of path, even if it is unconventional and less traveled.

In fact, the possible reasons for a Right to Left shift are limited in the following sense. I have already indicated that in the key personality traits or mental frameworks from Chapter 3 (i.e., pragmatist vs. idealist, opportunist vs. egalitarian, absolutist vs. relativist), the normal progression is toward features associated with the Left to Right drift. Personality changes in the other direction can occur on occasion, but I suspect they are rare. No, I believe that political switches from Right to Left are primarily caused by significant life experiences that engender a re-evaluation of political axioms. These would be very similar to those described in the "personal experience" section earlier in this chapter—except that the event causes a political shift to the Left instead of to the Right. What form might they take? Well, if I may coin a phrase, "a liberal is a conservative who has been mugged by the market." An individual who gets beat up in the stock market or in business or in real estate may decide that laissez-faire is not all that it is cracked up to be and that the benevolent hand of government might ease the pain. Immigrants or handicapped people or perhaps minorities (or other natural constituents of the Left) who, nevertheless, initially have a non-collectivist approach to life, but are having a hard time navigating the shoals of society, may come to the view that a centralized, managerially-oriented organization of the country is more desirable. Another possibility is a radicalizing experience. For example, while working in a charitable organization you decide that your clients are beyond the help of the meager resources that your organization can bring to bear and only the full weight of the federal government can save them. And of course, the possibility of a calamitous mentor always exists. It may not be common, or even occasional, but radicalization of a conservative does happen and I would be remiss not to acknowledge the possibility.

Now before going on to my two special environments, let's look back at the four patterns I listed at the beginning of the chapter. I will rephrase their statements to read more like phenomena than patterns, then I will expand the list by two, and finally comment on the frequency of occurrence of each phenomenon. Here are the six:

A.   creating young liberals;

B. creating young conservatives;

C. converting liberals into conservatives;

D. converting conservatives into liberals;

E. remaining liberal;

F. remaining conservative.

The main thrust of the book encompasses the assertion that A, C, and F are "natural phenomena." The justification for that assertion is presented in Parts I and II. So those three phenomena (A, C, F) are what you expect to see and generally what you do see. The remaining three phenomena, (B, D, E) might then be characterized as unusual or even perhaps unexpected. In this chapter we have given some plausible reasons to account for the occurrence of B and D. But in fact I think the most interesting phenomenon is E because it is, on the one hand, against the grain, but on the other, very common. It certainly bears close examination and that is what we'll do in the next chapter.

Now let's move on to Jews and academicians, who are disproportionately represented in A and E, and are largely missing from B and F. I'll comment on those momentarily, but first what about C and D? We've already agreed that phenomenon D is relatively rare; moreover, neither Jews nor academic faculty are playing any prominent role there. Phenomenon C is the one place where the paths of Jews and faculty have diverged to some extent. Specifically, Jews are rather heavily represented among the neocons, and while some faculty have taken the neocon road, they are not nearly as numerous, vocal or prominent as the Jewish neocons. Now all that I've said so far in this paragraph is self-evident to anyone who is paying attention. The interesting question of course is why. Why are Jews and faculty so reliably liberal? And why do they remain so? Well, as I've said several times, you could write a book; in fact, two books, one for the Jews and one for faculty. That is not my purpose here. But the questions are too interesting to ignore completely. So let me offer some partial answers for each of the two communities. Moreover, I will do so in a careful way so as to not impinge on the more general material that I will present in the next chapter. The reasons I will offer will not be of a general variety (like those in the next chapter), but will be specifically targeted to the two communities. Finally, they will be focused more toward explaining why the members of the two groups are receptive to adopting a liberal stance rather than why they tend to stay liberal indefinitely.

I will consider the Jews first, but with an immediate qualification. The Jewish community is fractured into subsets according to the religious branches of Judaism: orthodox, conservative and reform. At least these have been the commonly acknowledged categories for many years. But I think this categorization no longer applies very well, and it absolutely does not apply toward a political classification. First of all, the number of branches has been growing to include Reconstructionist, gay, some would add messianic, but also—what may be the largest group—the unaffiliated. Next, for my purposes, that is, political grouping, the classification is actually much simpler—namely, orthodox on the one hand and everyone else on the other. What I will say next applies to non-orthodox Jews. The orthodox Jewish community is much more politically conservative than the rest of the Jewish community. But since the orthodox are estimated to be no more than 10% of the Jewish population (actually, I find it hard to believe it is not substantially larger), my comments apply to the great majority of the Jewish people living in the USA. That said, I will now offer five (interrelated) explanations for the overwhelmingly liberal bias of (non-orthodox) American Jews.

Prophetic tradition. The history of the Jewish people is characterized by a constant tension between the *universal* and the *particular*. In the former, the outlook is outward rather than inward. The Jewish people must pay close attention to its assigned role in the world, to the nature of its interactions and dealings with the Goyim, and to the effect that those interactions have on both the Jews and the Goyim. As a guide for this outlook the Jews look to the books of the prophets in the Bible and in this regard Isaiah, Jeremiah and Ezekiel are the heroes and teachers. In the latter framework, the mindset is more inward than outward. The Jews are the chosen people of God, destined to live apart, a holy people whose mission is to observe and obey the word of God in as strict a fashion as it can. In addition to the Torah (the five books of Moses in the Bible, which constitute the Law), the guide is the Talmud, the book of commentaries on the Law written by Rabbis and sages nearly two millennia ago[1], and which dictates the details of the life of an observant Jew down to the minutest detail.

You don't have to be Sherlock Holmes to guess that orthodox Jews have adopted the inward (Talmudic) approach, whereas the non-orthodox Jews (i.e., just about everyone else) tend to favor the outward approach. And you don't have

---

1. Actually, there are two versions, one crafted in Jerusalem and the other in Babylon. The latter is the more influential.

to be Hercule Poirot to assay that the Talmudic approach goes more comfortably with a conservative political outlook while the prophetic tradition aligns much more easily with a liberal political view. Pretty easy, huh? Well, maybe I've over-simplified a bit, but I believe there is a great deal of validity to this explanation. The vast majority of American Jews see their role in America, if not the world—that is, if they see themselves at all as Jews who have a role to play in the world—as, to use another well-known phrase, "a light unto the Goyim." It is the job of the Jews to be a moral beacon, to light the way toward a more perfect world. Does that sound idealistic and/or utopian to you? It does to me. So, small wonder that we vote 80% for liberal/Democratic candidates. Given that the orthodox only account for 10% of us, one wonders why it is not 90%. Maybe the discrepancy is the fault of the neocons.

Tikkun ha' olam. That's Hebrew for "fix the world." This explanation is closely related to the first, but is not exactly the same. Let me explain. Being a "light unto the Goyim" is mainly a matter of setting a good example—for instance, leading a moral life, obeying the ten commandments (well at least numbers 5-10 since 1-4 are a bit more problematic), exhibiting holy qualities (like goodness, mercy, compassion, tolerance) that would impress any good Christian. Fixing the world is more activist. It is more than just setting a good example. It means putting on your overalls and getting your hands dirty in doing God's work to improve the world. It means righting wrongs, correcting injustices and helping your fellow man. This meddling, universalistic attitude clearly conflicts with the particularistic, inward view of the Talmudic tradition, but it dovetails with the prophetic vision excellently. At its most effective it can be seen in the enormous contributions individual Jews have made to mankind. I am thinking of: Einstein, Freud, Salk and Sabin, Jesus of Nazareth and, dare I say, Karl Marx. Boy did he fix the world! In any event, the connection between this mantra and the propensity of Jews toward liberalism is easy to see.

Protectors. In our wanderings over the last two millennia, we Jews have become very adept at enlisting protectors. These would be people (or institutions) at the highest rungs of society—kings, nobles, dukes and princes, even bishops or the Church—who had great power and would spread their cloak of protection over a local Jewish community in exchange for some special service that that community could provide. Generally it was business oriented items like capital, loans, scientific expertise or trade contacts that the noble lacked and to which he was having difficulty gaining access. So he made a deal. The Jews supplied the desired commodity in exchange for protection from the hoipoloi. The hoipoloi was usually a Christian or Muslim rabble who saw the Jews as infidels and/or economic or social threats that they would just as soon deal with by killing, expelling or converting them. But they were enjoined from acting on their bad intentions by the power of the noble. Jews became very skilled at finding protectors. Today, American Jews see the US Government as their protector, and they expect it to keep all those right-wing, fundamentalist evangelicals from imposing their will on the poor, powerless Jews. The services the Jews provide are exactly Salk, Sabin, etc. Historically, when the protector didn't need the services of the Jews any longer, he threw them to the wolves. I don't think that will happen in the USA. But as our numbers dwindle and our influence ebbs … Nah, this is America!

Fear of the rabble. This and the previous explanation go hand in hand. But whereas the previous item focused on whom the Jews were protected by, this one concentrates on whom the Jews were protected from. Certainly the history of danger from the mob is tragically full of relevant examples. Jewish communities have been sacked and looted, their members raped and killed by mobs too many times—during the Crusades, during the Chmielnicki Rebellion in Poland, on Kristallnacht, etc. It was to forestall such events that the Jews sought the powerful protector. But in modern times, the greatest threat has come from the potential protector, namely from the government itself. The vast death and destruction inflicted on the Jewish people during the last century was by the German government, and to a lesser extent, by the governments of the Soviet Union and tin pot dictators in the Arab world. This suggests that the old strategy of government protectors is no longer viable.

Now let us reinterpret in terms of American Jewry. In light of the ghastly world history of Jew hatred, the Holocaust, the vilification of modern Israel, world-wide anti-Semitism, it's always in the back of our minds that we may not be completely safe—even in America. Moreover, in a laissez faire environment who will restrain the rabble? We need the protection of the federal government. A key strategy we have employed to secure that protection is to be ardent supporters of the strongest possible separation of church and state. This will keep the government totally secular and therefore both receptive to and capable of ensuring the protection of our community. Is this a winning strategy?

Identifying with the persecuted. This one is a no-brainer. With our people's history of persecution, we have natural sympathies for the underdogs of the world. We resonate to the dreadful history of slavery in the United States. We feel for the poor and huddled masses yearning to come here—like we did—even if they employ illegal means to do so. Knowing what it is like to be a minority community, we identify with minority populations in the US. Any blow for the persecuted is a blow for ourselves. Yet again, it is not hard to see how this mindset skews our attitude toward liberalism.

Next we move on to the university and especially its faculty, another seemingly impenetrable bastion of liberal strength. Everyone has seen the data compiled from voter registration rolls, which show Democratic preference among faculty to be as high as 75 or 80%, reaching as high as 90% or even more in the liberal arts and socials sciences. It is somewhat less in the science schools, and still less in the Engineering and Business schools. But the overall liberal tilt in the faculty is unmistakable. Again I will offer five explanations.

Secular Humanism. The conflict between faith and reason goes back to the dawn of civilization. The conflict sharpened during the Enlightenment and the gap between those who profess faith and those who worship reason has not narrowed. The liberal arts colleges and departments in the universities of this country are repositories of the latter. Furthermore, I used the word "worship" for a reason. The fundamental belief of those who reject religious faith, who are secular in their outlook, is that the rules by which human behavior should be governed are not to be decided by an unseen deity, but by human beings here on Earth. Thus the name *secular humanists*. The truths they seek, the beauty of nature that they discover, the mysteries of the human spirit that they divine are expressed in the poetry, literature, music, history, language and philosophy that they create as members of humanities faculties. Two points to emphasize: (i) their discoveries, which are of course the work of human beings, are not of God's law, nor of the mysteries of nature governed by scientific laws, but rather the ideals of beauty and truth that their instincts and intellect guide them toward; and (ii) the beauty and truth that they unlock are changeable—for they depend on time, space and the observer. Therefore, idealism and relativism are part and parcel of the humanists' nature. So, once again, it does not take a Solomon to fathom the natural tendency toward political liberalism among humanities faculty.

But what about the social sciences and the hard sciences? I'll deal with the latter in the next item. As for the former, social science is somewhat of a misnomer. Just because you pursue a discipline in which statistics is used heavily does not make you a scientist. I think Social Arts would have been a better term, or even the old label Social Studies. Regardless of the umbrella term, we are still left with the question about why the political proclivities of social scientists are so liberal. The practitioners are psychologists, sociologists, economists, anthropologists, and the species who populate criminology and government and politics departments. Certainly the mindset of many of the faculty who teach and do research in the social sciences is little different from that of the humanists. The overlap is reflected accidentally in the location of all the "Studies" departments (Urban Studies, African-American Studies, Women's Studies, etc.), which are inconsistently situated, sometimes in humanities colleges and sometimes in social science colleges. Furthermore, although the truths and phenomena that social scientists seek are more in the realm of human behavior than natural beauty, idealism and relativism are still prominent components of the investigator's approach. Therefore, it is not surprising that many social scientists, like their humanities brethren, are fervently liberal. But there are also niches and corners of social science colleges where the faculty do deport themselves more like scientists. We'll deal with them, together with the physical and life scientists, in the next section.

The Scientific Method. The conflict between science and faith, while perhaps as old as the one between faith and reason, is not as intense. For its adherents, secular humanism serves as a "religion" that substitutes for religious faith. On the other hand, many scientists have found the means to compartmentalize their scientific work and their religious faith, thus allowing them to coexist. But let's go a little deeper. The method that governs a scientist's work is not difficult to describe. She observes or is aware of a phenomenon—whether it be physical, chemical, biological, social, statistical, quantum, celestial, subatomic, ... She formulates a theory (usually in the form of a mathematical model) that she hopes will describe the phenomenon, more specifically, quantify its past behavior and predicts its future behavior. She tests the results of the theory against observations or measurements of the phenomenon. If the data match, she congratulates herself on a job well done and pronounces the phenomenon understood and described. Others will repeat her experiments and hopefully replicate the conclusions. If, on the other hand, the data don't match, then it's back to the drawing board, rework the theory, and start testing again. If the data never match, the phenomenon remains unexplained. But even if a successful reconciliation is achieved, time may eventually require a reworking of her theory because powers of observation may improve, measurements may get more precise, certain simplifying assumptions that were made may need to be removed, or it may be discovered that the results of the theory contradict another phenomenon, which was thought initially unrelated to the original. The process begins again. The theory might or might not have to be adjusted. It is in the nature of the scientific method. In principle, opinions play no role in the process, only dispassionate, unbiased and objective scientific investigation. It is an ideal toward which we scientists constantly strive, and sometimes we even achieve it.

Now throw faith into the picture. It's not very scientific. When you take something on faith, for example the existence of God, there is no way to check. You can't test the theory with experiments or measurements. The scientific method does not apply. It can neither prove nor disprove the hypotheses that your faith has stipulated. But I think that limitation irks many scientists—that is, the uncertainty, and the inability to resolve the uncertainty, goes against their scientific mindset. Faith does not violate their scientific senses the way it does the humanistic senses of their liberal arts colleagues. It just kind of rubs them the wrong way. It's not any idealistic, egalitarian or relativistic traits that are being violated; it's just the lack of cold hard facts. Here's an oversimplified way of expressing my point: humanists are often atheists, whereas scientists are only agnostics. Of course, religion is far from the sole determining factor in driving one to a position in the liberal/conservative divide, but it plays a big role. Thus summarizing the effect of the first two items then, science faculty have a tendency to be liberal, but arts faculty have an overwhelming tendency in that direction.

Confidence in the elite. Faculty see themselves as members of the elite. They may not be paid as well as corporate executives, athletes, entertainers or successful entrepreneurs, but that doesn't shake their confidence that they are among the cream of American society. They view their research as uncovering new knowledge, revealing the complexities of human nature, explaining the mysteries of the universe and leading to outcomes for the betterment of mankind—for example, cures for disease, improved widgets, better human services and stronger infrastructure. The whole point of socialism lite—er, ah, that is the liberal agenda—is that the key decisions on the economy, social justice and war and peace will be made by the country's elite. This dovetails very nicely with the faculty's liberal leanings for they believe in the concept of an elite and, moreover, they see themselves as part of it.

On the take. The pervasive role of government in higher education is well documented. Three generations ago, that role was largely confined to the support of state universities by state governments. That specific role has actually declined slightly, but the federal government has more than picked up the slack. Today the federal government supports faculty research (through salaries, graduate students, posdtdocs, travel, computers, purchase of major instrumentation, etc.), curriculum development, student tuition, fees and expenses, research institutes, campus buildings and much more. Moreover, they do this for the vast majority of the nation's campuses and medical schools. In short we are all on the take. Now how can you plausibly adopt a stance in favor of limited government in a milieu like that? It would be tantamount to biting the hand that feeds you.

Mentors. This last explanation has to do with the special nature of faculty training. It may be the closest thing around these days to an old guild-style apprenticeship. How does it work? When you are a graduate student, after a relatively brief period of general education in the broad strokes of your discipline, your focus eventually becomes very narrow. You must produce an original piece of research or scholarship in your chosen field. To do that, you have to develop the highest level of knowledge in one (usually very narrow) area of specialty. You are led in the process by a faculty member who has already scaled that peak and proven it by throwing down from on high a long series of erudite books and articles on the area of specialty. To you, he is a God—and a meal ticket. You attempt to soak up his wisdom and then push the envelope a little further—even if only in one very narrow corner of his subject. When you think you have succeeded, he ratifies your achievement and welcomes you to the fraternity of specialists in his area. Having witnessed (and led) this process many times over my academic career, I am still amazed at how the student learns from the master not only the subject matter, but also how to think, how to work, and how to arrange priorities. In short, we faculty are pretty good at cloning ourselves. This helps to explain why once the liberals took over the academy, it's been relatively easy for them to keep it that way. Students do not realize that they are being programmed to replicate their mentors in more than just scientific expertise.

> *November 9, 1989—the day that the Berlin Wall fell; December 26, 1991—the dissolution of the Soviet Union. Two glorious dates in the history of human freedom. Together they mark the end of WWIII and signal victory for the United States and Western Civilization over the Soviet Union in that titanic clash. So why aren't those dates national holidays? They don't even carry the same weight in our society as the dates that mark the ends of WWI and WWII. November 11—Veteran's Day, which is celebrated primarily as a shopping day, is the successor to Armistice Day, which commemorated the end of WWI in 1918. And*

actually May 8, 1945 (VE Day) and August 15, 1945 (VJ Day) are essentially no longer celebrated; but I remember clearly their being observed annually in the US for roughly 20 years after the end of WWII. Personally, I feel privileged to have witnessed the events of those two days a decade and a half ago. Like most who came of age during the beginning of the Cold War, I imagined that it would last for 100 years. What a splendid surprise to see it end a <u>mere</u> 45 years after it began.

One wonders why we do not celebrate our triumph over the Soviets more vigorously. Maybe it's too soon. It took more than 50 years to build the FDR Memorial and nearly 60 years to construct the WWII Memorial. There should be a WWIII Memorial and also one to Ronald Reagan. And perhaps a museum to honor the millions of people murdered by Lenin, Stalin and Mao. I'm not holding my breadth. However, instead of telling you other reasons why I think these memorials might be delayed, or offering other personal memories of the close of WWIII, I am going to devote my space here to talking about holidays. I have a proposal that I have been itching to make for years and this seems like a good spot.

We have botched up our holidays in the US pretty badly. Thanksgiving and Independence Day are in good shape. But virtually all the others (MLK Day, Presidents Day, Memorial Day, Labor Day, Columbus Day, Veterans Day, even New Years Day) are little more than excuses to shop and stay home from work. Christmas provides the ultimate shopping exercise and progressively less and less of its true meaning survives. I first became aware of the magnitude of this problem when I lived in Israel. Israel doesn't outshine the US in too many areas, but in holiday celebration, it is no contest. Israel has three kinds of holidays. First are the eight festival holy days of the Jewish calendar (Rosh Hashanah [2], Yom Kippur, Succot, Simchat Torah, Pesach [2] and Shavuot). These are national holidays. More than half the country celebrates them in the traditional ways (synagogue, family gatherings and the special trappings that go with each). The remaining secular population often goes to the beach, but the sense that the country is observing an ancient and hallowed festival is ubiquitous. There are no Simchat Torah sales. The second set of national holidays commemorates modern events: Independence Day, Remembrance Day, Holocaust Day and Jerusalem Day. All are national holidays, although businesses are only closed on the first of them, which commemorates Israel's' birth on May 14, 1948. Remembrance Day is analogous to our Memorial Day (honoring fallen soldiers), Holocaust Day is self-explanatory and Jerusalem Day commemorates the liberation and reunification of Jerusalem on June 7, 1967. These days are observed on a specific date in the Hebrew calendar each year, not moved annually to mesh with weekends. The activities are special, well-identified, constant from year to year, and celebrated by nearly everyone. The third set comprise the minor holidays of the Hebrew calendar (Chanukah, Purim, Tu B'shvat [Arbor Day], Tisha B'Av [commemorating the fall of the ancient temple]). Businesses are open but many special activities are scheduled—especially in the schools. It is all very well done. Each holiday has specific content, is widely celebrated, occurs on a fixed date and has meaning for a large portion of the population.

Well, I can't tikkun the olam, but here's a proposal for tikkuning the American chagim (holidays). First of all, why do we celebrate Labor Day and not Business Day? Labor Day was a sop to a union movement that is no longer powerful. Why not celebrate the date that Adam Smith published the Wealth of Nations or the date that the NY Stock Exchange first opened its doors? Next, Armistice Day has vanished into a duplicate of Memorial Day (and of course shopping), probably because very few are even aware of its historical significance. No one pays any attention to Columbus any more—after all, he's just another DWEM (Dead White European Male). I'm sorry, but Martin Luther King was not the most important American in the history of our country—a conclusion that a foreigner might well come to since he is the unique person whose birthday we celebrate. Here's my proposal for a more meaningful set of eight American national holidays:

- *Thanksgiving, Independence Day, Christmas and New Years Day remain as is.*

- *One day celebrating freedom's global victories and honoring our fallen soldiers.*

- *One day celebrating our democratic, constitutional, rule-of-law form of government.*

- *One day celebrating America's greatest heroes.*

- *One day celebrating our free market economic system.*

Here's the interesting part. The actual dates on which the last four celebrations would occur will rotate from year to year. For each of those four, we would have a list of 3-5 <u>candidates</u> and the actual date celebrated each year would rotate among the members of the list. Possibilities include:

- *Freedom Day (November 11—Armistice Day; May 5—VE Day; August 15—VJ Day; November 9—Berlin Wall; December 19—Cold War victory). God willing, we will add another candidate when Islamofascism is laid to rest.*

- *Great American Day (the birthdays of Washington, Jefferson, Lincoln, FDR, MLK, Reagan)*

- *Economy Day, or Business & Labor Day (Labor Day, birthday of Samuel Gompers, Publication date of The Wealth of Nations, opening of NY Stock Exchange)*

- *Constitution or Law Day (date of ratification of the Constitution, date of ratification of the Bill of Rights, Flag Day)*

Then we would declare a host of minor holidays. Businesses and schools would be open, but the days could be appropriately commemorated by whatever groups felt the desire to celebrate them. Retailers are always free to declare them shopping days. For example: Columbus Day, dates of religious significance (Rosh Hashanah, one of the feast days associated with Ramadan, Easter or other Christian holy days), Halloween, Arbor Day, or maybe the solstices and equinoxes. I'm a little fuzzy about whether there should be an official list of the qualifying minor holidays, but knowing the American character, said list would be hard to maintain. On the other hand, the eight major holidays would be fixed by Congress and there would have to be a rigorous process for choosing the candidates, altering the lists over time if warranted, and selecting the actual dates of celebrations over a long period of calendar years.

One sticking point: Mondays! Moving holidays to Mondays probably helps the economy; and both employers and employees favor it. But it dilutes the meaning of our holidays. We have resisted the temptation to do this for the big four. If we want to reinvigorate our holidays, infuse them with meaning and galvanize the people to celebrate them other than by going shopping, we need to retire the practice for all eight.

11

Aging Liberals

We arrive finally at our consideration of aging liberals or, as I've been known to call them in less than flattering fashion, "liberals who won't grow up." I will do two things in this chapter. First, I will try to establish that the less than flattering phrase has some validity. Second, I will offer explanations for the occurrence of incurable liberalism. Both are important for the following reasons. First of all, the occurrence is commonplace, or to repeat a comment from the last chapter: although aging liberalism is in some sense against the grain, it is nevertheless exceedingly common. I already remarked that for every David Brock there are 10 David Horowitzes. But, for every David Horowitz, there may well be 100 Dan Rathers. Next, they are the power in the liberal movement. Indeed the liberal ship is not steered by youngsters. While, among the conservative leadership, there is a fair amount of representation by young people and also by former liberals, this is not so in the liberal leadership. It is comprised of people who have been liberal all their lives. So its constituents are old, some would say sclerotic. Third, it is important to know thine enemy. I believe it is crucial for conservatives to get inside their opponents' heads. If conservatives can understand how liberals got that way, and why they stay that way, it may help conservatives to negotiate with liberals and perhaps even to convert them or at least shake their confidence.

To summarize, aging liberals are numerous, powerful and often a mystery to conservatives. Actually, to a great extent we conservatives can understand how they got that way. Simply put, the idealism of their youth led them down that path. What we don't understand is why they fail to get over it. Our job here then is to speculate on some reasons.

But first, why is the pejorative description "won't grow up" legitimate? Now I confess that some of what I am about to say concerning liberals may sound harsh, even insulting. However, it is not my intention to smear liberals gratuitously.

Indeed, at the risk of sounding frivolous, some of my best friends are liberals. Actually, now that I think about it, most of my friends are liberal. Ah, so be it. I have to call `em as I see `em. So why do I think of aging liberals as people who won't grow up—at least politically?

Let me start by asking you to think about an adult that you know who has not grown up. The person often behaves like an adolescent, expresses opinions that seem naïve and unsophisticated, lacks self-control, and overall just creates the impression of an immature individual for whom the maturation process has gone awry. What are some of the typical traits or signature qualities of an overgrown adolescent? Here are a few:

1. He does not learn from his mistakes.

2. He does not take responsibility for the consequences of his actions.

3. He is prone to temper tantrums and fits of whining.

4. He thinks his 'elders' are stupid.

5. He behaves recklessly.

6. He is totally self-centered.

Next I am going to list various prominent liberal people and some of the policies they espouse, which manifest precisely these traits in an unmistakable manner. Moreover, these cases are the rule, not the exception. Altogether they will bolster my contention that the phrases *aging liberal* and *overgrown adolescent* fit nicely together in the same context. Ooh, that was a zinger. OK, here goes.

1. **Failure to learn from mistakes.** When the energy crunch of the late 1970s hit, the arch liberal Jimmy Carter responded by rationing gas. Of course in this action he was only following the example set by his pseudo-liberal predecessor, Richard Nixon, who did exactly the same thing in response to the Arab oil embargo of 1973-1974. The predictable consequences ensued: shortages, misallocations, skyrocketing prices, consumer inconvenience and hardship. By these actions they revealed their lack of understanding of our market economy. When a commodity is in short supply and/or high demand, the market forces adjust the price upward to deal with the shortage. The higher price dampens demand and encourages competing suppliers to increase production. The higher price level will prevail until market forces respond to planned and unplanned palliatives—e.g., alternate sources are generated, consumers switch to alternate prod-

ucts, or other forces cause the original supply shortage or excessive demand to ameliorate. That's how it's supposed to work. That's how it does work. If you don't understand it, just read *Basic Economics: A Citizen's Guide to the Economy* by Thomas Sowell (Basic Books 2000), the most elementary and clear-headed explanation of the economic laws of a free market system that any citizen—and certainly any politician—should know. Rationing or government edicts directing supplies or prices interfere with the normal, corrective market response to the crisis and thereby make it worse. This was completely obvious to any dispassionate observer of the government-caused debacle in both crises in the 1970s.

Did either of Mssrs. Nixon or Carter apologize for their folly? Of course not. But worse, did any of the liberals who advocated rationing learn anything? It would appear not. Because in the energy crisis of 2005 caused by Hurricanes Katrina and Rita, liberals had the standard response. Namely, berate the oil companies for the resulting high prices—which is of course what is supposed to happen—and advocate rationing and price controls. Fortunately, the Republican administration and Congress were not persuaded and did not comply. Eventually the market responded to corrections,[1] as any rational person knew it would, and prices and supplies returned to very close to the levels seen before the crisis.[2] Had we heeded the liberals' plans for dealing with the crisis, we would have had the same dreadful consequences that we had three decades earlier. The liberals learned nothing from those experiences.

Raising the minimum wage causes increased unemployment among those earning salaries at the minimum wage level. It does not raise the wages of many workers earning minimum wage salaries—it puts them out of work. No self-respecting economist disputes this assertion. And every raise in the minimum wage level has had exactly that consequence. But liberals never learn. They are constantly advocating raises in the minimum wage level, despite the fact that this action often hurts precisely those whom it is supposedly targeted to help. Moreover, liberals are apoplectic when it is pointed out that the whole concept is flawed. It is another well-known fact that many, if not most, minimum wage workers are purposefully part-time employees, very young or very old workers

---

1.   which, in this case, was largely just a matter of time until the refineries affected by the weather returned to normal production. Also, some consumers parked their SUVs for a while.
2.   Prices went up again two years later, but for different reasons. The liberals' hysterical response is the same of course.

who are not in it for the money, seasonal workers, (il)legal immigrants, or others who are just glad to be working for any wage. By not allowing employers to pay below some artificial wage floor, the net effect is to remove job opportunities for these and other potential workers who would indeed work for what liberals deem inadequate salaries. Well, just as your home is worth exactly what someone is willing to pay you for it, or your football team is worth exactly what someone is willing to pay you for it, so is your labor worth exactly what someone is willing to pay you for it. We do not have minimum levels set on home sales or football teams (although I suppose the liberals wish we did—at least for the former); why should we distort the market by setting artificial minimum levels for salaries? Because it makes the liberals feel good when they do it! But it accomplishes little that is worthwhile. Is anybody learning anything here?[3]

Here are two examples that should be near and dear to the heart of the citizens of the People's Republic of Maryland (PRM) in which I reside. In this regard, let me take as the fundamentally flawed action, from which nothing was gleaned, the luxury tax enacted in 1991. In furtherance of the never-ending liberal desire to punish success, a tax was enacted on certain luxury items—e.g., airplanes, very expensive jewelry, but especially on new boats. This tax was intended to help ensure that "the rich pay their fair share." Good old Marxism-Leninism. Apparently the fact that the top 10% of earners already pay more than 96% of all federal income tax (2001 data) means they are paying less than their fair share. Anyway, the luxury tax had the predictable effect. Since a luxury item is by definition not a necessity, many who could afford it nevertheless decided to skip the purchase. Sales of the targeted items plummeted. This hit the boat industry particularly hard. In fact, it just about closed down the small shipbuilding industry in the United States—throwing lots of laborers out of work of course. Can you say "tyranny of good intentions?" The luxury tax was repealed in 1993. OK, how did the geniuses who dominate the Maryland State Legislature (which is more than 2-1 Democratic over Republican) process this information? They made two brilliant moves in the 2005 session:

(i) They decided that HMOs in Maryland were making too much money, so they passed a special 2% tax that applied only to HMOs. Then they were surprised when the HMOs passed on the entire extra cost directly to their customers in the form of higher fees. So who gets slugged—the public of course. Incidentally, in the PRM, the State government is huge and there are lots of State

---

3.   Apparently not, Congress recently voted an increase in the minimum wage.

employees—full disclosure, I am one of them. Also, the State picks up much of the medical insurance costs of its employees (although not as much as it used to). So the revenue from the HMO tax will be offset to some extent by the higher subsidies the State needs to provide its employees for the higher insurance fees. I imagine the State will respond that it must raise other taxes to cope with this unexpected "shortfall." The dim bulbs who run the legislature can't figure this out. Actually, maybe they can. I may be wrong in attributing their foolishness to ignorance and stubbornness; it may be due to duplicity and nefariousness.

(ii) They passed the so-called Wal-Mart tax. It places a special tax on any company with a certain (high) number of employees that is not spending a certain percentage of its wage base on health care subsidies for its employees. Wal-Mart is the unique company in the PRM to which the law applies. The tax was clearly designed to punish Wal-Mart, a favorite target of liberals for its non-union practices. The tax was thrown out by the courts, but the consequences had it survived would have been crystal clear. Wal-Mart would scale back its operations in the PRM. In fact, Wal-Mart has already announced that it is rethinking its plans to build a major distribution center on the rural eastern shore of the State. Having learned nothing about basic economics, the liberals have punished the State's economy, not Wal-Mart.

Then Governor Ehrlich, a Republican, vetoed both bills passed by the Democratic-controlled legislature. The overwhelmingly Democratic legislature overrode both vetoes. The legislators will either profess to be surprised by the damage to the State's economy these bills will cause or they will deny that their actions had any deleterious effect. They learned nothing from the luxury tax fiasco.

2. **Unwillingness to accept responsibility**. A sustained, prolonged and extremely vigorous campaign by the liberal movement eventually caused the withdrawal of American forces from Vietnam in 1973 without a victory. Less than two years later, liberals in Congress engineered the cessation of all assistance to our South Vietnamese allies who had continued the fight. As a direct result of those actions, millions of people died. They died in rickety boats in the South China Sea, in re-education camps established by the North Vietnamese, and in the killing fields of Cambodia. To the best of my knowledge, Jane Fonda hasn't connected the dots yet. However, I can't imagine that there aren't plenty of Americans who were active in the anti-war movement and yet understand that our defeat in Vietnam led directly to the death and destruction that followed. But the number who have publicly acknowledged the connection is pitifully small.

On the contrary, the non-contrite majority is busy advocating that we commit the same error today in Iraq.

Now don't mistake me. The decision to *enter* both wars, Vietnam and Iraq, can legitimately be questioned. In the case of Vietnam, those who took us to war there saw it as a battleground in the ongoing Cold War with the Soviets, or WWIII as I've referred to it.[4] They feared that if we did not contain Communist expansion across Asia, the Soviets would continue to gain territory, resulting in even greater difficulties for us later on. They subscribed to the Domino Theory, that is, each country or region that fell into the Communist orbit became an inducement for its neighbors to befall the same fate. But opponents argued that the Vietnam conflict was really a civil war, that it was far away and not of strategic import to the US, that it was a guerilla struggle in an inhospitable jungle environment, in which we could not prevail regardless of the amount of resources we might devote to it. The arguments on both sides were legitimate. But the point is that by 1968, the argument was moot. Rightly or wrongly, we had decided in favor of entering the war and half a million US troops were engaged with Communist forces throughout Indochina. The argument was no longer about whether the US should enter the war, but rather how we could win it. That was a debate that the Left chose not to enter. Instead they advocated a precipitous withdrawal, which they justified by claiming that our entry was illegal. But it should have been obvious that if we were to just cut and run, there would be a human disaster of calamitous proportions. Well it took the liberals more than half a decade and the toppling of two presidents, but they eventually prevailed. And the slaughter followed predictably. No apologies to the families of the deceased millions have been forthcoming.

The situation is eerily similar in Iraq—up to a point. As I've argued, the Bush administration feared that the madman Hussein was in possession of WMD and that he might make them available to Al Qaeda or other Islamofascists—who had proven that they would not hesitate to use them against us. The administration decided that war was necessary to prevent that horrendous possibility. Again, there were cogent arguments against such a war. There was no hard evidence that Hussein was in cahoots with Bin Laden; moreover, we should be concentrating on the latter not the former—indeed a war in Iraq would drain resources from

---

4.   I'm not sure who gets credit for the nomenclature I've used: WWIII = Cold War; WWIV = war against Islamofascism. I believe it is Norman Podhoretz.

the more critical war against Islamic terror. Next, fearing that nation-building was on the program—as indeed it turned out to be—they argued that the Arab/ Muslim world was not ready for democracy and it would be a fool's errand to try to export it to them. More worrisome was the likelihood that the Iraqis would not greet us as liberators and that our effort would destabilize the Arab world and engender increased hatred for America. Once again, legitimate opposing arguments—but, as in Vietnam, eventually beside the point. For at a certain juncture, we found ourselves at war rendering the orginal arguments moot. To the war critics' credit, many of the difficulties that they foresaw came to pass. And not unexpectedly, the liberal solution is, once again, to cut and run. Duh! Haven't we made that tragic mistake once already? If we cut and run, the ensuing bloodbath will make today's casualties look like a tea party. And when that happens, I doubt apologies will be forthcoming.

There is another obvious item in the category of unacknowledged responsibility—namely, federal entitlements. Social Security, Medicare and Medicaid should be thought of as, if not a runaway train speeding toward a brick wall, then as a balloon into which air is incessantly being pumped. Either way, the imminent explosion is going to be spectacular. It is already the case that these programs account for more than half the federal budget. I have argued against these entitlement programs from the point of view that the federal government has no constitutional mandate to be providing retirement funds or health services to the public. But like the anti-war zealots in the last item, I have already lost the *a priori* argument. The entitlements may or may not have been a good idea. It doesn't matter because the country opted to deploy them. They are here and now we have to deal with them. In fact, however well-intentioned Social Security may have been, even if you think Medicare was the right thing to do, if Medicaid fulfills your (utopian) vision of how America should be run, it cannot be denied that these programs are not sustainable in anything remotely resembling their present form. I wonder if any of the originators could foresee the demographics that are derailing these programs. If they could and argued for them anyhow, they were unscrupulous. It is more likely that they did not. But anyone with half a brain can see them now. People are living much longer than the years allotted to them by the programs' designers. Setting it up as a "pay as you go" system was exceedingly unwise. The ratio of workers to recipients has diminished precipitously. In not very many years, the finances of these programs will implode. Either taxes will have to be drastically increased, or benefits will have to be drastically cut, or massive government borrowing (i.e., deficit spending) will be required, probably all three. It will be a calamity that could destroy the nation's economy.

I cannot think of anything more irresponsible than the Democrats' stonewalling on Bush's (fairly feeble) attempt to start dealing with Social Security, which arguably is in the least perilous shape of the three. And yet they frustrated his efforts rather easily. Apparently the country refuses to deal with the imminent earthquake until it is one minute to midnight. That may be too late. Here's a prediction. The liberals, who set up these programs and won't accept the fact that they are collapsing, will not apologize to those who are injured by that collapse.

One more example: the Alternative Minimum Tax (AMT). Enacted in 1969 as yet another "punish success/soak the rich" scheme, the AMT was designed to extract extra tax revenue from those folks who were *legally* invoking the absurd intricacies of the regular tax system to minimize their tax liability. For you see, our Rube Goldberg-like federal income tax code has long been a maze of loopholes, contradictions and a patchwork crazy quilt of exemptions, deductions and credits. *Everyone* tries to game the system. "Wealthy people" are particularly adept at the game for two reasons: first, they are highly motivated since a lot of money is at stake and; second, they can afford to hire tax attorneys and accountants to mine the contraption for every penny. But make no mistake: the multitude of middle class tax payers does exactly the same. It's just that without the resources of the wealthy, the average Joes do the best they can on their own. Middle class taxpayers pay very close attention to well-known deductions such as State income tax, real estate tax, home mortgage interest, medical expenses and charitable contributions. People with more assets seek more esoteric loopholes such as credits for child care and elder care, municipal bonds, capital losses, business expenses and other more arcane features of the tax code. The lunatics who set this up and perpetuate it should be ashamed. The worst feature of this despicable system is the way it corrupts the public. It sets up an honor system and then provides endless encouragement for taxpayers to behave dishonorably. It causes disrespect for the law, contempt for the lawyers who created it, and bewilderment at its inconsistent enforcement. And despite endless talk about reforming it or abolishing it, Congress does nothing but make it more complicated almost every year. The latest insanity was to pass tax laws with sunset clauses. For those in the know about the estate tax (or as conservatives call it, the death tax), plan on dying in 2010 and not in 2011. You could look it up, as Casey would say.

Anyway, surrendering to one of their frequent spasms of desire to tinker with the tax code, Congress established the AMT. Basically it created an alternate tax system for those with lots of exemptions, deductions and credits. The precise details need not concern us here; suffice it to say that those who could legally hold down their tax bill by means of appropriate exemptions, deductions and credits were subjected to an alternate system that applied high rates to an adjusted gross income figure that was inflated by the loss of these exemptions, etc. More egregiously—if that is possible, although it looks now like more of an oversight than a planned time bomb—they didn't index the AMT to account for inflation, as has been the case in the regular tax system since 1979. (Note: this postdates 1969.) Today, more than 35 years later, the time bomb is getting ready to explode; inflation (rampant in the 1970s, more modest since) has caused the AMT to ensnare millions of taxpayers (it's original goal was to catch hundreds, perhaps thousands), and very soon it will apply to tens of millions. Which liberal politician, then or now, has admitted that the AMT was a mistake and is now a calamity? What have they done to fix or abolish it? Why don't they at least index it? The answers: no one, nothing, and that would be admitting a mistake. Well, in fact, they may actually "fix" this. That is because the AMT victims are heavily concentrated among moderate to high income liberals in blue states (limousine liberals in New York, Hollywood lefties all over California, and hip DINKs in the Pacific Northwest and New England). Like the luxury tax, this abomination will eventually go to its graveyard when its pernicious effects are sufficiently appreciated. But no one will issue a mea culpa and it won't guarantee that a future liberal-controlled Congress won't do something equally creative.

3. **Whining and temper tantrums**. This entry is very short. Namely, is there a bigger political whiner than Al Gore? And the phrase "temper tantrum" should be Howard Dean's middle name.

4. **Those who think otherwise are stupid**. When my eldest son was approaching the end of his college career, he visited my wife and me one evening. Without preamble, he began a sentence, "You know Dad, you were right about ..." My wife and I did not allow him to complete the thought. We shrieked, ran for the recorder and asked him to repeat his words. What I was right about was unimportant. The fact that I was right about anything was astounding. Neither my wife nor I had been right about anything at all for at least five years. We were overjoyed to finally be emerging from our state of stupidity.

What I have just described is a familiar story in the homes of America. Parents of young teens grow incredibly stupid as their children progress through their middle and late teen years. It's true. Any teen will tell you so. But the disease is reversible. Recovery usually occurs in the post teen years—sometimes earlier, sometimes later, it depends on the perception of the youngster, and on his rate of maturation. That we were beginning to recover when my son was only 20 or so was very encouraging. And I am pleased to say that in his and his younger brother's eyes, we long ago returned to a normal state of intelligence. We're definitely not cool, but at least we are not stupid anymore. Incidentally, my son now has a child who is approaching double digit age. I've warned him that he will inevitably descend into stupidity before too many more years pass.

The persistent insistence of liberals on labeling Republican presidents as stupid is a damning piece of evidence supporting my argument that liberals behave like overgrown adolescents. Let's examine that evidence. Actually, I don't think they ever called Ike stupid. After all he did successfully lead the greatest military force in the history of the world. It would have been stupid to charge him with stupidity. They did charge him with laziness and lack of diligence in pursuing the duties of the presidency. I still remember one of my parent's favorite jokes, namely that: President Eisenhower was careful to ensure that his presidential duties did not exact too heavy a personal toll by always taking two two-week vacations every month." I guess political humor was less sophisticated then. Liberals also did not call Nixon stupid. They settled instead on evil, criminal and devious. But beginning with Ford, every Republican president has been characterized by liberal Democrats as stupid. For example, it was "common knowledge" that Ford could not walk and chew gum at the same time. Chevy Chase's devastatingly funny, but also deeply irreverent and condescending, portrayals of a confused, inept, bumbling, clownish and clueless President Ford on Saturday Night Live are still memorable today.

Then came Ronald Reagan, a moderately successful movie star, a very successful president of the Screen Actors Guild, and a phenomenally successful Governor of California before he ascended to the Presidency. The magnificent campaign he ran against Jimmy Carter, in which he eloquently and passionately described his conservative beliefs, propelled him to a landslide victory. Nevertheless, liberal Democrats were absolutely convinced that he was stupid, at best an amiable dunce. (The sweet adjective was their way of conceding that he was charming.) They held him in contempt. Who but an idiot would believe in supply side economics baloney? Does he really think that tax cuts will jump start the economy and promote economic growth? How idiotic! What a jerk he is to think the Soviets will be frightened by his Star Wars nonsense. What is this "morning in America" crap? What a simpleton! Gorbachev will have him for lunch in Reykjavik. How could he be so stupid as to demand that the Soviets tear down the Berlin Wall? To this day, liberals seem to be convinced that Reagan was lucky, but not terribly intelligent. Unlike my son, they are not emerging from their adolescent trance. When will they grow up?

Of course there have been two more Republican presidents since Reagan, and they have fared no better. Liberals did not despise George Bush senior like they did Reagan, but they did hold him in contempt. They saw him as the second coming of Gerald Ford—an inarticulate, wimpish, scatterbrained, intellectual lightweight, whose defining moment was when he upchucked on the Japanese Prime Minister. In fact, Dana Carvey's impersonations of him on Saturday Night Live were just as funny and just as contemptuous as were Chevy Chase's of Ford 15 years earlier. Finally, we come to Bush junior, whom the liberals truly hate, even more than Reagan. I've already explained the reasons earlier. A sign of their visceral hatred is that the common epithet for him is not stupid, but moron. Now I am forced to state the obvious. George W. Bush is clearly not a moron. How juvenile to make such an accusation. W is a graduate of Yale and Harvard, a reasonably successful businessman, a very successful Governor of Texas, and a war president who has made many difficult and courageous decisions. You might not like his policies. You might not like him. But when you call him a moron, you exhibit adolescent behavior. Will you please grow up!

Aside. In the PRM we elected in 2002 a Republican governor for the first time in more than 30 years. He was not very conservative; rather a big government, moderate Republican. But the ultra-leftists, who dominate state politics, portrayed him as somewhere to the right of Attila the Hun. Oh and many of my colleagues assured me that he was a moron.[5]

5. **Reckless behavior.** This is another short entry. Which would you say is more reckless: cavorting with mob hookers or having oral sex with an intern under the desk in the oval office? Actually, I think it is the former, but Kennedy didn't get

5.   He was defeated for reelection in 2006.

caught while Clinton did. Slick Willie treated the White House like a College fraternity house, demeaning its tradition and cheapening its aura.

6. **Self-centered**. When my children were in their early teens, my wife and I used to refer to them and their friends as *little centers of the universe*. In their minds, everything revolved around them. Not an uncommon trait among American teens. And also among left-wing Hollywood "stars." People such as Barbara Streisand, Rosie O'Donnell, Alec Baldwin, Sean Penn and Harry Belafonte are so full of themselves that there is no room in their universe for anything but the brilliance of their own sun. They preen, prattle and pontificate, issuing political proclamations unmindful that their pathetic thoughts should not command the attention of a 4-year old. They are actors. They have no more political wisdom or insight than any truck driver, middle level corporate manager, hairdresser, auto assembly line worker, or farmer. Yet they are completely convinced of the superiority of their utopian opinions, in which they are buoyed by the liberal press that encourages their strutting, and accords them accolades for their political acumen. Talk about centers of the universe.

Now the relevance of these observations to my argument is exactly this. Hollywood and liberal Democrats are in bed together—literally and figuratively. Liberal Democrats court the stars, invite them to the White House (when it is in their hands), raise gobs of money from them and with their assistance, and accord their daffy opinions respect. It is a symbiotic relationship, as strong as the love between two teenagers. The politicians get to appear on Jay Leno, the entertainers get to testify before Congressional committees. Both preen for the camera, secure in the knowledge that they truly are centers of the universe. They deserve each other. But we don't deserve their adolescent claptrap.

To reiterate, the point of the previous six sections was to illustrate the connection between incurable liberalism and adolescent behavior. Next, we turn to the second main objective of the chapter—a presentation of what I see as the most plausible explanations for lifelong or incurable liberalism. So picture your average aging, lifelong liberal: his head is graying, his stomach is growing, his wallet and house are increasing in size, he has more and more stuff to conserve and protect, his kids are doubting his values, and finally the hard realities of life are chipping away at the idealism of his youth. Nevertheless, he remains steadfast and true to the liberal dogmas that he developed or adopted in his youth, unwavering, unquestioning, faithful and without doubt. What preserves him in this persistent state of liberal piety? I will offer five possible reasons. These reasons are general in nature, not specific to any particular liberal group, as were the explanations in the last chapter, which applied specifically to Jews and faculty. Incidentally, here is a good exercise for some of you who might be so inclined. I am thinking of those of you who belong to a group, which is well-known to be dominated by liberals, but who also have the sagacious misfortune to actually be conservative. Examples might be trial lawyers, media types, government workers, foundation executives, etc. Here's the exercise: try to write an analog of what I wrote in Chapter 10, that is, an explanation—based on the special features of your group—for why its membership is so overwhelming liberal. It's an instructive exercise that will help you to build confidence that your conservative views are worth defending, even in the deep sea of liberalism in which you swim. But let's get back to our immediate task—general explanations of incurable liberalism.

Ignorance. I don't intend that this label should imply stupidity, only lack of knowledge of or exposure to ideas other than those found in the rigid liberal programming to which too many Americans are subjected. This occurs throughout the American public education system, from kindergarten up through high school, college and graduate school. Children are taught little about free market economics, but a great deal about the need for and wisdom of a government-regulated economy. They are taught about evil robber barons, the inequities created by the industrial revolution, and the rape of the third world by colonial empires (including the United States). They are also told that: Western Civilization denigrated women and minorities; the inherent flaws of capitalism caused the Great Depression, but the country was rescued by the enlightened programs of the New Deal; globalization results in the outsourcing of vital domestic jobs; our wasteful society is destroying the Earth's atmosphere; American culture is no better than any other; American history is irrevocably stained by slavery, unwarranted limits on women's rights, the internment of Japanese-American citizens, anti-Semitism, homophobia, and discrimination against minorities; left to its own devices, business is inherently untrustworthy and will collude and conspire to rob American workers of their honest due; the practice of capital punishment is proof that our society is hopelessly violent, even barbaric; and that religious Christian fundamentalists pose the gravest threat to the fabric of our society. I could go on.[6]

---

6. As an aside I might mention that they are also not taught anything about rudimentary economics and personal finance; a glaring lack that can now be overcome by reading my book, *You Can Do the Math: Overcome Your Math Phobia and Make Better Financial Decisions*, Praeger Press, 2004.

Now I will refute these teachings on a point-by-point basis, by indicating that students are usually *not* taught that: our free market economy has created the richest society in the history of the world; the wealth created by the "robber barons" generated jobs, housing, education and recreational opportunities unmatched by any other country; at the end of the industrial revolution, the United States—although then little more than a century old—was already the richest country on Earth with the highest per capita income; many third world countries, freed from the imperialist yoke, have subjected their people to far greater brutality than they experienced under their colonial rulers; while it is true that the US often did relegate women and minorities to second class status, it has corrected those injustices and now provides full opportunity for all; the Great Depression was caused by foolish economic policies, was not inevitable and would have had a shorter duration than it had if government hadn't unwisely intervened; the modern global economy is generating wealth, knowledge and capital all over the globe, and is creating more jobs than it is destroying; the air over American cities is cleaner, the forests are thicker, and the rivers less polluted than they have been in a hundred years; American culture, which celebrates the rule of law, individual freedom, religious tolerance and the absorption of immigrants is indeed one of the most enlightened in the world, and that it promotes human freedom, economic opportunity and, while not perfect, it corrects its mistakes; the main objective of business is to make a profit and in order to do so it must create products and services that please its customers, not screw them over; Osama Bin Laden is the barbarian, not state officials who carry out legally sanctioned executions as punishment for heinous crimes, only after a fair trial, decades-long appeals and intensive gubernatorial scrutiny; and that without a grounding in religious morals our society would degenerate into unwieldy and ungovernable chaos—likely analogous to the socialist paradises created by godless communists—a point that our founders knew well and emphasized often.

Well maybe I'm wrong and the liberal programmers are right. But how could anyone know if their ideas are not fairly tested against mine? If the information offered to students in public and higher education is overwhelmingly skewed to one side, and if you are the product of such an educational system, you may not be equipped to adequately weigh the merits of the opposing arguments. The natural outcome is hardcore liberals who instinctively think that conservative ideas are wrong, maybe even stupid or deviant. Now that's a good word. It expresses the assessment that incurable liberals often make of conservative ideas—ideas about which they have been largely ignorant all their lives.

The liberal ignorance that is fostered by a biased educational system is reinforced by three features of our society. First and foremost is the mainstream media, which has been totally devoted to a liberal outlook. Until recently, the airwaves were thoroughly dominated by the liberal press (led by the New York Times), the liberal networks (CBS, ABC, NBC, CNN, PBS) and the left-wing entertainment industry. Therefore, incurable liberals had their skewed educations constantly reinforced and reconfirmed. It is a deadly combination. During one's formative years, the mind is inculcated with an agenda that is then ratified by all the sensory input one receives as life progresses. What a *brave new world!* The second reinforcing feature of the society is that so many incurable liberals live, work and play in homogeneous environments whose occupants are programmed exactly the same. Like minders all around you are reinforcing your beliefs. I am thinking of course of entities like university humanities departments, network news rooms, clubs where trial lawyers hang out, and the like. In such an environment only one channel has been and is being received. It's a rare bird who can block out the channel and find some new reception.

There is a third factor that abets liberal ignorance—namely, the large number of immigrants and foreign born members of the society. Unfortunately, such people often labor under language barriers, lack of intimate familiarity with American laws, customs and culture, and a need to depend on special organizations to help them acclimate to and make their way in society. Those organizations are often well left of center and it's not hard for the leaders of those organizations to steer their charges into liberalism. It takes an independent and questioning mind to escape that kind of political programming.

Immaturity. There are two components to this explanation. I have already explained one in the first part of the chapter. Namely, there is a propensity for liberals to behave like adolescents. Well if so, then why not hold onto your adolescent beliefs and values as well? Why not indeed! But here I want to concentrate on the second component, which is better described by the word *inexperience* instead of immaturity. In this regard I would like to hearken back to a comment I made in the *Academic Issues* section of Chapter 4. Namely, faculty come in many flavors, but priests, soldiers and businessmen are not among the typical varieties. The point is that those soaked in liberalism just don't have the opportunity to experience situations that might cause them to question the liberal axioms that govern their lives.

This can take place in various milieus. A prominent one is of course higher education. It really is a very sheltered life—one that shields its occupants from the kinds of experiences that might contradict the utopian ideals of a liberal axiom system. For example, faculty don't have to worry about the company making a profit. They don't have to worry about being fired. They don't have to worry that the parent company is going to go out of business, or transfer them to Kalamazoo. Can you say, "Ivory Tower!" I have given a somewhat idealistic picture of university life in Chapter 4. And while it is a rewarding, often productive life, which I have enjoyed, it is also insular and helps to foster the preservation of aging liberals.

University life may be the perfect incubator for incurable liberalism, but there are other equally effective, if not perfect, environments. In this regard I would include: public school systems, government offices, labor unions, most law schools, and Hollywood studios. In those environments you can easily maintain your political ideology without anything upsetting your liberal apple cart. Actually, you can achieve that level of political comfort even if you're not in one of those environments. Here are a few examples. Suppose you're a salaried worker all your life. Your paycheck comes regularly—replete with all those insane deductions, but you don't think about them. You only pay attention to the net amount. Moreover, you understand relatively little about your employer's business—especially if it's a non-profit organization. You are a small cog in a big machine; you inhabit your own little corner of the work world and big brother takes care of everything else. It is not surprising that you have little appreciation for the business world, but great respect for benefactors—like your employer or the US Government. Liberal philosophy fits very well into the small space you allot to political opinion.

Here are two other "lifestyles" that lend themselves to a lifetime of liberalism. Consider people who rent apartments all their lives, never owning their home. They never worry about the countless details of maintaining a house that every homeowner copes with on an endless basis. The landlord takes care of all of it for you. If you're comfy with that arrangement, you may also be comfortable with Uncle Sam taking care of all the other details of your life. The last illustrative example is the category of people who are comfortable as recipients of goodies disbursed by the nanny state: welfare recipients, those living on housing assistance or subsidized farms, people who live off of government grants, or the score of people whose existence is dependent upon government largesse—and who are psychologically *comfortable* with it, who think it is natural or OK. Can you imagine anything other than a liberal mindset here? (There is some overlap between this point and the self-interest rationale below.)

Stubbornness. This explanation differs from the previous two in that it is anchored in personality or instinct as opposed to external circumstances. I have entitled it "stubbornness," but actually that is only one of three traits or instincts I will describe that can steer one toward a lifetime of liberalism. The first of these is indeed stubbornness. Thus some of us fall into a certain way of thinking about things or doing things and then we stubbornly cling to that way merely because it is our nature. I don't claim that liberals have a greater tendency to be stubborn than anyone else. But for those with that propensity, clinging to their liberalism represents nothing more complicated than this personality trait at work. At an early point they decided that liberalism is the way to go and they refuse to revisit the issue.

I will summarize the second type of instinctive behavior that might contribute to lifelong liberalism in the phrase "sheepishness." More precisely, it is a tendency to surrender to the herd mentality. If you happen to be embedded in a liberal milieu and you are the type who doesn't like to buck the majority—especially if it is a large majority—then you'll go along to get along. This is not the same scenario as stubbornness, which is an individual decision based on the force of one's own personality not to change path. The second instinct is governed by the fact that you haven't the will to challenge the majority and so you let them decide in which direction the political currents will carry you. Incidentally, this can manifest in two ways. In one, the strong urge to blend in comes about not because you have thought about the alternatives—you just want to look like everyone else. The urge to blend is the dominating a factor. In the other, you have thought about the alternatives but you worry that if you adopt any of it, this would make you stand out. The friendship of your liberal comrades is so important to you, that you fear that the manifestation of any conservative tendencies would make you look cold-hearted, not compassionate, not a good person. That's not something you could cope with, so you stick with the herd. The fear of being different, even if there is an inclination to be so, is paramount here.

Stubbornness and sheepishness are not pretty, but the third trait is even worse—arrogance. You are convinced of your own moral superiority, which comes through as an arrogant self-confidence. As such you decide that you could not have been mistaken in your original adoption of a liberal paradigm. Then you proceed to infuse it with moral justification: how could an undirected market be more equitable than a directed economy; fair play must take preference over individual desires; liberalism is clearly morally superior to conservatism, therefore it must be the system for me. In this explanation, unlike the previous two, the adoption and retention of liberalism may not be unexamined. No such examination occurs when ignorance, immaturity or inexperience is governing reactions, but here, it's possible that the individual has explored the conservative alternative intellectually. But for one of the three stated reasons (stubbornness, sheepishness, or arrogance), conservatism is set aside and the individual continues to pursue an unalterable liberal path. Instinct takes precedence over logic or rationality.

Self-Interest. Some of what we present here is related to a few points raised in the previous explanations. But unlike the first two, which are largely determined by external circumstances, and unlike the third, which involves instinct or personality, this explanation emanates from cold-blooded calculation. The individual considers the political philosophies and assesses which better serves his own interests. He decides that his interests will be better served in a liberal political environment and so that is what he chooses to promote. Here are some of the ways this can occur:

- You're on the take. You're a scientist working for a beltway bandit that lives exclusively off federal grants. Your company builds military equipment and your sole customer is the US Armed Forces. You work for an office supply company whose prime contract is with 10 federal agencies. You're on welfare. You are one of the 100,000 "new" policemen hired under Clinton's program to add cops to the beat. Your farm income is primarily derived from the federal government paying you not to grow something. You work for the US Park Service or one of a thousand other federal entities. You're a tax attorney. The list is endless. Cutting the size, scope and budget of the federal government is just not in your interest. It would take a remarkably principled person to espouse conservatism in one of these situations.

- You're the kind of person who fears competition and dreads uncertainty. You like safety nets and being told what to do. Rugged individualism is not your cup of tea. It's in your self-interest to construct society in an orderly, top-down, directed fashion and that is what you support. (This is related to the previous explanation, but differs from it in the following sense: you want to arrange things not according to how you feel, rather according to what you believe better serves your needs.)

• You see yourself as part of the elite. You're highly educated, in a position of authority or influence; you have very definite ideas as to how things should be run and the self-confidence to carry out your ideas. It feeds your ego to have society organized centrally with you in a position to manage important matters.

Eureka! They Might be Right. When I planned this chapter, I originally scoped out four reasons for incurable liberalism, the four that you have just finished reading. Then I thought about some of my liberal friends with whom I could not legitimately associate any of those reasons. What followed was a bad moment for me. "Eureka," I thought, as I pondered the explanation for the lifelong liberalism of this last group of incurable liberals, "Could it be that they might be right?" For you see, this last group, for whom I have deep respect, consists of aging liberals who are not immature or inexperienced, are not plagued by any slavishness to a herd mentality, are not primarily motivated by self-interest, nor are they ignorant in any sense of the word. No, this last group is comprised of those liberals whose political principles are born of examination—self and societal, who are well-versed in and cognizant of conservative philosophy, who have compared the two systems and have decided—repeatedly, emphatically and as dispassionately as possible—that liberalism is superior to conservatism. They would argue that conservatism might have been appropriate for a pre-industrial society, but it does not suit an industrial or post-industrial society. The latter are simply too big, too complex and too dangerous for the little guy to navigate safely—unless he is protected by the State. A conservative, industrial America resulted in robber barons, repeated recessions, the Great Depression, colonialism and now globalization—forces against which a laissez-faire approach is hopelessly inadequate. To correct these flaws, to prevent their reoccurrence, to strive for the perfection of man, society must be arranged according to liberal precepts.

I reiterate that I am describing people who do not suffer from a lack of knowledge or a lack of experience, whose political philosophies are not governed by personality traits, and who can discern the difference between political conviction and self-interest. I am talking about liberals who understand what animates conservatives like me, who can appreciate the subtleties and nuances of my arguments, who are willing to listen to what I have to say respectfully and thoughtfully, but who think, nevertheless, that I am wrong. Faced with fair-minded conviction like that, it is inconceivable that I would not entertain the thought that they might be right. Perhaps liberalism is a more humane, equitable, compassionate and just system. Perhaps the conservative system of rugged individualism, free markets, economic competition and deep respect for tradition is just too hard on the average bloke. Perhaps conservatism is not the better route to freedom and prosperity. Might that be the case?

Nah! No way! I stand by all the arguments I have made throughout the book for the superiority of conservatism, and by my descriptions of the various tragedies that liberalism has inflicted on our society. I won't rehash them here. But what I will do is raise the following question. I have offered five reasons for incurable liberalism. Certainly you have divined my belief that the first four are excuses, while the fifth is a legitimate alternative to my way of thinking—let's call it *examined liberalism*. Now here is the question. The profile of a lifelong liberal must conform to at least one of the five explanations. I'm sure that all you liberals who have made it this far in the book are convinced that the last explanation encompasses you. I am not so convinced. My observation is that *substantially less than half* of the lifelong liberals that I've encountered have practiced examined liberalism in the way that I've described it. In short, I repeatedly encounter intelligent people who say the most unintelligent things. This convinces me that the explanation for incurable liberalism lies predominately among the first four possibilities that I've listed.

OK, here comes a paragraph in which the mathematician in me reveals itself. As we have seen, there are ample reasons to remain liberal. Nevertheless, I believe two things:

- There is a natural tendency—even if it is only present in less than an overwhelming percentage of aging liberals—to become more conservative with time; and

- The sweep of history over the last half-century has revealed the inherent flaws of liberalism.

Now many people believe that the US population is now, or was relatively recently, in a state of political equilibrium, that is, the forces of liberalism and conservatism are equally divided in strength in the nation. But suppose, as I believe, that among those who will change their political stripes over time, say 51% will go from Left to Right, while the remaining 49% will proceed the other way. The (mathematical) point is that it may take a while, but eventually the tide will be unmistakable. In fact, I think the changes over the last 25 years that I've outlined demonstrate that the trend is already clearly visible. We'll carry this argument further in the last chapter.

Next, let us re-state some of the questions we asked at the beginning of the book and set down the answers we have arrived at:

1. Is there a correlation between age and political philosophy? *Yes, with age, political philosophy has a greater likelihood of moving from Left to Right than vice versa.*

2. Is it a strong correlation? *Probably not.*

3. Can the trend be bucked? *Yes, for the many reasons we have outlined in this chapter.*

4. What's the long term trend? *To be answered; see the next chapter.*

Now I want to reemphasize a point I've made several times in regard to #3 above. Despite the Left to Right trend and the great success conservatives have enjoyed—coming back from near oblivion to, if not majority status, then equal status with favorable future vectors—liberalism is still forcefully defending its turf. One very important reason is that, despite the conservative's political successes, the opinion-making organs of society remain firmly in liberal hands. University faculty, much of the judiciary, the legal profession, mainstream media, Hollywood and certain segments of the mainline churches, large corporations and philanthropic foundations are still staunchly liberal; this acts as a powerful check on the rightward migration of the US population.

Here's an intensely personal observation. I think the saying "a conservative is a liberal who's been mugged by reality" is particularly pertinent here. In my personal reminiscences, I outlined four traumas, two of which were deeply personal, that helped me along in my voyage from Left to Right. Well, life in America may be cushier for most aging liberals. They have not had a large enough dose of reality, not enough life-changing experiences that cause a questioning of axioms. Failing that, it's just too easy to go on believing what you (and your parents or mentors) have always believed—all evidence to the contrary.

And here's a final thought for this chapter. There are two competing philosophies struggling for the privilege to direct the American destiny. In that struggle, adherents should state their philosophy and argue its merit robustly, openly and honestly. I happen to work in an environment (academia) where the terrain has been made inhospitable for one side. After beating my head against the rocks for a decade and, as a consequence, occasionally suffering the scorn of my colleagues, I decided that it wasn't worth the anguish. I shut up. It has made my professional life less stressful, but upon reflection, it was a mistake. In effect, I cooperated in my own muzzling. (I imagine this is a fairly common story for conservative faculty all over the US.) I regret the mistake. With the publication of this book I have taken off the muzzle.

In the spring of 1991 the Dean of the College of Computer, Mathematical and Physical Sciences at the University of Maryland appointed a new Chair of the Mathematics Department. For a long time I had assumed that that person would be me. It was not; the Dean appointed one of my colleagues instead. When the news of the appointment reached me, I was shocked and greatly disappointed.

The chairmanship of the Mathematics Department had attracted very talented people over the years. Between my arrival at Maryland and the painful decision in 1991, there had been four chairs. Those individuals went on to be, respectively: Dean of the Graduate School and Provost of the University; Provost and President of the University and, following a stint as President of another State University, Chancellor of the University System of Maryland; Dean of the College (twice); and Provost of the University and Provost of an elite private university. I saw myself in the same mold until the fateful decision.

Perhaps a word of explanation on the method used to select a Chair will be helpful. The Dean appoints a search committee, comprised mostly of Mathematics Department faculty, to elicit nominations from the remaining Math faculty for the position. Naturally, the Dean is careful not to place potential candidates on the search committee. Some faculty nominate themselves, but the stronger candidates are usually nominated by colleagues. In a large department like the Mathematics Department, there may be 4-6 nominees, or more. The search committee then conducts a popularity contest of sorts, involving interviews, testimonials, perhaps an open departmental forum or debate, and the like. The committee then forwards 2-3 names to the Dean for his consideration. With those names, the committee will typically provide the Dean with a report indicating the strengths and weaknesses of the finalists as assessed by the Department and filtered through the eyes of the search committee. The choice is then the Dean's. However, if the search committee report makes clear that the faculty strongly favor one candidate, the Dean rarely goes against their wishes. It is an unwise Dean who ignores a consensus expression of the faculty as to who they wish to be their leader. On the other hand, if there are multiple, viable finalists, then before making a choice, the Dean will consult with key people (in and out of the Department), interview the finalists (individually, of course), review the records, and talk to his boss, the Provost.

I was stunned when this process resulted in a selection other than me. Why? I had spent years preparing for the post. I had enjoyed successful terms in the two key administrative positions under the Chair—namely, Associate Chair for Undergraduate Studies and Associate Chair for Graduate Studies. I had long been an influential member of the Department in matters of hiring, research initiatives, curriculum, administrative structure and university affairs. I was one of the leaders in the Department in curriculum reform and had lobbied effectively for the introduction of technology into undergraduate courses. My teaching credentials were impeccable and my research career was flourishing and included books, scholarly journal articles, invited lectures and financial support from the National Science Foundation. This will sound bombastic, but I was absolutely convinced that my professional credentials (education, research, administration and leadership) so far exceeded the other two finalists that it was not even a fair fight. So to put it mildly, I was quite surprised when the Dean chose someone else.

I spent a great deal of time and energy trying to diagnose what went wrong, why the decision went against me. I spoke to colleagues, staff and campus administrators. Four reasons were cited, although of course which ones were ultimately the cause I couldn't know. The two persons who really knew, the Dean and the Provost, wouldn't tell me—as was within their privilege, and of course the correct course of action on their part. (The President, who was a good friend, probably knew too, but I didn't ask him.) Thus I could only speculate. Here are the four reasons that were offered:

1. *Exuberant youth. When I arrived at Maryland I was part of a vanguard of talented young people who were hired to elevate the stature of the Mathematics Department to a higher plane. (There's that immodesty again.) The Chair at that time had embarked, with the faculty's support, on a venture to move Maryland Math from somewhat more than mediocre to closer to truly excellent. I took my role in that quest seriously and argued at every opportunity for higher standards, tougher hiring and promotion criteria, strict emphasis on merit in salary considerations and a departmental focus on the most important areas of*

research in modern mathematics. In the familiar style of exuberant youth, I was occasionally intemperate in expressing my dissatisfaction with what I saw as second class mathematics. Naturally, some of the older faculty, who had been hired and promoted under different standards, thought me a bit too exuberant. Thus, despite the fact that my youthful exuberance occurred two decades prior to the Chair search, and despite the fact that I had long since learned to temporize my public exhortations for higher quality, it was suggested that people have long memories. The recollection of my firebrand youth may have caused some to be at best tepid in their support of my candidacy. And yet, the most influential people in the Department were not among the few old-timers still around; moreover, the Dean had only arrived on campus a year earlier. So I had difficulty attaching much credence to this reason.

2. *Politically conservative. A natural thought was that my out-of-step political views might not have endeared me to my liberal colleagues. In fact, I found this suggestion insulting to me, but even more so to my colleagues. In all my years of doing verbal battle about politics in the Math lounge with my colleagues, I never once sensed that my minority views were ever held against me in academic or administrative decisions made in the Department. I was entrusted with the two most responsible positions below the Chair, my word on academic matters was respected and my salary was in the top percentiles. I think they found my conservative politics more amusing than a threat. I know that in many humanities and social science departments around the country faculty (and students) are unfairly punished for holding conservative views. That was not the case in the Mathematics Department at Maryland, nor do I think it is common in science and engineering departments in general.*

3. *Nonchalance. Now I will be more critical of my colleagues. There was a commonly held opinion that it didn't really matter that much who was Chair. This view stemmed from three factors. First, some faculty—unfortunately, some of our most talented faculty—did not want to be Chair. They saw it as a distraction from their research, entailing duties that they were ill-trained to discharge, and not particularly the way they wanted to spend their time. They were happy to have someone else do it, almost anybody else. Second, many faculty were overconfident that the administrative and academic structures that had been estab-*

lished in the Department were so successful that it didn't really matter who was steering the ship. Any competent person could do the job. This was related to the third factor. The faculty harbored no intention to change the Department's fundamental nature, neither the way it approached the design of its curriculum, nor the way it chose to prioritize or pursue its research endeavors. Their devotion to traditional mathematics as they understood it was unlike the approach to their disciplines taken by the campus's physicists or computer scientists or engineers, who are much more entrepreneurial, open to change and aggressive about pursuing activities that mathematicians would consider diversions, like research partnerships with industry or government labs, fundraising, outreach to public schools, professional programs, and the like. No, mathematicians worship tradition, are insular, are unconcerned if the public sees their discipline as abstruse, and not disturbed when it is pointed out to them by other scientists that their objective for themselves seems to be a clone of the Math Department in Princeton in 1955, or Göttingen in 1932, or Oxford in 1898. Now it's not that they saw me as a radical who wanted to take them to places that they did not want to go; they never actually asked me where I wanted to lead them. The issue had little import for them, since they did not expect more than basic managerial skills from the Chair. Leadership skills were not critical, and so they just didn't attach that much importance to the selection of a Chair. Which, as we shall see, plays right into the last reason.

4. *Diversity.* The credentials of the colleague who was selected did not match mine—in particular, his salary which was no more than 75% of mine, reflected that. But he had one thing that I did not. He was black. Now before you get all bent out of shape, let me say that this was, by far, the reason most often cited to me—by people of all political stripes. To paraphrase the sentences I heard over and over, "Ron, once you were not the consensus choice of the Department, you didn't have a prayer. All other things being perceived as equal, how could they pass up the opportunity to appoint a minority Chair of the Math Department!"

Now here is the moral of the story. I had some bad months, but I got over it. I supported the new chair in any way he asked; and later I accepted an appointment to the third deputy-like position in the Department (Associate Chair for Faculty Affairs—thereby earning the distinction of being the only person in the

history of the Mathematics Department to hold all three Associate Chair posts).
Eventually, I was appointed Associate Dean of the College and then Senior Asso-
ciate Dean, my current position. Maryland has continued to be an encouraging
and hospitable home to my academic and administrative talents and I expect to
retire from here very satisfied with the career I built. What actually happened in
the chair search I will never know. Which of the four reasons was paramount?
Who knows! Maybe there was a fifth reason or other reasons of which I am
unaware. The point is that I certainly entertained the plausibility of the idea that
the choice was motivated by racial considerations. What a horrible thought! For
my colleague as well as for me. To think that a decision like that could be made
not on academic grounds, not based on research, educational or leadership cre-
dentials, but upon the color of one's skin, was deeply unsettling. Even if not true,
the fact that I and, more importantly, others gave it credence tainted my col-
league's achievement. This is one of the twin horrors of <u>diversity</u>.[7] It was indeed
clear that many colleagues believed the selection was influenced by race, even
without their being able to know for sure whether it was or not. The United
States of America has atoned for historical injustices by deciding that, legally and
morally, discrimination <u>against</u> anyone on the basis of race, gender, religion, etc.
is wrong and impermissible. Well, discrimination <u>for</u> someone on any of those
grounds is just as morally reprehensible—even if in our temporary blindness, we
have made it legal. All over the country, well-qualified minority candidates have
legitimately earned positions that other people suspect were conferred solely
because the candidate belonged to a favored minority. It cheapens their accom-
plishments. We should cease the unsavory and biased processes that are the cause
of these unwarranted assumptions.

---

7.   The other is that it too often results in the passing over of a more qualified non-
      minority candidate, which is grossly unfair to that person.

12

The Liberal/Conservative Divide in the USA; The Future

Our final task is to conjure up some prognostication of what lies in store in the near future regarding the liberal/conservative divide in the USA. Ever mindful of the famous dictum, "Predictions are difficult, especially of the future,"[1] we shall restrict the size of the window into the future to no more than 20-25 years. Even that length is problematic because of the breathtaking pace of change in certain areas of human history. I will mention three. First, the recent political/economic changes in the world's configuration have been dramatic: the fall of communism, the rise of Islamofascism, the globalization of the world's economy and the looming presence of two new colossuses, India and China. It is very difficult to see what new and equally dramatic political and/or economic changes might occur that will make the world of today look as out of date in 25 years as the world of 1981 looks to billions of people today.[2] Second is the accelerating rate of technological progress in classic areas of human endeavor: communication, medicine, transportation, information retrieval, etc. And third, aside from the new tech widgets that may revolutionize the aforementioned traditional domains, we stand at the cusp of new fields that could drastically change the world, even the nature of human beings. We've all heard the buzzwords: nano science, bio-engineering, quantum computing. Unforeseen developments in these or other incipient areas

---

1. Unlike the phrase that inspired the book's title, which is generally ascribed to either Churchill or Disraeli, the authorship of this phrase has been attributed to dozens of wits. Try googling it to get an idea.
2. Twenty five years ago we were at the height of WWIII, which is little noted by people currently under the age of 25. Will WWIV be red hot or long concluded in 25 years? It is impossible to tell now.

could alter the fundamental nature of human interaction, the relationship between citizens and their government, and the shape of political entities. One doesn't know whether to await the future with great anticipation or paralyzing dread, whether to stand in wondrous awe or quake with fear.

Whichever way one is inclined to contemplate the future, it is highly likely that many of the basic questions we ask today, as well as the problems that confront us and the key decisions we think we face, will be trivial, irrelevant or inconsequential in 25 years and certainly in 50 or 75 years. So in this final chapter, we'll adopt a limited time frame—20-25 years, and in actuality probably no more than 10-12. Also we shall approach the future as we did the past, namely, we'll interpret political change in light of how we understand matters today.

The basic context of this book has been the struggle between political liberalism and political conservatism as we understand those terms today. Therefore, when contemplating the future, we would want to address questions like: Which of the two movements will grow in strength, presumably at the expense of the other, over the next 10-12 years? over the coming 20-25 years? Will the changes be modest or drastic? Will all change be in the same political direction, or will the future fortunes of the two competing political movements oscillate? I will address these below. But before I do so, we need to be sure that we understand the relationship between where we are today and where we were 25+ years ago. As we mathematicians say, it's not enough to know the position vector, we need to know the velocity vector too. (I'll comment about the acceleration vector also.) Now what I say in the next few paragraphs will encapsulate points that were made in Chapters 5 and 8, as well as other parts of the book. But before I say it, let me state that I believe that the points of commonality (in Chapter 2) will remain in force whether or not my specific prediction about the future of the liberal/conservative divide proves to be true.

Before the liberal movement began to crack up in the 1970s, it controlled the American political agenda in a comprehensive way, a fact that it managed to conceal rather effectively. But indeed, liberalism was the political religion of the country, so much so that its policies—some of which were quite Left—were viewed as totally mainstream, with the attendant effect that classic conservatism was relegated to the extreme Right flank. The liberals controlled all three branches of government, they dominated virtually all the elite, opinion-making organs of society—universities, media, foundations, the entertainment industry, the legal profession, government bureaucracies, unions, mainline churches and a surprisingly large part of big corporations. Even Republicans professed to be Keynesians (a mild euphemism for collectivist economics). Domestically, the liberal hegemony was taking the country steadily Left—usually slowly, but occasionally quite rapidly. The Great Society was a natural successor to the New Deal. On the other hand, internationally, the liberal movement was undergoing a powerful reversal: the aggressive, anti-totalitarian, militarily-oriented, unilateralist approach of Roosevelt, Truman and Kennedy was supplanted by the passive, military-averse, multilateralist outlook of McGovern and Carter.

Now it is rather dramatic to compare where the country was politically in the late 1970s to where it is today. The liberal hegemony has been shattered. Conservatives—although they are not nearly as conservative as the liberals were/are liberal—share control of the executive and legislative branches of government and are making a serious push on the judiciary as well. The elite, opinion-making organs still remain to a great extent in liberal hands, but conservatives have risen to challenge that control on many fronts. Talk radio, internet bloggers and Fox News have hammered the liberal bias of the mainstream media. The union movement's power has receded dramatically under the assault of modern business models. Evangelical church membership is skyrocketing while that of the mainline churches is plummeting. Right wing think tanks (like the Heritage Foundation and the Cato Institute) have grown in stature and influence and now challenge liberal foundations like Ford and Rockefeller. Small business, populated with conservative, free market aficionados, contributes as dynamically to the American economy as does big business, which is often led by liberal CEOs. In other areas (universities, government bureaucracies, and the entertainment industry) the liberals still run the asylum, but if any of my colleagues have gotten this far in the book, maybe change is in the cards there too.

Economically, the rightward drift may be even stronger than the political current. Hardly anyone is a Keynesian any more. All but the willfully blind can see, from the concrete experiences of the century past, that a centrally-directed economy cannot compete, even minimally, with the market-driven economies. (Although, when it comes to the scope of government's role in the economy, much less in the society in general, putative conservatives are finding it very hard to practice what they preach.) Milton Friedman, Alan Greenspan, Thomas Sowell and Walter Williams have more credence than any left wing economist. One can only hope that Friedrich Hayek's *The Road to Serfdom* and Adam Smith's *The Wealth of Nations* will be a standard part of the public school curriculum soon.

Now that we've reviewed where we've come in the last 25 years, let us reiterate the kind of basic questions that we would like to answer in this final chapter about the next 25. Is the country moving to the Left or to the Right? Is the conservative movement gaining strength at the expense of the liberal movement or vice versa? How strong are these trends? And over what time frame? Only a Nostradamus could give precise answers to these questions. Instead, let us reformulate as follows. In the next period (choose 10-12 or 20-25 as you see fit), I see only five possibilities for the evolving shape of the liberal/conservative divide. We shall fulfill the task I set for this chapter by assessing the likelihood of each possibility. The choices:

1. There is an overwhelming shift back to the Left and liberalism once again regains its totally dominant role in the political life of the United States.

2. There is a significant, but not overwhelming, move to the Left. Liberalism again becomes the clearly stronger force in American politics, but it does not achieve the dominance that it once had.

3. The needle oscillates in a fairly narrow range around the political center—now conservatism is up and liberalism is down, then vice versa, with perhaps several swings over the next generation. This would be characterized by the Republican and Democratic parties trading the White House and Congress several times over the next two decades or so.

4. The current move to the Right continues, perhaps even strengthens a bit, but no huge shift to the Right occurs. Conservatism becomes the clearly stronger voice in American society, but does not approach the kind of dominance liberalism had in its heyday, or conservatism enjoyed in the nineteenth century.

5. There is an overwhelming shift to the Right and conservatism reigns supreme.

I will argue that there is virtually no chance of (1) and little chance of (3) coming to pass and therefore, our political future lies along one of the paths (2), (4) or (5). Then I will assess the relative likelihood of these three.

Why should we take (1) and (3) out of consideration? Well, we cannot experience (1) for the following two simple reasons. First, the age of liberal hegemony is just too recent. Those who experienced it and remember it are still with us in great numbers. An age of liberalism cannot be dangled before us as a novel, fresh and exciting idea. We've been there, done that. Now couple that with the second reason: liberalism's failures, colossal and small, have been exposed for all to see. Let's revisit some of them:

- Socialism, even of the lite variety, is completely discredited. The hardcore Marxists instituted totalitarian regimes and bled their people into poverty, and the soft-core socialists of Western Europe have produced stagnating economies that pale by comparison with America's (not totally) free market economy.

- What socialism we have instituted here, that is, Social Security, Medicare and Medicaid, have been revealed for the unsustainable Ponzi schemes that they are. The fact that we don't have the courage to repair the damage does not change the fact that these welfare programs are doomed to failure.

- Secular humanism, the religion of liberalism, has led our sister countries in Europe to demographic suicide, cultural upheaval and a general malaise of spirit. Where it has taken hold here, the results are the same.

- Liberalism increasingly means pacifism and the denial of the portion of the American creed that asserts it is our nation's destiny to lead the cause of global freedom. Once again, if Europe is the example, this line of thinking is leading to political suicide as those societies no longer seem able to defend themselves against an invasion by peoples who do not share the spirit of Western Civilization. The same symptoms are again present here. Western Europe can get away with it for a while because we are able to protect them—at least from outside invasion. Who will protect us?

- Liberalism increasingly means environmental lunacy that has led us into an energy crisis of potentially staggering proportions.

The fact that these failures are *evident* and *recent* ensures that path (1) is not in our future. The flaws of the age of liberalism were numerous and *we remember them.* We're not doing that again—at least not for a very long time.

Next, why is possibility (3) also ruled out? Here is the main reason. It goes against the grain of our nation as a people. Americans are decisive, value strength of purpose and appreciate the advantage of unity as our nation confronts its destiny. It's hard to imagine us wishy-washy for an extended period of time. Therefore, I think one side or the other will establish supremacy in relatively short order. The current situation is marked by indecisiveness, confusion and the acrimony I described in Chapter 9. This vacillation bewilders our friends and delights our enemies, and is contrary to the American character. I don't think continued vacillation is in the cards; the political tide will shift one way or the other, with some degree of permanence. Actually, I have another reason for ruling out this possibility. What kind of a chicken-hearted predictor would I be if I just said things are going to stay the way they are? It is more interesting and exciting to go out on a limb and predict a specific new path. If I do, you and I can revisit the book in a decade or two and decide whether I was right or wrong.

A liberal resurgence. Having ruled out paths (1) and (3), let's now consider the remaining three. In this section we examine path (2). I am willing to entertain the possibility that, although liberalism will not become dominant again, it could regain the upper hand in American politics. Perhaps the election of 2006 (and the widely anticipated result in 2008) supports that possibility. There are some pre-existing models around the globe. I am thinking primarily of Canada and Latin America. Canada moved distinctly to the Right in the 1980s—in part under the strong influence of Reagan. This followed many years of liberal dominance in Ottawa. But the Conservative Party cracked up and the liberals regained power more than a decade ago. The recent election of a minority conservative government suggests that the path our northern neighbor is traveling is more accurately characterized as (3) rather than (2). I'm not so sure. I don't want to attempt a detailed analysis; let me just say that I see strong trends north of the border that bespeak a much greater affinity for a European style society than an American one.

Latin America provides many more examples. After an extended period of authoritarian government—in some places considered Left, in others, Right, but always despotic (see the next section for more on the distinctions)—a great portion of Latin America turned to democracy, free markets and conservative policies. The influence of Reagan again cannot be denied. This trend lasted perhaps a decade, but recently, in one country after another, Leftists—both of the radical and moderate variety—have come to power. Conservatism is in retreat in Latin America and the Left is reestablishing control.

Can that happen here? I wish I could say no. For the reasons already enumerated, I think the chance of a major leeward resurgence resulting in a renewed and complete liberal dominance is virtually nil. But I also believe that the country could turn Left again, and perhaps stay that way for a while. In fact, many so-called conservatives seem to be working hard to bring exactly that about. To wit:

- Government spending has exploded under Republican tutelage.

- Republicans have failed to enact tax reform, entitlement reform or to reign in the size and scope of government.

- Conservative government has not protected our borders, and George W. Bush's immigration policy is appalling.

- The level of corruption in government, often too high under liberal Democrats, is no better under conservative Republicans.

- George W. Bush has taken down a brutal regime in Iraq, but clearly his administration had inadequate plans for what to do there next.

- Iran has not been adequately addressed; China is off the radar screen; Russia is backsliding; Osama is still at large and Islamofascism shows no signs of abating.

- No true conservative successor to Reagan was groomed; both Bushes have been disappointments—faux conservatives are how I have characterized them.

- Eminent domain is out of control; government still oppresses small businesses that run afoul of the EPA, OSHA, or the "diversity police"; and in general, the whole liberal gestalt seems to still be in place and operational.

Reasonable people might think, "Why have fake liberals when we can have the real thing." As I already said: hardcore liberalism is thoroughly discredited; right wing bloggers and the other populist features of the conservative revolution are not going to go to sleep; the mainstream media can no longer steer the nation's agenda as it did during Watergate and Vietnam; and secular humanism is the religion of no more than a quarter of the country. A liberal avalanche is not coming. But the disappointments and failures of the faux conservatives who have been running the country might send real conservatives to the political sidelines to await the next Reagan, thereby enabling liberals to once again gain the upper hand. That's what happened in 1992. If the Democrats choose wisely in 2008, then maybe they will not only regain power, but also, by establishing a true Center-Left government, hold it for a while.

However, I don't think this scenario is highly likely. It is possible, just not very likely. It is unlikely because the Democratic Party is totally controlled by its extreme Left wing. And we know that true Lefties' desire to win is eclipsed by their desire for purity. The country may not be as Right as I would like, but it is nowhere near as Left as the radicals who try to pass themselves off as mainstream think it is. We may go Left, but it will definitely not be hard Left.

Conservative dominance. Next we consider path (5), a conservative dominance. Could we have a society whose political, economic and social agendas were thoroughly dominated by conservative ideas and practices? Could conservatives control the scene to the same extent that liberals did 50 years ago or that conservatives themselves once did another 75 years earlier? To arrive at an answer, let's ask, as we did in the last section, what are the recent models? Of course, nineteenth century America is an excellent model, but it's not recent. One strives mightily to find a legitimate recent model. Hong Kong before its takeover by the Peoples Republic of China comes to mind, but I am hard pressed to supply another good example. At which point many people, especially liberals, would say, "What about all the Right-wing dictatorships the world has endured since WWII?" Which brings me to an important aside in this book—the nature of societies under the rule of a dictatorship. You will have to excuse me for momentarily interrupting the flow of this chapter's discussion, but there are some important, and germane, points to be made.

First, dictatorships come in two flavors, *authoritarian* and *totalitarian*. What's the difference? In a totalitarian regime, the government completely controls all political, economic, social and cultural systems. That is the "ideal" toward which such a regime aspires. The thirst for human freedom being what it is, such regimes usually cannot achieve total control, but a few have come quite close. The two most (in)famous totalitarian regimes of modern times were Soviet Communism and German Nazism. Now I venture that most people, if pressed to classify those regimes as Left or Right, would say that Communism was of the extreme Left and Nazism was of the extreme Right. Ridiculous! They were both extreme Left wing forms of government. Why do I say that? Well of course by extreme Left or ultra Left wing we mean liberalism carried to its most extreme, and by extreme Right or ultra Right wing we mean conservatism carried to its most extreme. Now if I am forced to reduce the difference between liberalism and conservatism to a single issue or a unique fundamental tenet, I would have to say: *the scope of government.* The key distinction is that conservatives believe the powers of government should be kept as limited as possible beyond the absolute basics like preserving the currency, defending the nation against foreign enemies and ensuring the rule of law. Liberals, on the other hand, believe that government should not only be responsible for the aforementioned basics, but it should also be heavily involved in solving virtually all of the problems, common and uncommon, that confront its citizens.

Limited government vs. unlimited government. Having identified that as the litmus test for identifying a system as conservative or liberal, it is clear that any totalitarian regime is ultra Left wing. The system of a society under total control by the government is an ultra Left wing system. An ultra Right wing system would be the opposite, one in which there is virtually no government, that is, *anarchy.* Now, can you think of a society that has chosen, or has had imposed on it, anarchy as the method of organizing society. What passes for a society in the Gaza Strip these days might qualify. Certain third world countries, where warlords and bandits control vast acreage, also present themselves as candidates. Nazi Germany, on the other hand, does not qualify. There was no anarchy in the Third Reich, just cold-blooded government-sponsored mass murder. It was an ultra Left wing regime, as were/is Soviet Russia, China under Mao, North Korea, Hoxta's Albania, Fidel's Cuba and Khomeni's Iran. They are all correctly labeled totalitarian and Ultra Left wing. Lenin may have taken his inspiration from economics while Hitler took his from perverted racial theories, but they both created ultra Left wing, repressive, totalitarian regimes in which the government controlled almost every aspect of the lives of its subjects.

Now a key point is that the same analysis applies to authoritarian regimes. What is the usual distinction drawn between the two types of dictatorships? A typical answer will be that an authoritarian regime, unlike a totalitarian regime, only controls the political agenda—albeit, ruthlessly of course. In such a regime, the government may leave economic, social and/or cultural agendas substantially outside the boundaries of its powers. The authoritarian government either doesn't want or is not powerful enough to control all aspects of life. In a totalitarian society, nothing a citizen does is outside the scrutiny and purvey of the government. But in an authoritarian society, if you keep your nose out of politics, you may be able to run a business, plan a cultural event, or worship God without governmental interference. But to identify any such regime as one of limited government is absurd.

Nevertheless, people usually persist in characterizing authoritarian regimes as Left wing or Right wing. Franco's Spain, Greece under the generals in the 1970s, and Pinochet's Chile are normally classified as Right wing while Peron's Argentina, Nasser's Egypt and Tito's Yugoslavia are labeled as Left wing. Sometimes I think these nonsensical attributions proceed according to whether the dictator is presumed to have a greater affinity for Hitler or Lenin/Stalin. Alternatively, but not consistently, an authoritarian regime is classified as Right or Left according to whether the dictator emerged from a military or civilian background. It is all nonsense. If the government controls all forms of political expression in the society and is not responsive to the will of the people, then it represents extreme liberalism, and must be classified as ultra Left wing. All authoritarian regimes do not meet the most fundamental requirement of a conservative society—limited government.

"Oh beautiful," my liberal friends are saying, "You've arranged your definitions so that all evil regimes are on the Left." Well if the shoe fits. No, just kidding. However, if one takes the fulcrum of the liberal/conservative divide to be the role of government in society, then dictatorships must be on the Left. Unless the dictator is a benevolent despot, and we all know how many of those there have been. By the way, there is no comfort to be had on the extreme Right either. Societies afflicted by anarchy can be just as dangerous to human health as those run by dictatorial tyrants. But it's hard to imagine a stable society in the grip of anarchy. People want order; that is why they agree to be governed. Those places in the world that have degenerated into anarchy have always experienced wanton slaughter. (The aforementioned Gaza Strip and several locales in Africa are examples; some would add present day Iraq.) Anyway, authoritarian regimes, while ghastly, can be stable—at least for a while. So, since dictatorship is more common than anarchy, there are more unsavory regimes on the extreme Left than there are on the extreme Right—but not because either is preferable to the other.

Now an indisputable fact is that even away from the extremes, there are more societies that tilt Left than Right. Even in the advanced industrial world, there are many more liberal societies than conservative ones. In fact, the former are legion all over Western Europe and Latin America. But you can name the latter on the fingers of one hand—the US, Hong Kong, maybe Singapore, Ireland lately, a few others; but no very large country except for the US. Maybe this will change. The Founding Fathers of America laid out an excellent blueprint for a conservative society in the US Constitution. And we followed it rather effectively for a long while. But starting a hundred years ago (more or less) it came under attack, an attack to which it succumbed to a substantial degree. Although, as we've shown, there's been a pretty strong counterattack and resurgence of conservative sentiment in the last 25 years.

Could this resurgence increase further in strength? Could the US reemerge as a fundamentally conservative society in which conservative ideas and practices dominate political, economic and social life? I think it's possible—but not likely. Why?

- The apparatus of liberalism is so deeply ingrained in US society that it would take a tremendous upheaval to undo it. It is almost unimaginable to contemplate: the complete privatization of Social Security and health care; the dismantling of the gargantuan regulatory machine; or the institution of a flat tax.

- Secular humanism is very strong, even if limited to say a quarter of the population.

- We live in a time of rapid and profound change—technologically of course, but also in social and economic ways. It is extremely difficult to sustain a traditional society in an era of constant tumult and turmoil.

Nevertheless, it is not impossible. But here's what it would take to realize such a conservative society in the United States. We would have to witness:

- A true conservative successor (or better, successors) to Ronald Reagan.

- The diminution and perhaps disappearance of the Democratic Party, to be replaced by a more centrist entity.

- A Congress that is able to police itself, that is, one that embraces the notion of limited government and controls its addiction to spending.

- A judiciary that tempers its predisposition to legislate, and restricts itself to interpreting the law.

- The growth of the ownership society to 85-90% (the percentage of Americans who own stock, which is currently somewhat in excess of one half).

- A reestablished broad consensus on defense policy (which existed in the 1940s and 1950s under the liberal hegemony).

- A religious revival.

Like I said, this is possible, just not very likely. When the country produces a conservative Walter Cronkite,[3] then we'll know the conservative millennium has arrived.

Tacking Right. We have described two paths, liberal hegemony and political oscillation, that are definitely not coming to pass, and two paths, conservative hegemony and liberal ascendancy without domination, that are potentially possible in our future, but not likely. That leaves the remaining path, conservative ascendancy without domination, as the winner by default. But there are also some good reasons why this scenario is most likely in store for us in the near-term future. Thus let me offer a few observations, which suggest that our country will continue to move modestly to the Right over the next decade or two. There are four.

1.   Twentieth century liberalism is a spent bullet. Liberals are out of ideas. They bring little to the current political debate beside whining, complaints, negativism, and stale, rehashed plans for more government, higher taxes, wealth redistribution and increased regulation. Seventy five years ago liberals had a ton of new ideas. We've tried them. Most are counterproductive. The few that are worthy have been institutionalized. (Unfortunately, we've institutionalized far too many of their ideas that are unworthy.) The liberals of the Democratic Party are as pathetic today as the conservatives of the Republican Party were 50-60 years ago. The voters of America rejected the Republicans then and they will continue to reject the Democrats now.

Continuing the analogy, in that dismal past for the conservative movement, it was the liberals who were confident, optimistic and brimming with ideas and policies that they desperately wanted to turn into practice. The voters entrusted them with that responsibility and privilege. Today the roles are reversed. In contrast to the defensive, pessimistic and boring liberals, it is the conservatives who exude confidence, optimism and passion for institutionalizing their ideas. The voters have increasingly turned the baton over to them and I believe this will continue and possibly accelerate.

---

3.   Walter Cronkite is a famous (retired) journalist who, despite the fact that his transparent opinions were clearly rather Left, earned the reputation as the "most trusted man in America." Of course this was in an era when the equation *Left* = *mainstream* was operational.

2. Liberals are their own worst enemies. Conservatives have certainly given liberals ample opportunity to stage a political comeback. Conservatives have not remained true to their bedrock principles; they have behaved in as cocky and corrupt a manner as their liberal predecessors; they have not been overwhelmingly successful in bringing freedom to the Middle East; and they have alienated many of America's allies. But liberals are too busy stewing in their anger at the loss of their hegemony, so they have missed every opportunity to step into the breach that conservatives have opened for them.

    • They have selected leaders like Howard Dean, Harry Reid, Nancy Pelosi, Ted Kennedy and of course Al Gore and John Kerry, who are bitter, angry and shrill. Their ill-tempered criticisms and vicious attacks on Bush and the Republicans reveal their paucity of new ideas and turn off the public.

    • They continue to move further to the Left in the formulation of their program and they pay homage to radicals like Jesse Jackson, Al Sharpton, Cindy Sheehan, Michael Moore and Julian Bond, while they reject moderates like Joe Lieberman. They act like the moderate Left, much less the Center, is radioactive.

    • They give absolutely no credence to the possibility that some conservative ideas might have merit, and might be effective in promoting the economy or enhancing freedom. They brook no compromise with their "till death do us part" devotion to liberal principles. They choose ideological purity over open-minded political compromise.

    • They don't learn from their mistakes. I've already discussed this point, but let me point out that liberal diehards continue to lionize villains like Che Guevara, Ho Chi Minh, Mao and Fidel—preferring to see them as liberal icons rather than the criminal mass murderers that they are.

3. Conservatives are learning to play the game. It has not been pretty, but conservatives are slowly learning how to exercise power after several generations in the political wilderness. They have learned how to market their ideas through think tanks (the Heritage Foundation), newspapers (the Washington Times), the media (Fox News), the internet and via direct mail. They are working hard to recapture the judiciary that was kidnapped by the liberals 50 years ago. They have learned to pay attention to their base and not take it for granted. When they violate that

credo, as they did in the Harriett Meyers affair, their feet are held to the fire quickly. They have learned how to enlist political volunteers, stir up the grass roots, turn out their base on election day, and disseminate their message more effectively. They had a very difficult time learning how to run Congress; one hopes for better performance in the future. They are starting to challenge in the elite, opinion-making organs of society (such as the universities) in which they took a ferocious beating over the years; but there is a long way to go in this arena. And perhaps most importantly, under the tutelage of Reagan, they have learned to be optimistic, forward looking, and confident. They are trying to convert young people, minorities and other natural constituents of the liberal base, occasionally with surprising success. As a movement, conservatism is formidable and dynamic, and that bodes well for its future.

4.   My last observation is that conservatism is fundamental to the character of the American people. We look to the heroes and ideals of the American Revolution, not the French Revolution. In short we are a conservative people. Our founding documents are conservative. Our creed is conservative. America is as much an idea as a nation. To be American, unlike say to be Polish, does not mean primarily having ancestors who lived in the same land, or having the same ethnic heritage, or speaking the same language (although English is a powerful unifying force), or following the same religion, or deriving from the same geographic region. Being an American is, at the core, to be faithful to a political idea: the belief in human freedom, individual liberty under the rule of law, administered by a government whose powers include only those that the people grant to it. It's a conservative notion. And if we ever take back the organs of opinion-making in society, then not only will the US tack Right, but a conservative hegemony will be in the offing.

Now to finish up this chapter (and the book, except for the final reminiscence), I will briefly explore three more thoughts: (i) having won in 2006, what if the Dems also win in 2008, what will be the effect on my prediction; (ii) two caveats to accompany that prediction; and finally (iii) an inescapable reason why my prediction will in fact be fulfilled.

What if. At this writing, in the summer of 2007, the pundits' prediction of the Democrats taking back Congress has been fulfilled. And with no obvious Republican successor to W, much less to Reagan, the Dems are also licking their chops at the prospect of the presidential election in 2008. Suppose their optimism pans out. What would such an event have to say regarding my prediction of a continued, if modest, move to the Right in America?

In fact I think that the election of 2006 and the probable Democratic triumph in 2008 will have no more permanent effect than did the election of Bill Clinton in 1992. If anything his ascension to the presidency may have hastened the pace of the drift to the Right. Recall that his first presidential act was an attempt to render the military gay-friendly. It was followed quickly by large tax increases and the thrust for nationalized health care (HillaryCare). These Leftists maneuvers probably were the triggers that led to the Republican capture of Congress in 1994. Thereafter, Clinton's policies were somewhat more conservative (free trade agreements and welfare reform, e.g.). And don't forget that Clinton's election, and reelection, was aided by his self-portrayal as a Centrist.

Despite the slow learning curve of the Republican Congress, and despite the faux conservative nature of George W's administration, both of which have opened a door for the liberals, I think that even if the Democrats win in 08, it will not herald a halt to the nation's shift to conservatism. There are two reasons. First, as was the case in 2006, for the liberals to be successful in 2008, they will have to moderate their positions. As I already pointed out, the Democratic Party continues to veer sharply to the Left. If this persists, then even though there may be an open door for them, the American voters will not invite them through that door. In order to succeed, the Dems must come back toward the Center. I have strong doubts that they are capable of doing so. In fact, there are barely any signs that they recognize this fact, or even if they do, similarly few signs that they are willing to do anything about it.

The second reason is as follows. Suppose they do tack Right a little and succeed in 2008. Well, that just reinforces my point that the country is continuing to move Right. Moreover, in short order, three things will happen. First, voters will forget or forgive what caused their displeasure with Republican performance. Second, voters will decide that they would rather have real conservatives lead them than the fake kinds the Dems will have that are impersonating conservatives. And third, the conservative base will be reenergized by a candidacy that we cannot foresee at the moment. So any liberal success in the later years of this decade will prove illusory and the conservative march will reassert itself in the teens.

Two huge unknowns. There are two developments, one ominous, the other merely portentous, that could throw my analysis and prediction into doubt. The first is another major defeat in the war against Islamofascism, meaning that the enemy manages to hit us again, one or more times, in some dramatic fashion. It is very difficult to predict how the country would react to such an occurrence. Will we be even more resolute in hunting down and killing or capturing the perpetrators and their leaders; or will we adopt a more European approach of appeasement and isolation? I really don't know and I hope we don't find out. But if it does happen, which way we go could dramatically affect the overall political course of the country. So I will hedge my bet a little: my predictions are suspended, at least in the near term, if this awful eventuality does come to pass. However, in the long term, I am confident that we will prevail in WWIV. It just might take longer than the time frame I've specified for my predictions. Incidentally, dare we entertain the thought that there won't be a WWV, that Islamofascism is the last global menace that we have to eradicate? We can only hope.

The second unknown is more difficult to specify precisely and is not something that would occur suddenly like a terrorist attack—which of course could happen between the time I write and when you read. Moreover, not only is the second development not imminent, if it does happen, it will not be so evident that it has occurred. I am referring somewhat cryptically to the political effect on the country that the massive immigration we are now experiencing, both legal and illegal, could have.

In Chapter 5, I explained how the huge immigration from Eastern and Southern Europe of the late 19th/early 20th century had a slowly developing but profound effect on the politics of the USA. In fact, I attributed part of the success of the mid 20th century liberal movement to those immigrants, and especially to their children. My point was that, although those immigrants, like all other immigrant groups that preceded them and—so far as one can tell—those that succeeded them, bought into the American creed, assimilated, and became American in the sense of pledging allegiance to the political idea I described earlier in this chapter, they also imported a strain of Leftist thinking that had profound effects on the political course of the nation. Will history repeat itself?

The current mass immigration is largely from Asia and Latin America—two areas of the globe that don't exactly nurture the conservative ideals of our Founding Fathers. Actually, I have no doubt that they and their children will assimilate into the American melting pot. I know that some of my conservative brethren dispute that. They worry about Hispanics who preach *reconquista* and Muslims who promote a world-wide caliphate. But the pull of the American ideal is exceedingly strong, especially on those who come seeking a better life—a description that fits the vast majority currently raining down on our shores. They will assimilate. In fact there are already some encouraging signs: nearly 50% of the Hispanic community voted for Bush in 2004; Hispanic children are speaking English with greater frequency; and Asians are successfully imitating past European immigrant communities.[4]

So they will indeed assimilate. But will they wreak the same kind of (perhaps not so) subtle changes on the political course of the nation as did the immigrants of a century ago? It is impossible to say. And it may take some time to shake out, perhaps longer than the relatively short time frame I've specified for my future window. But maybe not. Everything else is speeded up in our breakneck society. Perhaps the political ripple effects of a new generation of immigrants will appear quickly. If so, this could also affect my predictions. The Democrats dearly hope that it will. Only time will tell.

On the Right side of history. Following the last section, which was a bit of a downer, I choose to end this op/ed book on a positive note. Here are three of the greatest ideas in human history:

1. Ethical monotheism.

2. All men are created equal ... they are endowed by their Creator with certain unalienable Rights ... among these are Life, Liberty and the Pursuit of Happiness ... to secure these rights, Governments are instituted among men, deriving their just powers from the consent of the governed.

3. The principle of *enlightened self interest*, as captured by the metaphor of the *invisible hand*.

---

4.   A tangentially related observation is that the number of black conservatives is increasing markedly. Actually, the black community is in many ways socially quite conservative. If they can get the blinders off, maybe they will give up their blind allegiance to the Left. And if they do, then maybe there is hope for the Jews also.

1. Ethical monotheism was articulated by the ancient Hebrew tribes sometime in the neighborhood of 3500 years ago. It is an idea that was either whispered into their ears by God, or it was a self-inspired notion that they attributed to a Creator. It says that God has given man free will, but He is interested in the choices that man makes. He instructed man as to which are the good choices and which are the bad ones. And although He does not make any choices for man, presumably He is keeping score. He may not be keeping individual scores, or even group scores, but He is tracking the progress humanity is making towards selecting better choices. He threw in the towel on humanity once, but reconsidered. It is very difficult to know whether or not He is pleased with our progress. But each individual is enjoined to enhance the goodness of the world by conducting his affairs and making his choices in accordance with God's instructions.

2. The powerful words of the Declaration of Independence are only 230 years old, but their effect on humanity matches that of the words of the Hebrew Bible. The ultimate authority is again the Creator, but this time instead of specifying mankind's obligations to God and one another, He offers up what He is putting on the table for us, namely, our Right to Life, Liberty and the Pursuit of Happiness. Moreover, He clearly commands that, in order to guarantee that those rights are implemented, governments are constituted to serve man, not the other way around.

3. The principle and the metaphor are due to Adam Smith, coined in his book *The Wealth of Nations*, published providentially in the same year as our Declaration of Independence, and arguably the most important book on economics ever written. If you google it, up pops a fascinating Wikipedia entry with the following passage(s) from the book:

> *It is not from the benevolence of the butcher, the brewer, or the baker that we expect our dinner, but from their regard to their own interest. We address ourselves, not to their humanity but to their self-love, and never talk to them of our own necessities but of their advantages. As every individual, therefore, endeavours as much as he can both to employ his capital in the support of domestic industry, and so to direct that industry that its produce may be of the greatest value; every individual necessarily labours to render the annual value of society as great as he can. He generally, indeed, neither intends to promote the public interest, nor knows how much he is promoting it. By preferring the support of domestic to that of foreign industry, he intends only his own security; and by directing that industry in such a manner as its produce may be of the greatest value, he intends only*

his own gain, and he is in this, as in many other cases, led by an invisible hand to promote an end which was no part of his intention. Nor is it always the worse for the society that it was no part of it. By pursuing his own interest he frequently promotes that of society more effectually than when he really intends to promote it. I have never known much good done by those who affected to trade for the public good. It is an affectation, indeed, not very common among merchants, and very few words need be employed in dissuading them from it.

The invisible hand, its automatic pricing mechanism, the actions of millions of independent individuals acting in their own self interest, unrestricted by artificial constraints, are infinitely wiser and more benevolent than any conceivable cadre of government officials could ever be. This system came to be known as *capitalism*; today it is more common to say *free market economy.*[5]

Three ideas that have animated humanity for hundreds of years, and in one instance, thousands of years. Three basically conservative ideas. The individual's political interests are not to be constrained by government. Nor are his economic interests to be constrained by government. However, his behavior is constrained by God—morally, not politically or economically. If the American people remain faithful to these ideas, then how can we not go in a conservative direction? I believe that our commitment to these principles is very strong and that we will restore the conservative nature of American society. It won't be exactly as it was in the nineteenth century, but it will take a form that will help us to continue to go forward proudly as one of the freest, richest and morally sound nations in world history.

It's a trite expression by now, but the events of September 11, 2001 are seared into my memory. The only other comparable day for me is November 22, 1963, JFK's assassination. My parents always spoke about Pearl Harbor Day, December 7, 1941, in the same way and my grandparents recalled Black Tuesday, October 29,1929. But the Stock Market Crash of 1929 was really spread out over more than one day and the percentage of Americans affected <u>on that specific date</u> by the crash was relatively small. The attack on Pearl Harbor occurred far away from the population centers of the American mainland and there was no live TV; although, everyone understood immediately what lay in store for the nation following the attack. The assassination of JFK was also not broadcast live,

---

5.   In part because starting with Marx and continuing with today's Left, the original word has been turned into a pejorative.

but the events that followed immediately thereafter (including the murder of Oswald and JFK's funeral) were. Part of the horror of the day was the uncertainty of its meaning and implications for the future. On September 11 we all saw the plane hit the second tower live on TV. This horrific event, clearly the worst military calamity on the American mainland since the Civil War, combined the national trauma of Black Tuesday, the military disgrace of December 7 and the agonizing uncertainty of November 22.

I remember vividly the emotions that engulfed me as I watched the burning towers, the victims jumping to their deaths, and the civilians lucky enough not to be trapped inside fleeing the carnage. Those emotions were rage, shame and determination. First there was the pure, unadulterated rage at and hatred for the barbarians who had planned and executed this hideously evil deed. I had no thoughts about why they did it, nor did I care. Nothing could justify this fiendish act of unspeakable cruelty. The people who dispatched those maniacal hijackers had to be caught and executed.

Next came shame. How could we get caught so unawares? After a decade of warnings, both veiled and transparent, how could those low budget crackpots inflict such death and destruction on our powerful nation? How disgraceful that we were unable to prevent it. Our government failed at its most basic duty—to defend the nation from foreign enemies.

The third emotion was determination. Our nation could no longer labor under the delusion that this latest threat to world peace—Islamofascism—was a nuisance that could safely be ignored. With their heinous act, the Islamofascists declared war on the US. I was determined that they would get their wish—but henceforth on our terms. In short we would hunt them down in their nests and kill or capture them. Furthermore, we would dismantle the regimes that gave them succor. Of course, I was in no position to act on this emotion. But I assumed that my determination was shared by the overwhelming majority of my fellow citizens, and that those who were in a position to act would do so. That may not have been a completely accurate assumption.

To see why, fast forward to the next day, September 12. On that day, two events occurred on campus that troubled me and raised doubt in my mind that my determination was indeed a reflection of a universal, nation-wide determination to avenge our innocent dead. First, there was a memorial service—the kind of ceremony that was happening all over the country. There were several solemn speeches. But here's the thing. If you were a visitor from outer space who landed at the service taking place at the University of Maryland on September 12, 2001, knowing nothing about what had happened a day earlier, you would have concluded from the speeches that some natural disaster had befallen the US—maybe a horrible flood or earthquake, or a bridge collapsed or some such thing. The word terror was not spoken. Nor was there talk of murder, a foreign attack, war, evil or Islam. Those bastards crashed hijacked airliners into US buildings, on the orders of their Al Qaeda masters, with the express intent of killing as many American civilians as they could, and they likely hit those buildings screaming Allah Akhbar. Our space visitor would not have learned any of those details from the speeches. It shocked me to see that not everyone was experiencing the same emotions that I was. Instead of rage, shame and determination, I saw sorrow, disappointment and feeble attempts to "understand what happened and why."

The second event that disturbed me that day was a special meeting of campus administrators that I attended. Its purpose was to plan how to deal with a problem that the university was worried would arise in the coming days. Namely, they wanted to ensure that the Muslim community on campus would be treated with respect by faculty, students and staff. In fact, I was offended by the unstated implication that those of us who were not Muslim could not be trusted to differentiate between law abiding Muslim students, say, and the murderers in New York and Washington who happened to share their faith. Of course Muslims should be treated with respect—as should Christians and Jews, whose treatment the university did not seem to be equally concerned about. But the meeting had a second, even more shocking purpose—namely, to plan how to shield Muslim students and postdocs on campus from the expected horde of federal agents who would soon descend on our (and all other) campus(es) to seek out Islamic traitors and spies in our midst. Now don't get me wrong: we shouldn't make the same mistake we made with Americans of Japanese extraction in WWII. But let's be realistic; the events of the previous day revealed that the Al Qaeda murderers had been able to hide in the open in the US for months (in some cases years), aided by certain sympathetic US residents. If we were to prevent repeat occurrences of 9/11, clearly those Al Qaeda safe havens had to be destroyed. The FBI would have a delicate, but legitimate role in discharging that duty. The idea that this sacred duty was eclipsed in importance by a concern for potentially minor disruptions to the Muslim portion of our community was ludicrous. At a time when the university might have exhorted its members to organize a help campaign for those wounded in the catastrophe, or the families of the brave firemen that ran into those buildings, or their neighbors who died in the Pentagon, it was more con-

cerned with Muslim sensitivities.[6] As events would prove, this attitude did not augur well for our effort in WWIV.

But once again, let us not part on a negative note. The greatest joy of my life is my three grandchildren. These youngsters will, God willing, live to see the latter part of the 21st century and, if medical science continues its rapid advance, perhaps even the beginning of the 22nd. In my more Reaganesque moments, I am very optimistic that throughout their lives they will live in a vibrant, prosperous and free United States of America, and that their country will continue to shine a beacon of freedom to illuminate the world's dark corners. I feel privileged to be a citizen of a country whose people believe in the three great ideas I described in this chapter. I subscribe to Ronald Reagan's description of the US as "the last best hope for a mankind plagued by tyranny and deprivation," and it is an honor to strive to uphold the ideals that are the source of that hope.

I am especially privileged to be part of two communities that have played a large role in this story—Jewish Americans and university faculty. Despite my occasional criticism of the university and Jewish communities in this book, I want to reiterate what I said in the Introduction, "I love mathematics and the academic life in which I pursue it [and] … I also treasure my Jewish life." The universities of America are the envy of the world. The education of youth and the pursuit of knowledge are noble callings. It is a worthy way to live one's life. I feel lucky to have done so. It is no secret that the Jewish presence in the university is substantial, as it is in so many other important areas of American life. How fortunate I am to have experienced the greatest haven (outside of Israel) that the Jewish people have enjoyed in their long history. The continued flourishing of Jewish life in America, indeed the continuing existence of Jews in the world, is testimony to God's ongoing presence in the world. I would like to close by citing Reagan's image of America as "a shining city on a hill," (adopted from the first Massachusetts Bay Colony Governor, John Winthrop, who lifted it in part from the Book of Matthew). When my grandchildren reach my age in the second half of this century, I would be pleased to know that they will also speak in glowing terms of their Jewish and American heritages. It would be doubly pleasing if they do it from a university campus that honors the memory of Ronald Reagan.

---

6.   To its credit the university behaved more admirably after Hurricane Katrina when it generously took in many students and some faculty from Tulane University.

Bibliography

1. Bartlett, Bruce. *Imposter: How George W. Bush Bankrupted America and Betrayed the Reagan Legacy.* Doubleday: New York, 2006.

2. Bennett, William. *America: The Last Best Hope*, 2 vols. Thomas Nelson: Nashville, 2006 & 2007.

3. D'Souza, Dinesh. *Letters to a Young Conservative.* Basic Books: New York, 2002.

4. Friedman, Milton & Friedman, Rose. *Free to Choose.* Harcourt: Orlando, 1990.

5. Frum, David. *Dead Right.* Basic Books: New York, 1994.

6. Fukuyama, Francis. *The End of History and the Last Man.* The Free Press: New York, 1992.

7. Gingrich, Newt. *To Renew America.* HarperCollins: New York, 1995.

8. Goldberg, Bernard. *Crazies to the Left of Me, Wimps to the Right.* HarperCollins: New York, 2007.

9. Grafton, John, ed. *The Declaration of Independence and Other Great Documents of American History.* Dover: Minneola, 2000.

10. Hayek, F. A. *The Road to Serfdom.* University of Chicago Press: Chicago, 1994.

11. Hazlitt, Henry. *Economics in One Lesson.* Crown: New York, 1978.

12. Johnson, Paul. *A History of the Jews.* Harper & Row: New York, 1987.

13.————. *A History of the American People.* HarperCollins: New York, 1997.

14. Kestler, Charles & Rossiter, Clinton, eds. *The Federalist Papers*. Signet: New York, 1999.

15. Murphy, Robert. *The Politically Incorrect Guide to Capitalism*. Regnery: Washington, 2007

16. Sowell, Thomas. *Basic Economics: A Citizen's Guide to the Economy*. Basic Books: New York, 2000.

17. Steyn, Mark. *America Alone*. Regnery: Washington, 2006.

18. Vazsonyi, Balint. *America's Thirty Years War*. Regnery: Washington, 1998.

19. Williams, Walter. *More Liberty Means Less Government: Our Founders Knew This Well*. Hoover Institution Press: Stanford, 1999.

20. Woods, Theodore, Jr. *The Politically Incorrect Guide to American History*. Regnery: Washington, 2004.

About the Author

Ron Lipsman is Senior Associate Dean and Professor of Mathematics in the College of Computer, Mathematical and Physical Sciences at the University of Maryland. He has a Bachelor of Science degree from the City College of New York and a Ph.D. in Mathematics from M.I.T. He is the author or co-author of eleven books dealing with mathematics and computing. He has also published more than 70 scientific research articles and is the editor of numerous mathematical research volumes. Recently, he published *YOU CAN DO THE MATH: How to Overcome your Math Phobia and Make Better Financial Decisions*, a financial self-help manual for the math-challenged people of America. He divides his time between College Park and Garrett County in Western Maryland, and his interests oscillate between math and science on the one hand and politics and history on the other.

Index

978-0-595-46320-6
0-595-46320-7

www.ingramcontent.com/pod-product-compliance
Lightning Source LLC
Chambersburg PA
CBHW030252290526
45785CB00001B/56